T0146715

BECAUSE WE

LOVE

HIM

EMBRACING A LIFE OF HOLINESS

CLYDE CRANFORD

Multnomah® Publishers *Sisters, Oregon*

BECAUSE WE LOVE HIM
published by Multnomah Publishers, Inc.
© 2002 by Jordan Thomas

International Standard Book Number: 1-57673-865-5

Cover design by The Office of Bill Chiaravalle
Cover image by FPG International

Italics in Scripture quotations are the author's emphasis.
Unless otherwise indicated, Scripture quotations are from:
New American Standard Bible © 1960, 1977 by the Lockman Foundation

Other Scripture quotations:
The Holy Bible, King James Version (KJV)

The Holy Bible, New International Version (NIV) © 1973, 1984 by International
Bible Society, used by permission of Zondervan Publishing House

Multnomah is a trademark of Multnomah Publishers, Inc.,
and is registered in the U.S. Patent and Trademark Office.
The colophon is a trademark of Multnomah Publishers, Inc.

For information:
MULTNOMAH PUBLISHERS, INC.•POST OFFICE BOX 1720•SISTERS, OREGON 97759

Library of Congress Cataloging-in-Publication Data
Cranford, Clyde.
     Because we love Him : embracing a life of holiness / by Clyde Cranford.
         p. cm.
Includes bibliographical references (p.   ).
   ISBN-13: 978-1-576-73865-8
   1. Holiness--Christianity. I. Title.
   BT767 .C812 2002
   248.4--dc21

To Dr. L. Reginald Barnard,
who taught his students always to seek the loftiest view of Christ.

And to Carolyn Marshall, who was a shining
example of what a true Christian should be.

TABLE OF CONTENTS

Part Five
Pleasing God—The Fire of Love

Foreword

Clyde Cranford went to be with the Lord on August 3, 2000.

Clyde Cranford was a gentle, unassuming, and true friend, a man clearly shaped by God. For many years, we worked together from time to time. I would preach and he would sing. But more than that, we shared our hearts about biblical and practical discipleship.

God gave Clyde great insights in answer to prayer, which he would faithfully share with all those God entrusted to him to disciple. He loved his Lord, Jesus, and lived an uncomplaining and uncompromising life of integrity before God and man.

He carried in his heart a simple but profound vision of his life as a disciple of Jesus in our day. He passed this vision on to his friends, especially men to whom God had granted a similar heart. His life will continue to speak through them until Jesus, whom he loved, comes again. Indeed, had Clyde never put a single word on paper, their changed lives would have been an abundant legacy.

But Clyde Cranford *did* put words on paper, except that he put much more than words alone. This book amounts to a lifetime of meditation and prayer, poured out onto these few pages and backed up meticulously by the Scriptures Clyde so obviously studied for so very long.

Clyde was often called a "walking biblical encyclopedia," but he was much more than that. He was a man of profound insight, a man of unique perspective, a man of astonishing clarity of mind, a man of boundless faith.

To those around him, Clyde was a gift of God, granted for a little while. Through him, God changed hundreds of lives.

Through this book, *Because We Love Him,* our Lord will change many more. Most likely, you will be in that number.

Dr. Henry Blackaby
November, 2001

PREFACE

For a few short years it has been my joy to be a discipler of men. My approach has been that of an older disciple of Christ helping younger disciples become better disciples.

I have sought to teach what the Lord has taught me, but never in a formal discipleship setting, by which I mean one-on-one mentoring and teaching. Some teach that every believer should have a "Paul"; I did not. I believe this was God's sovereign design for me, though not for everyone. He very carefully locked me up to Himself and taught me to be abundantly satisfied with Him alone. Yet He also gave me a desire to teach others what He was teaching me.

My father died when I was very small. Somewhere along the way, God changed my profound desire *for* an earthly father into a desire to *be* a father. And yet, He never gave me a family of my own. Instead, He called me to the gospel ministry and gave me a parental heart and a desire to invest my life in the lives of others as a nurturer.

I believe I can understand the apostle Paul's heart toward the Thessalonians when he wrote: "But we proved to be gentle among you, as a nursing mother tenderly cares for her own children. Having thus a fond affection for you, we were well-pleased to impart to you not only the gospel of God but also our own lives, because you had become very dear to us" (1 Thessalonians 2:7–8).

Three verses later, Paul continued the parental analogy: "Just as you know how we were exhorting and encouraging and imploring each one of you as a father would his own children, so that you may walk in a manner worthy of the God who calls you into His own kingdom and glory" (1 Thessalonians 2:11–12).

I also believe that I feel toward those under my care what Paul felt when he said, "For who is our hope or joy or crown of exultation? Is it not even you, in the presence of our Lord Jesus at His coming? For you are our glory and joy" (1 Thessalonians 2:19–20); and further, "For now we really live, if you stand firm in the Lord" (1 Thessalonians 3:8).

Truly, those whom I have had the opportunity to teach are an enormous joy to me. The material in this book is the substance of what I teach "my guys." Several years ago, some of them went together and bought me a word processor for Christmas. They wanted to encourage me to write down what I had taught them. I also felt a prompting from the Lord. So, with real fear and trembling, I embarked on this writing project. I first thought that I would try to write a discipleship manual. But as I prayed, organized, and wrote, it seemed right for the book to focus on one central theme—*holiness*.

This has been a huge, overwhelming task, for which I have often felt inadequate. Yet as Paul told the Corinthians, "our adequacy is from God" (2 Corinthians 3:5). God has chosen to use the foolish, weak, and base things of this world that He might receive all the glory (see 1 Corinthians 1:27–29). It is my prayer that He will use this meager offering to that end.

Ecclesiastes 1:9 tells us that there is nothing new under the sun. And yet, each person has a unique life context into which he receives whatever he learns. Each person interprets things a little differently than another. The truths of God are old, but they become new and different in the context of each unique life.

The things I teach are certainly not new; they are simply truths that I have received into my own life. I teach from that context; he who receives my efforts eventually teaches others from yet another context. Thus the old remains old but becomes new over and over again. This is part of the creativity of God.

I commend this book to you with the prayer that, in the context of your own life, it will be a help and an encouragement to be holy as your heavenly Father is holy.

And I offer this book to You, Father, with blushing face, tear-filled eyes, and a captive heart. Only You are glorious. Only You are holy.

ACKNOWLEDGMENTS

My sincere thanks to all
who have supported Life to Life Ministries through the years.
Without their help, this project
would never have been realized.

INTRODUCTION

In His call to holiness, God has set before us a high standard and also a great prize—conformity to the image of the Christ we love. Most Christians in our society today have set their sights far too low. They have compromised holiness and conformed to the complacency and worldly mindedness that typify the church today. Yet God's Word is uncompromising: Without holiness, none will see the Lord (see Hebrews 12:14).

At certain times in history, holiness was recognized by Christians and non-Christians alike as an essential distinction of true Christianity. It was understood that one who became a Christian began a life marked by an unflinching pursuit of holiness, that this pursuit was the responsibility of every professing believer, and that it was unthinkable for one to call himself a Christian without taking seriously this responsibility.

But alas, today the distinguishing mark of a Christian is thought to be some one-time, individual experience that might or might not result in a changed life. To this idea we must say plainly: Repentance that is not ongoing is not genuine; faith that does not involve surrender is not adequate; a life in which holiness does not develop is not Christian.

Sadly, we live in an irresponsible society in which sins are often excused as phobias. For example, a recent television talk show segment was devoted to the problem some men have in committing to marriage. The guests were heterosexual couples who were actively involved sexually but not married because the men were unwilling to commit. Instead of being rightly assessed as immoral, immature, and irresponsible, these men were said to have a "commitment phobia," as though this excused their sinful lifestyles.

In our culture, people are encouraged to see themselves as victims of either the system or their environment. They must not be held responsible for their actions no matter what they do. But this is far from the way God sees it. We cannot hide behind our excuses and justifications for sin when we are in the presence of our holy God. "And there is no creature hidden from His sight, but all things are open and laid bare to the eyes of Him with whom we have to do" (Hebrews 4:13). God holds us responsible for our behavior even if we do not. His very holiness is our standard of conduct.

Nevertheless, in Western evangelical Christianity, the trend has been to ignore God's call to personal holiness. Indeed, for all our care in defending the authority and authenticity of Scripture, we have virtually abandoned one of its central, fundamental teachings. The average pew-warmer hears very little preaching on personal holiness and seems quite content to know equally little of God's demand for it.

We live in a self-centered, self-absorbed society in which self is nurtured, pampered, indulged, and even worshiped. Self-obsession has so engulfed the church that the biblical concept of self-denial, which is simply saying *no* to self, seems strange and unfamiliar to most, even though this is the very entrance into the Christian life.

Christians who should live in the wondrous reality of God have bought into Satan's lie that reality is too grim or too boring to be dealt with directly. More and more they fill their lives with unreality—if not through drugs or alcohol, then through sexual fantasy, constant activity, or worldly entertainment. It seems that what people fear most is boredom.

Such Christians have succumbed to the notion that happiness is more in keeping with God's desire for them than holiness. But happiness is a fleeting thing and much overrated. Happiness depends on what happens *to* us. It is circumstantial. When things are "happening," as we used to say in the sixties, we are "happy." But happiness goes out the window when adverse circumstances come along.

Adversities are tools in the hand of God to give us something far greater than happiness. They are part of what He uses to discipline us, so we might share in His holiness. A Christian who pursues holiness knows a joy that surpasses mere happiness, for there is joy in the Lord regardless of circumstances. Oh, that we might lose our fascination with happiness and be consumed with a desire for holiness!

Much theology in America today is man-centered rather than

God-centered. God is reduced to a servant who exists to meet man's needs. It is wonderfully true that Jesus Christ "'did not come to be served, but to serve, and to give His life a ransom for many'" (Matthew 20:28). But this simply shows the awesome humility of almighty God. It does not mean that man is the center of God's universe.

God Himself is the center of the universe. Even God's command to be holy is a God-centered command. God does not say, "Be holy because of what it will do for you," but rather, "Be holy because I am holy." Yet God, in expressing His infinite humility, has made man the object of His infinite love and has called him to share in God's own holiness. This is what man was created for to begin with; thus it remains his only true source of joy and fulfillment.

We should be greatly humbled by these truths, which should motivate us to live holy lives as God expects. But instead, pride has caused us to think better of ourselves than we ought and to embrace the world's philosophy of self-exaltation. This has dulled our influence on the world. The church of America was once salt and light. Now, rather than having any real impact on the world around us, we have become more affected than effective. Rather than being set apart from the world, we have sought to be like the world, conforming to its image rather than the image of Christ. We argue that by doing so we will win the world for God. Instead, the world and its values have rendered the church virtually impotent.

By imitating the world we have lost not only our influence but also our credibility. We are no longer a clear beacon pointing men to God. The world looks at the church and sees a cheap, amateurish imitation of itself, so it concludes quite reasonably that the church has nothing special to offer. The church has only one thing that the world does not have but desperately needs—Jesus. And He is everything.

Jesus said: "'And I, if I be lifted up from the earth, will draw all men to Myself'" (John 12:32). We must lift Christ up to a lost and dying world. But how can we lift Christ up if our focus is on ourselves? How can we lift Christ up if we are not living holy lives that illustrate the difference Christ can make?

PART ONE

DEVELOPING
PRACTICAL HOLINESS

*But like the Holy One who called you,
be holy yourselves also in all your behavior.*

1 PETER 1:15

In the preface to *The Pursuit of Holiness,* Jerry Bridges beautifully illustrates both sides of the development of practical holiness in the life of the believer: God's side and the believer's side. His illustration is that of a farmer who recognizes his own responsibility to plant and nurture his crop while acknowledging that only God gives life to the seed. Says Bridges: "The farmer cannot do what God must do, and God will not do what the farmer should do."[1]

Even so, as we grow in practical holiness we are responsible to read the Bible, pray, believe God, and love beyond ourselves. God will not pick up the Bible and open it in front of us, although He will prompt, convict, encourage, and stimulate us to pick it up for ourselves. He will not make us pray, although He will work within our individual circumstances to show us our desperate need for Him. He will not force us to deny ourselves and to invest our lives in the lives of others, although if we listen and observe He will teach us the meaning of John 12:24, that "unless a grain of wheat falls into the earth and dies, it remains by itself alone; but if it dies, it bears much fruit."

God will no more release us from any of His commands than He will release Himself from any of His promises. Yet He will create in us willing and faithful hearts that cherish pleasing Him above all else (see Psalm 51:10; Philippians 2:13). By His grace alone, God will enable us to obey His commands. And once we choose to obey, He will infuse our obedience with true spiritual life (see John 7:38). In just this way, practical holiness is developed in the life of every believer.

Bridges concludes his illustration by saying, "The pursuit of holiness is a joint venture between God and the Christian. No one can attain any degree of holiness without God working in his life, but just as surely, no one will attain it without effort on his own part."[2]

In the following three chapters we will first define what holiness is, then we will examine God's part, and finally, and throughout the remainder of this book, we will focus on man's part.

CHAPTER ONE

AN APPEAL TO LOVE

Be holy; for I am holy.

LEVITICUS 11:44

The best thinking time for me is late at night, when everything is still and the whole world has gone to sleep. I sit on the side of my bed with the covers turned down and read. As a rule, I'm plodding through four or five books concurrently—devotional writings, commentaries, biographies, or poetical works. So there's always something, either half finished or barely begun, into which I can sink my teeth. At times I find myself reading far into the night.

Eventually, though, I begin to fade; so I close the book, nestle down, and turn out the light. In the quiet moments that follow, God often speaks to my heart in gentle yet profound ways, burdening me to pray, convicting me of sin, driving home some truth by letting me see it in a new light, or just reassuring me of His love.

One such night, in that stage between waking and sleeping where dreams begin, part of a verse of Scripture came into my half-conscious mind and nudged me fully awake. "'Be holy; for I am holy'" (Leviticus 11:44). This was a familiar note, but it sounded in a way I'd never heard before.

To be honest, my inmost reaction to this command had always been one of frustration, fear, and resistance: frustration because the standard seemed so high and unattainable; fear because, if holiness really is what God expects, I could never hope to please Him; resistance because "nothing good dwells in me, that is, in my flesh" (Romans 7:18). There is no denying this obstinate pull within me in the opposite direction, which balks at being told what to do even by God.

Yet God has every right to expect unwavering obedience from me simply because of who He is, not to mention what He has done for me by His grace. However, that night there was no authoritative tone in His words. Instead, they seemed to appeal to *love*. The message was not, "Be holy because I *said* to be holy," but rather, "Be holy because I *am* holy, and if you love Me, you will want to be like Me."

The reaction of my heart was a longing for holiness that I had never known before. I was overwhelmed with God's great love and the thought that *my* love should matter to *Him!* Truly it is "to the praise of the glory of His grace" that He has chosen unholy, unworthy sinners to be "holy and blameless before him" (Ephesians 1:4–6). These phrases from Ephesians speak of our position in Christ, but I believe they also speak of what God wants to see manifested in our daily lives, as loving tributes to His matchless love for us.

HOLINESS PURSUED

Is holiness really possible in the life of the believer? Surely God would not call us to so high a standard without also aiding us in its pursuit.

God has commanded holiness not only within the context of the Mosaic law, which was given as a tutor to show us our sinfulness through our failure to keep the Law (see Romans 7:7–11; Galatians 3:22–25), but also in the heart of the New Testament's instruction on right living. "But like the Holy One who called you, be holy yourselves also in all your behavior; because it is written, 'You shall be holy, for I am holy'" (1 Peter 1:15–16).

Christ said: "'The things impossible with men are possible with God'" (Luke 18:27), so some degree of holiness must be within the realm of possibility. But how is it possible? And, even more fundamentally, what is holiness exactly?

Does holiness reside on some mysterious, mystical plane of spiritual existence that can be reached only through great suffering or severe self-abasement? The apostle Peter said:

Therefore, since Christ has suffered in the flesh, arm yourselves also with the same purpose, because he who has suffered in the flesh has ceased from sin, so as to live the rest of the time in the flesh no longer for the lusts of men, but for the will of God. (1 Peter 4:1–2)

These verses suggest that suffering is an aid to holiness. They teach that suffering sobers us and alters the way we live our lives. But they do not teach that suffering initiates us into some elite stratum meant only for the chosen few. Neither is holiness a reward for suffering, as the medieval monastics mistakenly thought.

Surely, true spirituality does begin with self-denial. Christ Himself said: "'If anyone wishes to come after Me, he must deny himself, and take up his cross daily, and follow Me'" (Luke 9:23). But here, self-denial really means turning the back on self, ignoring it rather than controlling it through any form of self-discipline.[1]

In contrast, self-control, a fruit of the Holy Spirit (see Galatians 5:22–23), is the ruling of self by the power of the Spirit. As Elisabeth Elliot said so succinctly: "As we give ourselves to His rule, He gives us grace to rule."[2] But any discipline apart from the Holy Spirit is self-generated, rooted in pride and unbelief, and "of no value against fleshly indulgence" (Colossians 2:23). Thus holiness cannot be its result.

Some have insisted that holiness is composed of outward things such as dress, hairstyles, or the endless keeping of rules crafted by men. But holiness consists of something more profound than outward show, something which goes much deeper than mere externals (see Colossians 2:16–23).

When I was a child, growing up in what I would consider a typical Protestant church of the late fifties and early sixties, I knew the word *holy* was primarily attached to two other words: *ghost,* which frightened me for obvious reasons, and *roller,* which also frightened me because I envisioned people rolling around on the floor with no sense of impropriety or embarrassment. I now understand more clearly the deep enjoyment of the presence of the Lord and the rejuvenating influence of the Holy Spirit on the soul of man. Nevertheless, I must argue that holiness cannot be characterized by some state of hyperspiritual enthusiasm, nor by displays of emotional adrenaline in a worship service.

Others have held that holiness is an eventual state of sinless perfection attainable in this life. But the clear teaching of Scripture is that, although we have been freed from the dominion of sin and have been given "everything pertaining to life and godliness" (2 Peter 1:3), we still cannot escape our own depravity. We will never be completely free from sin until we are with the Lord (see Galatians 5:17).

Often holiness is seen as a state to be reached, some future attainment, perhaps a far-off destination on the Christian pilgrimage obscured by many obstacles along the way. However, it seems from God's commands that He expects holiness from us *now*, today, not at some future time. So what does it mean to be holy right now?

To answer that question, we must first attempt a positive definition of holiness. We need to come to a basic understanding of holiness as it applies primarily to God, and then to man. Second, we must examine more specifically the concept of holiness in its biblical context.

GOD'S HOLINESS

God's holiness is a mystery of which man has caught only a glimpse. Infinite, immutable, transcendent, He who dwells in unapproachable light yet still condescends to look upon the things in heaven and on the earth (see 1 Timothy 6:16; Habakkuk 1:13; Psalm 113:6).

A. W. Tozer writes: "He is the absolute quintessence of moral excellence, infinitely perfect in righteousness, purity, rectitude, and incomprehensible holiness."[3] Because God is infinite, His holiness is limitless; because He is immutable, His holiness is always the same; because He is transcendent, His holiness is beyond the realm of man's mind.

Holiness stands above all the other attributes of God, yet it is simply that—an attribute. It does not stand above God as though it were some category under which He falls, along with other things. Holiness does not define God; God defines holiness; it belongs to Him alone. In Revelation 15:4 we read these words addressed to God, "'Thou alone art holy'" (see also 1 Samuel 2:2).

MAN'S HOLINESS

We can thus conclude that man has no holiness in himself. In and of ourselves, we are but wretched sinners who must shrink under the dazzling brilliance of holy God. What a tragically stark contrast is the degradation of our sin. "'Woe is me, for I am ruined! Because I am a man of unclean lips, and I live among a people of unclean lips; for my eyes have seen the King, the LORD of hosts'" (Isaiah 6:5).

Like Isaiah, when we suddenly comprehend the holiness of God, we are immediately filled with dread and horror over personal sin. Only when we see the holiness of God can we see the blackness of our own sin. The apostle Peter, confronted with the reality of who Jesus really was, fell at His feet and cried: "'Depart from me, for I am a sinful man, O Lord!'" (Luke 5:8).

Yet the word *holy* is used over and over in Scripture in reference to man, in two very distinct ways: *positional holiness* and *practical holiness*.

Positional Holiness

The word *saints,* or *holy ones,* as used in reference to all believers, denotes our *position* in Christ. We see this, for example, in the salutation of Paul's letter to the Philippians: "Paul and Timothy, bondservants of Christ Jesus, to all the *saints in Christ Jesus* who are in Philippi" (Philippians 1:1). We are only holy if we are in Christ (see Ephesians 1:4), and we are in Christ not by our doing, but by God's alone.

Indeed, as Paul puts it, Christ Himself has *become to us* sanctification (see 1 Corinthians 1:30). Just as the righteousness of Christ is imputed to us, so His holiness is imputed as well. Furthermore, we were called with a "holy calling" (see 2 Timothy 1:9); called as "saints" (see 1 Corinthians 1:2; Romans 1:7); declared to be "a chosen race, a royal priesthood, a holy nation, a people for God's own possession" (1 Peter 2:9).

We have been made holy according to the will of God through the sacrificial death of the Lord Jesus Christ: "By this will we have been *sanctified* [made holy] through the offering of the body of Jesus Christ once for all" (Hebrews 10:10; see also Hebrews 10:29; 13:11).

"For by one offering He *has perfected* for all time those who are sanctified" (Hebrews 10:14). But in this last verse, the tense used with the word *sanctified* implies an ongoing action; those who are *being sanctified*, those who are *being made holy*.

Practical Holiness

Scripture also speaks of holiness in reference to man as a goal to be accomplished in the *practical* realm of daily living. We must pursue this goal with all our hearts. Peter adjures us, "Like the Holy One who called you, be holy yourselves also in all your behavior" (1 Peter 1:15). The book of Hebrews tells us to *pursue* "holiness, without which no man shall see the Lord" (Hebrews 12:14, KJV).

A great portion of Scripture is devoted to instructing us in this pursuit, and we are assured that we are not left to ourselves, but our efforts are fueled and energized by the sanctifying discipline of God.

> Now may the God of peace Himself sanctify you entirely; and may your spirit and soul and body be preserved complete, without blame at the coming of our Lord Jesus Christ. Faithful is He who calls you, and He also *will bring it to pass*. (1 Thessalonians 5:23–24)

It is fundamentally God's work to make us holy in this practical sense, just as it was in the positional sense, and He uses whatever means He sees fit to discipline us into holy living (see Hebrews 12:10). God includes us in the process by enlivening our wills and our energies after holiness (see Philippians 2:13). But even this practical holiness is possible only by an impartation of His divine holiness. "He disciplines us for our good, that we may *share His holiness*" (Hebrews 12:10). Thus Christ's holiness is not only imputed to us in a positional sense, but also *imparted* to us in a practical sense.

Hence we do not have a holiness *like* God's; we have God's *own* holiness, both positionally and practically. Positionally, we wear on our hearts an identifying mark; the mark of God's image, of God's likeness. This mark is holiness. In an outward, behavioral sense, if we are not merely moral but truly holy, it is because the very life of the Holy One is being manifested through us. Thus both positionally and practically, holiness is our likeness to God.

Now this does not mean that we are to sit back passively and wait for God to "animate" us with His holiness. Instead, we are to pursue holiness; we are to strive after holiness of character and holiness of conduct. This is *our part* in the process, for the holiness that was extended to us at conversion is not immediately evident in our daily lives. Yet as Paul told the Philippians, "He who began a good work in you will perfect it until the day of Christ Jesus" (Philippians 1:6). As we struggle and grow in the pursuit of practical holiness, it becomes evident to those around us that we have a likeness to God. "So, as those who have been chosen of God, *holy* [a state of being] and beloved, put on [an action] a heart of compassion, kindness, humility, gentleness and patience" (Colossians 3:12). In other words, you *are* holy so *act* like it.

Holiness is the very essence of our identity as believers. Holy is *what* we are, *who* we are, and what we *become progressively* as we pursue holiness on a daily basis. This effort on our part is what Paul called "perfecting holiness in the fear of God" (2 Corinthians 7:1).

HOLINESS AS SEPARATION

Now let's consider a specific, rudimentary definition of the word *holy*. This word has at its root the idea of *separation*. God is holy in that He is unique, infinitely above and set apart from all of His creation. Man is holy when he is set apart from the world and its lusts, from sin (thus holiness may sometimes mean *undefiled*), and from self.

In addition, holiness means to be set apart exclusively unto God for His purposes. Hence the word *saints*—holy ones—refers to believers who are changed into new creatures (see 2 Corinthians 5:17). They are somehow inherently different and separate from the world. What's more, they are sacred vessels set apart by God before the world began (see Ephesians 1:4), vessels that are holy to the Lord, from which the very life of God must shine forth.

The Dynamic of Depravity

Now, to say that believers are different is not to say they are inherently better or improved. The Christian retains his depravity throughout his earthly life. He cannot escape from it as he cannot escape from himself, nor can he improve upon it. He is thoroughly sinful; fundamentally disposed to pride, rebellion, and unbelief. He has no inherent goodness, nor will he ever develop any on his own initiative, because goodness is a fruit of the Holy Spirit (see Galatians 5:22).

Nevertheless, he is different in two ways. First, he was dead spiritually but now he has been made alive by the indwelling of the Holy Spirit (see Romans 8:9–10; Ephesians 2:1–7). Second, this indwelling brings with it a new desire. In the spiritual dimension of his being he was separated from God (death is not annihilation, but separation). Now he is spiritually alive with the capacity to experience and commune with the Holy Spirit of God. He didn't have this capacity before. This is what it is to be a new creature in Christ and sets the Christian apart from the natural world (see 1 Corinthians 2:14). Indeed, this is his holiness in a positional sense: He is a new creature with a new capacity in Christ.

SANCTIFICATION

This new capacity for God begins at conversion, when the Holy Spirit indwells the believer and renews within him the image of God, producing positional holiness. Then begins a process of achieving practical holiness, wherein the Holy Spirit works to conform the believer's will to the will of God and to conform his daily life—how he thinks, how he feels, where he goes, what he does—to the image of God (see Philippians 2:13). The Bible calls this process of conforming *sanctification*.

But the conformity of the will is more than just the *ability* to choose good over evil. This alone might imply an indifference to both good and evil. There must also be a new and growing *disposition toward* what is good. This is accomplished at conversion as well, when God removes the heart of stone and replaces it with a heart of flesh (see Ezekiel 36:26), alive and sensitive and inclined to love God. Thus the Scripture speaks of a circumcision of the heart: "'Moreover the LORD your God will circumcise your heart and the heart of your descendants, *to love the LORD Your God*'"(Deuteronomy 30:6).

We then see a gradual change based on a change of heart, or desire. This new desire is characteristic of the new life in Christ. It is not self-generated, but it is energized by the Holy Spirit within. There is no cancellation of depravity, either instant or gradual. The Christian does not outgrow his depravity, yet he need not live by its dictates.

A classic manifestation of depravity is that, apart from the grace of God, the Christian would run headlong into every form of wickedness. Yet the grace of God enables him to desire and obey. Grace, in this sense, is the inner working of the Holy Spirit on the soul. The believer sees more clearly his own wretchedness as the Spirit reveals more of the love of God and the beauty of Christ, yet by God's grace he also longs to please God. Thus he discovers a growing desire for holiness even as he develops a growing aversion to sin (see Ezekiel 36:31).

Yet to his shame, he cannot deny that within him there is also an innate love of *sin*—a love which the Puritans referred to as sin's "pollution." Hence he learns to cast himself more on the mercies of God, to rely more heavily on the grace of God, which alone can enable him to turn from his own way and follow Christ. The process of true Christian growth is not a development in personal goodness, but a deepening awareness of one's innate "badness" (see Luke 11:13) apart from Christ, and thus of one's great need for God.

The most holy person I have ever known was Dr. Charlie Culpepper, a missionary to China for forty years where he was greatly used of God in the Shantung Revival. I knew Dr. Charlie much later, as a teacher when I was a young seminary student. Once he spoke of man's depravity. He said that it was most evident in his own life when he would get behind the wheel of a car and find himself irritated with other drivers who got in his way. We students chuckled at this minor sin, until we saw that Dr. Charlie was crying so hard he could barely speak. This was no small or frivolous matter to him!

I also remember going to his office to pray with him and watching with amazement as this frail, little man got down on his knees and cried out loud over his own great sinfulness. But his prayers were also rich with the sweet joy of Christ. Dr. Charlie took seriously God's call to holiness, but he also rejoiced in God's mercy.

The most holy person is most in touch with his own depravity and, consequently, with the great mercy and kindness of God. In a sense he has grown downward, not upward; he is humbled, not exalted.

This ongoing growth process, of which the Holy Spirit is the agent, is *sanctification* (see 2 Thessalonians 2:13; 2 Peter 1:1–2). The word *sanctification* shares its root with the word *holy*. In sanctification the believer is *progressively* set apart from the world and unto God. The lifestyle that results is one of *practical* holiness.

This is not to imply, however, that we may reach some end to the process and from that point on live in a state of perfect holiness. Rather, it shows that as we are progressively set apart by God and as we pursue the development of holiness in a practical sense in our daily lives, we are holy. Our lives more and more exemplify the spiritual virtues and moral integrity that mark the true saint of God.

The Ongoing Struggle

Absolute sinlessness will not be realized until we are at home with the Lord. Still, the goal toward which each believer must strive, toward which the Holy Spirit enlivens us, is *perfect* holiness. This humbles us because it so keenly magnifies our sin, yet it propels us forward because its embodiment is our beloved Lord Himself (see Philippians 3:10–14). Hence we see the dynamic tension that marks the life of every believer. We are depraved, yet He has called us to be like Him, and He is holy.

Those who comfort themselves with the cliché, "Oh, nobody's perfect," should recall the admonition of Christ: "'Therefore you are to be perfect, as your heavenly Father is perfect'" (Matthew 5:48). The fact that we will not reach a state of sinless perfection in our earthly lives does not exempt us from striving after it with our whole hearts. Paul told the Corinthians: "Therefore, having these promises, beloved, let us cleanse ourselves from all defilement of flesh and spirit, *perfecting holiness* in the fear of God" (2 Corinthians 7:1).

Each of us is embroiled in an intense conflict between the Holy Spirit within us and our own flesh. Paul told the Galatians: "For the flesh sets its desire against the Spirit, and the Spirit against the flesh; for these are in opposition to one another, so that you may not do the things that you please" (Galatians 5:17). J. I. Packer says of this verse: "These words alert us to the reality of tension, the necessity of effort, and the incompleteness of achievement that mark the life of holiness in this world."[4] However, Packer goes on to say: "The born-again believer who is in good spiritual health aims each day at perfect obedience, perfect righteousness, perfect pleasing of his heavenly Father."[5]

In the words of John Calvin: "He is therefore said to be like God who aspires to His likeness, however distant from it he may as yet be."[6]

DEVOTION

Before holiness can be evidenced outwardly in our lives, it must be anchored deep within. There is more to it than merely living a moral life. Moral purity is involved, but morality alone cannot denote holiness. Morality may be simply a pharisaic adherence to certain rules of conduct—an outward thing that has nothing to do with true holiness.

Holiness is more than morality; it is separation from the world, which is first an attitude of the heart. It is devotion not to a creed or to a system of rules, but to a Person, and it is wrought by the indwelling Spirit of God. As He stirs our hearts to love God, our lives become more and more an expression of the holy life and love of Christ in us (see Galatians 5:22). Where there is no love, there is no holiness.

This brings me back to the appeal I sensed from God on the night previously mentioned. It seemed that He was pressing this on my heart: *Holy living is a matter of love.* How simple this is and yet how profound! Holiness is not the highest form of legalism. Holiness is the highest expression of love.

I used to wince at the word *holy.* I felt condemned because I didn't measure up. But love obliterates condemnation. "There is therefore now no condemnation to those who are in Christ Jesus" (Romans 8:1). Love, the supreme motivation in practical holiness, echoes the great love of God, and the form that echo takes is holiness.

The Attraction of the Cross

The supreme expression of God's love to us is the cross of Jesus Christ. How sacred the scenes of Calvary; how precious the flow of love from those wounds; what suffering and sorrow our Lord endured, not only to redeem us, but *to make us holy!* As Paul wrote to the Colossians,

"And although you were formerly alienated and hostile in mind, engaged in evil deeds, yet He has now reconciled you *in His fleshly body through death,* in order to present you before Him holy and blameless and beyond reproach" (Colossians 1:21–22).

Holiness cannot be separated from love; therefore, holiness cannot be separated from the cross. Paul said, "But may it never be that I should boast, except in *the cross of our Lord Jesus Christ, through which the world has been crucified to me, and I to the world*" (Galatians 6:14). This personal crucifixion is the essence of practical holiness.

Thus the life of the true believer reveals a growing detachment from the world that begins in the heart. To those who observe it, there is a sense about that life that the heart is attached to Christ. And this attraction of the heart is pictured beautifully in Song of Solomon 8:5, in a verse that may be symbolically applied both to sanctification and to holiness: "'Who is this coming up from the wilderness, leaning on her beloved?'"

The wilderness can represent the world; the one coming up from the wilderness could be the individual believer; and the beloved, of course, represents Christ. Here we see the believer with his back to the world. He has chosen to forsake the old life and cleave to Christ. But the believer is in a process; he is still in the world and must continue in it. However, the world is having less and less sway in his life.

Indeed, as the believer grows in love for God, he becomes more and more disenchanted with the world. The tender, intimate love relationship between the believer and his Lord is what draws him away from the world and toward true holiness. Indeed, at the end of his life, if he has learned to walk in tender intimacy with Christ, his heart echoes the cry of Samuel Rutherford:

> Oh! well it is for ever,
> Oh! well for evermore,
> My nest hung in no forest
> Of all this death-doom'd shore:
> Yea, let the vain world vanish,
> As from the ship the strand,

While glory—glory dwelleth
In Immanuel's land.[7]

The Persistence of the World

A true believer has made a clear initial choice; he has decided against
self and has surrendered to the love of Christ. He is not one who professes to love God while his heart still belongs to the world. Yet,
though he has been conquered by the love of Christ, there are still
times when "the lust of the flesh and the lust of the eyes and the boastful pride of life" overtake him and cause him to stumble (see 1 John
2:15–17). He is distracted by the deceptions of Satan and the allures
of the world, and his gaze on Christ is diverted. At those times he
finds maintaining his holiness a hard task.

Why? Because, although he loves God, the love of sin and the love
of self are still very strong in him. The world still holds some attraction. Were this not so, living a holy life would be simple. Only by
daily forsaking self (see Luke 9:23) and deliberately focusing his heart
on Christ can his love for Christ overshadow his love of self.

"Apart from Christ, let nothing dazzle you," wrote St. Ignatius.[8]
Christ must so captivate our souls and fill our spirits that, in contrast,
the attractions of the world grow pale and cheap. He must become to
us more precious and dear until He is "altogether lovely" (Song of
Solomon 5:16, KJV). Then will we be constrained by the love of Christ
(see 2 Corinthians 5:14)! Then will the mere mention of His name, in
favored moments, bring a lump to the throat and weeping to the
heart! Then will we feel that holiness is not so difficult after all.

Jesus, Thy boundless love to me
No thought can reach, no tongue declare;
O knit my thankful heart to Thee,
And reign without a rival there:
Thine wholly, Thine alone I am:
Be Thou alone my constant flame.
O grant that nothing in my soul
May dwell, but Thy pure love alone....[9]

THE ULTIMATE SOURCE

In God we have holiness, the essential "otherness" that is exclusively God's. This makes God's people peculiar altogether, each one singled out and set apart from the world. Man's holiness is not just "separateness," but *being in Christ,* who Himself is infinitely separate. In this relationship, which we have described as positional holiness, we find our fundamental likeness to God.

This separateness becomes more evident as God disciplines us toward practical holiness (Hebrews 12:10) and as we pursue this holiness in the fear of the Lord (Hebrews 12:14; 2 Corinthians 7:1). These themes of God's discipline and our pursuit set the course for the rest of our study.

Love is the well from which practical holiness springs: love for God, then love for men. This love is our humble response to God's great love for us. If we truly love Him, attaining to His likeness will be our heart's desire. And like Him we *will* be, if we are holy.

CHAPTER TWO

DISCIPLINE

He disciplines us for our good,
that we may share His holiness.

HEBREWS 12:10

Only God is holy. Man has no holiness apart from what belongs to God, extended to him in Christ. However, in a practical, day-to-day behavioral sense, holiness of character and conduct must be developed. God's responsibility in this process is to discipline. As the writer of Hebrews said:

"FOR THOSE WHOM THE LORD LOVES HE DISCIPLINES, AND HE SCOURGES EVERY SON WHOM HE RECEIVES." It is for discipline that you endure; God deals with you as with sons; for what son is there whom his father does not discipline? But if you are without discipline, of which all have become partakers, then you are illegitimate children and not sons. Furthermore, we had earthly fathers to discipline us, and we respected them; shall we not much rather be subject to the Father of spirits, and live? For they disciplined us for a short time as seemed best to them, but He disciplines us for our good, that we may *share His holiness.* (Hebrews 12:6–10)

Being disciplined by a superior is never a very appealing prospect. But the discipline of God toward His children is very precious. In the midst of the experience we might wish we were otherwise engaged, but the end result is worth the pain. Indeed, Hebrews 12:11 tells us that "All discipline for the moment seems not to be joyful, but sorrowful; yet to those who have been trained by it, afterwards it yields the peaceful fruit of righteousness."

When we speak of God's discipline, we mean something very different from punishment. God does not punish the sins of His children as He punishes the sins of a reprobate. Christ bore the penalty of our sin on the cross. As Isaiah said: "He was pierced through for our transgressions, He was crushed for our iniquities; the chastening for our well-being fell upon Him, and by His scourging we are healed" (Isaiah 53:5). We who believe have been made one with Christ; in Him we find pardon and peace with God. There remains no more of the wrath of God toward us (see Isaiah 27:4; Romans 5:9).

Nevertheless, God does chasten us as a father would his children. He disciplines us not for retribution, but for correction. The motivation for *punishment* is wrath, and the purpose of punishment is retribution. The motivation for *discipline* is love, and the purpose of discipline is correction and instruction. God disciplines with a father's love. His discipline shapes and molds us, bringing us into submission to His will, conformity to His mind, and oneness with His heart. Our lives thus reflect a union with Him, the essence of which is holiness.

God's discipline also *comforts* and *confirms* us. Was there ever comfort greater than being loved by God? God's discipline assures us of that love: "FOR THOSE WHOM THE LORD LOVES HE DISCIPLINES, AND HE SCOURGES EVERY SON WHOM HE RECEIVES" (Hebrews 12:6). The discipline of God confirms that *God* is our Father and that we are His children: "God deals with you as with sons; for what son is there whom his father does not discipline? But if you are without discipline, of which all have become partakers, then you are illegitimate children and not sons" (Hebrews 12:7–8).

Most pertinent to us is the outcome of God's discipline: holiness. Again, Hebrews 12:10 says, "He disciplines us…that we may share His holiness." God loves us and wants us to partake of His very nature on a practical, day-to-day basis. His part in accomplishing this is discipline.

Now let us consider *how* God disciplines the believer, the particular instruments that He employs to mold and shape the believer in holiness.

THE DISCIPLINE OF THE SPIRIT

First are the inner workings of the Holy Spirit, those sanctifying influences that He distills deep in our souls. How precise and exacting He is as He wields "the sword of the *Spirit,* which is the *word of God*" (Ephesians 6:17). The Word of God is "sharper than any two-edged sword...and able to judge the thoughts and intentions of the heart" (Hebrews 4:12). God misses nothing, for "there is no creature hidden from His sight, but all things are open and laid bare to the eyes of Him with whom we have to do" (Hebrews 4:13).

God breaks us with conviction and draws us with intimations of love. Then He takes the Word as bread and feeds it to our hungry souls, opening to us a world of precious insights and perceptions. He walks beside us, encouraging, correcting, instructing, guiding; our Helper, Intercessor, and Paraclete (see John 14:26; 16:13). Just as Christ promised, we are not left alone, but rather we have sweet communion with Him (see John 14:16; 15:26–27; 16:7; Romans 8:26–27).

By His indwelling presence, by wooing, encouraging, and reminding, the Holy Spirit reinforces His work of renewal within us (see Titus 3:5), changing our wills little by little, bringing them into harmony with the Father's and creating both the desire and the ability to follow that will. Philippians 2:13 says, "For it is God who is at work in you, both to will and to work for His good pleasure."

Herein lies one of the fundamental differences between Christianity and all other "religions" of the world. Those other religions are attempts by man to change himself from the outside in, through various systems of dos and don'ts. Man thinks that by adhering to rules of conduct and adopting certain philosophies, he can change his own heart. But the Scriptures tell us, "'The heart is more deceitful than all else and is desperately sick; who can understand it?'" (Jeremiah 17:9). Only God knows the heart of man, for "'God sees not as man sees, for man looks at the outward appearance, but the LORD looks at the heart'" (1 Samuel 16:7).

Man cannot change the inside no matter how much he may clean up the outside. That's why the Lord likened the scribes and Pharisees to "'whitewashed tombs which on the outside appear beautiful, but inside they are full of dead men's bones and all uncleanness'" (Matthew 23:27).

Jesus added, "'The mouth speaks out of that which fills the heart'" (Matthew 12:34). Indeed, from the heart flow the issues of life (see Proverbs 4:23). As the old saying goes, "What's down in the well comes up in the bucket." Whatever possesses the heart will be evidenced in what we say and how we live.

God does not ask us to change ourselves from the outside in; He changes us from the inside out. The Holy Spirit moves in and gives us a new heart (see Ezekiel 11:19). He replaces our cold, stony hearts with hearts that are tender, supple, and responsive; hearts that have been broken over the love of God (see Acts 2:37); hearts that desire to know God and to please Him. Then, deep within, He begins His transforming work, which can be seen progressively in how we live.[1]

RIGHTEOUSNESS

The practical manifestation of holiness is righteousness. Righteousness is a love for and a daily keeping of God's law, specifically the moral law represented in the Ten Commandments. It was summed up by Christ in these words: "'YOU SHALL LOVE THE LORD YOUR GOD WITH ALL YOUR HEART, AND WITH ALL YOUR SOUL, AND WITH ALL YOUR MIND.' This is the great and foremost commandment. The second is like it, 'YOU SHALL LOVE YOUR NEIGHBOR AS YOURSELF'" (Matthew 22:37–39). When we live by these two commandments, we keep the ten.

One may protest that we have been set free from the law, and indeed we are free from the responsibility to keep it as a *system of works* by which we attain to the *perfect righteousness* that God requires for salvation (see Romans 9:30–10:4). Further, if we are in Christ Jesus, we are free from the *condemnation* of the law (see 2 Corinthians 3:9), which we would otherwise incur from our inability to keep the law perfectly. We are free from the *curse* of the law, since Christ redeemed us from that curse by becoming a curse for us (see Galatians 3:13; 5:1; Romans 7:6). Thus we are now free to *keep* the law (see Galatians 5:13) as a response to God's love and as a rule of life.[2]

What is freedom? Is it irresponsibility and lawlessness? No. Such things lead to anarchy; true freedom comes only with obedience to the law. The lost man is not free; he is a slave to sin. And sin, according to John, is *lawlessness* or *unrighteousness* (see 1 John 3:4; 5:17). The Christian exchanges that slavery to sin for a slavery to righteousness; he keeps the law from a heart of love. Thus it is his *heart* which is enslaved, and in that he finds true freedom (see Romans 6:14–19).

One may further protest, "But I thought we were under *grace* and not bound to keep the law. Isn't that what Paul said in Romans 6:14?" We are indeed under grace, but does grace give us a license to sin, to be *lawless?* "May it never be!" said Paul a few verses earlier, "How shall we who died to sin still live in it?" (Romans 6:2).

If we can go on in a lifestyle of sin, we are not under grace; we are under a *delusion.* Grace delivers us from the curse of the law, but His love also *inspires* and *enables* us to keep the law as well—not as a means of salvation, but as a rule of life (see Romans 3:20; 10:1; Galatians 2:16; 3:11, 21; Acts 13:39; Hebrews 7:19; 10:1, 4, 11–14).

The Holy Spirit is the one who accomplishes this work of grace in our lives. This is evidenced in Galatians 5, where we first see a contrast between keeping the law as a means of justification (thus making ourselves righteous) and trusting in God for His righteousness *through the enabling of the indwelling Holy Spirit* (see Galatians 5:4–5). This is *imputed* righteousness, credited to our account through faith in Jesus Christ.

But the Holy Spirit, while enabling us to trust God for a righteous standing before Him, also disseminates within our hearts the grace of God, enabling us to keep the moral law of love. This is real-life *imparted* righteousness. Thus we see that grace is the instrument in the hands of the Holy Spirit by which He inspires (and enables) righteous living.

Further, Galatians 5:16 tells us that if we walk by the Spirit, in submission to His leadership, we will not carry out the desires of the flesh listed in Galatians 5:19–21. We will be enabled to keep the law *by the Spirit,* in spite of the enmity between our flesh and the Holy Spirit (Galatians 5:17). Thus if we are being led by the Spirit of God, we are no longer under the law as a means to eradicate the deeds of the flesh (see Galatians 5:18), but these deeds are being subverted by the fruit of the Spirit (Galatians 5:22–24; see also Romans 8:2–13).

The Holy Spirit's indwelling, and the righteous lifestyle which ensues from it, set the Christian apart from the world. This separation is practical holiness.

SPIRITUAL PERCEPTION

Now we must consider spiritual perception in contrast to intellectual comprehension. As in conversion, where there must be an opening of the spiritual eyes to truly see the gospel, so in the Christian walk there must be spiritual wisdom and discernment if we would truly know and please God (see Colossians 1:9–10).

When Christ says that He and the Father will come and abide with the believer and that He will disclose Himself to the believer, He is speaking of the indwelling ministry of the Holy Spirit, whereby the Spirit enables the believer to perceive God the Father and God the Son in a *spiritual* sense (see John 14:21–23). Thus the believer experiences God only through direct, spiritual perceptions.

These perceptions are always grounded in a correct understanding of God's Word; nevertheless, they are personal, vital, and actual. These perceptions are the very substance of eternal life as Christ defined it: "'This is eternal life, that they may *know Thee,* the only true God, and Jesus Christ whom Thou hast sent'" (John 17:3). Here, the word *know* means experiential, relational knowledge rather than head knowledge. The believer cannot experience the Father or the Son through his five senses, but he can experience them through perceptions communicated by the Holy Spirit. And he can experience these spiritual perceptions only because he has been made alive spiritually through the indwelling of the Holy Spirit. By this means the Holy Spirit knits our hearts to the Father and the Son, making our consciences tender and our wills submissive. He thus develops in us that holiness of heart without which no one will see the Lord (see Appendix A).

THE EXALTATION OF CHRIST

Paramount in the Spirit's sanctifying work is His exaltation of Christ in our eyes. "'He shall glorify Me,'" said Christ (John 16:14). The Holy Spirit takes every opportunity to point us to Christ, giving us insight into every aspect of Christ's glory, for His supreme New Covenant role is, as J. I. Packer says:

> To fulfill what we may call a floodlight ministry in relation to the Lord Jesus Christ.... It is as if the Spirit stands behind us, throwing light over our shoulder, on Jesus, who stands facing us. The Spirit's message to us is never, "Look at me; listen to me; come to me; get to know me," but always, "Look at Him and see His glory; listen to Him and hear His word; go to Him and have life; get to know Him and taste His gift of joy and peace."[3]

We can never have a high enough view of Christ, though we spend our whole lives in pursuit of a more lofty view. It is the Holy Spirit who aids us in this pursuit.

On a practical note, as we focus on Christ, having a heart to know and please Him, the Holy Spirit produces in us the fruits of the Spirit—love, joy, peace, patience, kindness, goodness, faithfulness, gentleness, and self-control (see Galatians 5:22–23), which Dr. Stephen F. Olford has called a "nine-dimensional configuration of the life of Christ."[4] Through the fruits of the Spirit, the Holy Spirit manifests in and through us the very life of Jesus Christ (see 2 Corinthians 4:10–11).

THE DISCIPLINE OF TRIALS

Another way to share in God's holiness is through the discipline of trials. God uses adversity to get our attention, to force us to consider what is really important, and to call us to a more separated life.

CONSEQUENCES OF SIN

Some of the difficulties we face in life result directly from personal sin. God does not punish His children as a vengeful dictator, but disciplines them as a loving father. One way He accomplishes this is through the discipline of consequences. Though He forgives, He does not remove the consequences of our sin. "Whatever a man sows, this he will also reap" (Galatians 6:7).

Some sins, of course, carry graver consequences than others, but even those which we consider insignificant are sins against God's holiness. With every sin comes the saddest of all consequences: the tragedy of *what might have been had we obeyed God.*

Some of the adversities that we endure are also direct or indirect consequences of someone else's sin. For instance, alcoholics often suffer certain consequences. But they are not alone; everyone around them suffers as well, especially any children they might have. Yet ours is a redemptive God who works to accomplish His sovereign purposes even through the sins of others. Such was the case with Joseph, who told his brothers (who had sold him into slavery): "'You meant evil against me, but God meant it for good...to preserve many people alive'" (Genesis 50:20).

Paul goes even further, saying that "God causes *all things* to work together for good to those who love God, to those who are called according to His purpose" (Romans 8:28). Whatever evil man has done to us, whether directly or indirectly, God is able to bring good out of it.

God is moving each of us toward a divine purpose, and He even uses wrong choices (willful or otherwise), failures, and defeats to bring that purpose about. God's master plan is to conform us to the image of Christ (see Romans 8:29), and the foremost facet of that image is holiness. It is a testimony to God's grace that He even uses the sins that we have committed, as well as the sins that others have committed against us, to humble us and draw us to a more separated life.

We are never closer to God than in repentance. There, in humility and shame, we partake of the matchless grace of God, and the result is a deeper intimacy with Him and a greater sensitivity to His desires (see Psalm 32). Suffering the consequences of another person's sin can also draw us closer to God (see Psalm 123) and provide an opportunity for us to grow in holiness.

When first wronged, we may have what Larry Crabb calls a demanding spirit toward the one who sinned against us, and we may feel quite justified in that spirit.[5] However, if we will look closely, we will see that behind a demanding spirit toward another *person* lies a demanding spirit toward *God:* "God, how could you let that person so abuse me?" Our false assumption is that we deserve something better. We do not see the absolute wretchedness of our own hearts before a holy God, so we exclaim, "God is not being fair!" But if God were completely fair with us, we would all spend eternity in hell, which is what we really deserve. Any sin that another commits against us has been exceeded by our own sins against God. Thankfully, God deals with us not with fairness, as men deal with men, but with mercy.

In Christ, the thing that we least deserve is that which we have been most freely given: forgiveness. How then do we dare not forgive those who have wronged us? The person who has sinned against us is no worse a sinner than we. Therefore, we must forgive.

This is not to deny or minimize the hurt caused by another's sin, nor is it to excuse that sin. The sin was wrong. Being wronged causes bewilderment and sorrow, especially when the one who hurt us is someone we love. Our natural instinct is to question *their* love for us. But the ultimate question for the Christian is, "Do I truly love them with a self-forgetful, God-kind of love—that 1 Corinthians 13 kind of love that is patient and kind and bears all things?"

Our love must be *magnanimous*—big-hearted, lion-hearted—like the love of Jesus Christ. We must rise deliberately above resentment, bitterness, and pettiness. This is the kind of love that led Jesus to the cross. If we love with this kind of love, remembering all that we have been forgiven, we will forgive others.

Thus a Christian is made distinct from the world. He is set free from hatred and vindictiveness and encouraged to exercise the holiness that is already his in Christ:

And so, as those who have been chosen of God, *holy* and beloved, put on a heart of compassion, kindness, humility, gentleness and patience; bearing with one another, and forgiving each other, whoever has a complaint against anyone; just as the Lord forgave you, so also should you. And beyond all these things *put on love,* which is the perfect bond of unity. (Colossians 3:12–14; see also Ephesians 4:32)

TESTING OF FAITH

Other adversities come purely for the testing of our faith and have nothing to do with the consequences of sin. Christians often think that their circumstances are subject either to chance or to the whims of the devil. Not so. Satan only does what he is allowed to do. Both he and our circumstances are subject to God.

After losing all of his earthly possessions, along with his children, Job did not say, "The Lord gave and the devil has taken away." Job said, "'The LORD gave and *the LORD* has taken away. Blessed be the name of the LORD'" (Job 1:21).

There is no such thing as chance. Every circumstance of life, whether good or bad, has been purposefully allowed by God. When adverse circumstances come we must remember that our God is bigger than those circumstances, and they are completely under His control. We sometimes say things like, "I'm doing fine, under the circumstances." The question is, why are we *under* the circumstances? God is above them and they are subject to Him. Therefore, we must be above them as well, no matter how difficult they might be.

James admonishes us with these words: "Consider it all joy, my brethren, when you encounter various trials, knowing that the testing of your faith produces endurance. And let endurance have its perfect result, that you may be perfect and complete, lacking in nothing" (James 1:2–4). *All Joy!* In addition to the difficulties of everyday life, those "little foxes, that spoil the vines" (Song of Solomon 2:15, KJV), these verses apply to the most devastating adversities, the most heart-wrenching hurts, the most disappointing losses. But the truth of God stands. We can rejoice, come what may; God and His Word are true.

At the same time, we cannot be ecstatic amid the horror of a crushing grief. But we can know the sustaining power of God's presence: "In Thy presence is fullness of joy" (Psalm 16:11). We can know the peace that passes all understanding (see John 14:27; Philippians 4:7). And we can rejoice *in Him* even in great sorrow, because joy is in the Lord, regardless of circumstances (see Philippians 4:4).

We also can rejoice that God's ultimate purpose is to test and prove our faith. Every trial is a test; as Amy Carmichael said, "Every test is a trust."[6] Whatever storm we may be in, we may rest assured that God has entrusted that storm to us for His good purposes. He is shaping, molding, and developing us into people of faith, which sets us apart from the rest of the world.

Trials test our faith in two fundamental truths about God: His *sovereignty* and His *goodness*. God wants us to know these truths by experience.

Sovereignty

Some trials specifically test our faith in God's sovereignty, which often is seen as a cold doctrine rather than the great source of comfort it actually is. To say that God is sovereign is to say that He is in absolute control of everything. And this is a great comfort if we know how truly good He is.

But some see His sovereignty as a contradiction to His goodness. "God is too good to allow evil; therefore, evil must be beyond His control." We would never say that God is the source of evil, in the sense that evil is inherent in God's nature; God is holy. But we must say that evil is under God's authority (see Lamentations 3:37–38; Amos 3:6; Job 2:10).

Lamentations 3:38 says, "Is it not from the mouth of the Most High that both good and ill go forth?" The word *ill* means calamity, which God initiates for His own purposes. Natural disasters and social catastrophes are not merely due to the law of cause and effect. God Himself put that law into motion, and He can and does overrule it whenever He chooses (see Isaiah 45:7; Amos 4:7).

God allows evil in those "spiritual forces of wickedness" that we war against (see Ephesians 6:12) and in the hearts of men (see Romans 7:21). He allows evil, at least within the confines of time, as a contrast to His holiness, and He does this for His own purposes. To say otherwise is to reduce God to something less than God.

Is this, then, a contradiction to His goodness? No. It testifies that God's purposes are often inscrutable to man. God by His very nature is harmonious within Himself and not full of contradiction.

But where did evil actually come from? This is one of the deep mysteries, hidden in God, for which we simply have no adequate answer. However, we can know that there is an answer, *because* God is sovereign (see Isaiah 45:9–10; Jeremiah 18:1–6).

Since God is sovereign, does He not have the power to prevent evil? No doubt God *does* prevent or disallow many evils and many adversities, and every tragedy provides evidence of His grace. But God has purposes beyond our immediate happiness. God wants us to trust *Him* in the face of adversity, to say with Job, "Though he slay me, yet will I trust in him" (Job 13:15, KJV).

Goodness

Some trials test our faith specifically in regard to God's *goodness*. In the throes of a devastating grief, as with a friend whose wife has just been told she has thirteen tumors, one might say, "I have no problem believing that God is sovereign, but deep in my soul I'm finding it hard to believe that He *is* good. Why would He allow this to happen?" Thus the trial becomes a test of faith in God's goodness.

In such a case, although he may never know all of God's purposes, the believer must determine to believe, in the face of every seeming contradiction, that God does indeed have a purpose and that all of His purposes are good and are born out of a heart of love.

Julian of Norwich said with profound simplicity, "All shall be well, and all shall be well, and all manner [of] thing shall be well."[7] Faith rests in the peace of knowing that God does all things well. He is worthy of our trust. In the words of Habakkuk:

> Though the fig tree should not blossom, and there be no fruit on the vines, though the yield of the olive should fail, and the fields produce no food, though the flock should be cut off from the fold, and there be no cattle in the stalls, yet I will exult in the LORD, I will rejoice in the God of my salvation. The LORD GOD is my strength, and He has made my feet like hinds' feet, and makes me walk on my high places. (Habakkuk 3:17–19)

God is good, though the very storm we are in may scream to the contrary. Here is where faith comes in; by faith we can know that nothing touches our lives that is not filtered through His fingers of love. Thus only a Christian *can* say, no matter what his trial, "This is my Father saying to me, 'I love you.'"

> This hath He done and shall we not adore Him?
> This shall He do and can we still despair?
> Come let us quickly fling ourselves before Him,
> Cast at His feet the burthen of our care...[8]

The sovereignty and goodness of God go hand in hand and can never be separated. They do not contradict, but complement one another. The sovereignty of God gives evidence of the goodness of God.

What comfort is there in believing that we are left to chance or the wiles of the devil? But there is great comfort in knowing that God is in charge of whatever trial may touch us and that there is a purpose toward us that is good.

The fourth verse of the great old hymn "How Firm a Foundation" speaks to these purposes beautifully:

> When through fiery trials thy pathway shall lie,
> My grace all sufficient shall be thy supply.
> The flame shall not hurt thee. I only design
> Thy dross to consume and thy gold to refine.[9]

God is not indifferent to our needs and our hurts. He loves us with an infinitely compassionate love. We can never go through any hurt that He has not felt, and when we suffer, He suffers right along with us. If we ever doubt this, we need only look at the Cross to restore our faith.

Amy Carmichael, in describing the life of a saintly friend who has suddenly been turned upside down by adversity, says:

> You see the life reel under shattering blows; perhaps you see it broken. And you look almost in fear. Thus suddenly discovered, what will appear? And no base metal shows, not even the lesser silver, but only veins and veins of gold. That gold is Christ.[10]

How different this perspective is from that of someone who does not know Christ! How different God's holy people are from those of this world! God uses the trials of this life to test our mettle and thus to establish us as holy.

THE PRIVILEGE OF SUFFERING

Sometimes a Christian is given the great privilege of suffering *for Christ's sake*. In our society we see very little of this because Christians are so much like the world. But when Christians pursue a life of real holiness, the world reacts with hatred (see John 15:18–21). Jesus called this a *blessing*:

> "Blessed are those who have been persecuted for the sake of righteousness, for theirs is the kingdom of heaven. Blessed are you when men cast insults at you, and persecute you, and say all kinds of evil against you falsely, on account of Me. Rejoice, and be glad, for your reward in heaven is great, for so they persecuted the prophets who were before you." (Matthew 5:10–12)

The apostle Peter said:

> Beloved, do not be surprised at the fiery ordeal among you, which comes upon you for your testing, as though some strange thing were happening to you; but to the degree that you share the sufferings of Christ, keep on rejoicing; so that also at the revelation of His glory, you may rejoice with exultation. (1 Peter 4:12–13)

Suffering for Christ's sake is a gift. Paul encouraged the Philippians with this truth: "For to you it has been *granted* for Christ's sake, not only to believe in Him, but also to suffer for His sake" (Philippians 1:29). This is not suffering for an ideal or for a cause, but for the God we love.

Suffering for Christ's sake gives us a unique opportunity to identify with Him. Jesus told His disciples,

"If the world hates you, you know that it has hated Me before it hated you. If you were of the world, the world would love its own; but because you are not of the world, but I chose you out of the world, therefore the world hates you." (John 15:18–19)

First Peter 4:1–2 says,

Therefore, since Christ has suffered in the flesh, arm yourselves also with the same purpose, because he who has suffered in the flesh has ceased from sin, so as to live the rest of the time in the flesh no longer for the lusts of men, but for the will of God.

Suffering gives us an eternal perspective, teaching us what is really important and weaning us away from the things of this world.

Suffering tests our allegiance to and love for God. More than any other aspect of suffering, this sets us apart unto Him. Such proof is not for God, but for us. Have we fallen in love with the good pleasure of God, no matter what that pleasure may be, just because it is *His* pleasure?

Hear an interpretation of His own quiet urging in this regard:

O thou beloved child of My desire,
Whether I lead thee through green valleys,
By still waters,
Or through fire,
Or lay thee down in silence under snows,
Through any weather, or whatever
Clouds may gather,
Winds may blow—
Wilt love Me? trust Me? praise Me?[11]

Finally, it is of great comfort to remember, that however much suffering we may go through, it is only temporary. In 1 Peter 1:6–7, we read:

Now for a little while, if necessary, you have been distressed by various trials, that the proof of your faith, being more precious than gold which is perishable, even though tested by fire, may be found to result in praise and glory and honor at the revelation of Jesus Christ.

And 1 Peter 5:10 says: "And after you have suffered for a little while, the God of all grace, who called you to His eternal glory in Christ, will Himself perfect, confirm, strengthen and establish you."

We must see all of life's difficulties as part of the discipline of God to make us holy. While imprisoned for his Christian convictions, Samuel Rutherford wrote: "Why should I start at the plough of my Lord, that maketh deep furrows on my soul? He purposeth a crop."[12]

God purposes a crop in our lives as well. What is that crop? According to James 1:4, it is "that [we] may be perfect and complete, lacking in nothing." According to Romans 8:29, He desires that we be "conformed to the image of His Son." According to 1 Peter 1:7, His goal is "that the proof of [our] faith...even though tested by fire, may be found to result in praise and glory and honor at the revelation of Jesus Christ." According to Hebrews 12:10, God's will is "that we may share His holiness."

THE DISCIPLINE OF GRACE

God uses what might at first seem an unlikely agent in disciplining us toward holiness: *grace*. Let us consider closely a short passage in Titus where grace is spoken of as a means of discipline, showing how it can be so potent a tool in the hand of the Holy Spirit:

For the grace of God has appeared, bringing salvation to all men, *instructing* us to deny ungodliness and worldly desires and to live sensibly, righteously and godly in the present age, looking for the blessed hope and the appearing of the glory of our great God and Savior, Christ Jesus; who gave Himself for us, that He might redeem us from every lawless deed and purify for Himself a people for His own possession, zealous for good deeds. (Titus 2:11–14)

The Greek word translated as *instructing* may also be translated as *disciplining*. God is so gloriously unpredictable. As with repentance, where kindness rather than wrath leads the way (see Romans 2:4), grace rather than coercion leads us to righteousness. But how does grace in the hands of the Spirit inspire or enable us to obey? The answer lies in a clear understanding of the word itself.

GRACE DEFINED

Grace is a multifaceted word, rich in meaning and hard to represent in a simple definition. The acrostic <u>G</u>od's <u>R</u>iches <u>A</u>t <u>C</u>hrist's <u>E</u>xpense expresses a wonderful truth but speaks more of atonement than grace. God's grace toward man invokes the broadest sense of "goodwill, loving-kindness, favor."[13]

More specifically, grace is the kindness of God toward the undeserving, *the unmerited favor of God.* However, man is not only not deserving of God's favor but very much *deserving* of the opposite. Our offense toward God was of infinite proportions, and the favor He has shown us required the very life of His own dear Son. Considering this great cost, *favor* seems to be a rather sterile word. Better to speak of an earnest, thoroughly selfless, sacrificial love, lavished on its objects; objects not only unmeritorious but contrary by nature to the holiness of God. Indeed, Paul refers to us as *enemies* of God before His grace found us (see Romans 5:10). So grace speaks not only of love but of the object of that love. Grace is God's love poured out on hell-deserving sinners.

One of my professors in seminary, Dr. Reginald Barnard, compared grace to Niagara Falls. Approaching the site for the first time, he saw a mist rising in the air. As he rounded a corner he saw the breathtaking falls, those magnificent torrents of water plunging down the cliffs and pounding on the rocks below, shooting huge sprays of foam into the air. Then he knew what had caused the mist he had seen at first.

The grace of God, Dr. Barnard said, is the undeserved, unearned, priceless love of God that plunges down into our rocky hearts and softens and breaks them, causing a response of love to rise like the mist from Niagara Falls. But how small is that response of love compared to the great rush of love poured out by God on guilty sinners? To a far greater extent, grace is *God* loving *me!*

Why would God love *me,* the *sinner?* There is certainly nothing in me to commend me, and no higher power that dictates to Him that He must love. He simply chose to love me, and in that choosing has lavished on me His infinite kindness. This is grace (see Ephesians 2:4–7). This is the good pleasure of God.

GRACE DEMONSTRATED

Now we will consider three great *appearances* of Christ in which the grace of God is demonstrated. First, let's go back to our passage in Titus 2:11, where it says that "the grace of God has appeared, bringing salvation to all men."

A Past Appearing

What a wonderful way to describe the coming of Christ into the world: *The grace of God has appeared!* In this first appearance of Christ, the grace of God brought salvation to all men. This is amplified in Hebrews 9:11–12:

> But when Christ *appeared* as a high priest of the good things to come, He entered through the greater and more perfect tabernacle, not made with hands, that is to say, not of this creation; and not through the blood of goats and calves, but through His own blood, He entered the holy place once for all, having obtained eternal redemption.

This is *the* demonstration of God's grace. The Cross, which is the ultimate expression of God's love, is the floodgate that opened to release the free grace of God, allowing His love to flood into our hearts for salvation. "For by grace you have been saved through faith; and that not of yourselves, it is the gift of God" (Ephesians 2:8).

Grace can also be pictured as a *river* which flows from the cross and leads to several different destinations. One of those destinations is *salvation.* Another destination is *blessing.* In fact, each blessing of life is a different destination along the river of grace. We deserve nothing, and yet He "daily loadeth us with benefits" (Psalm 68:19, KJV).

Another destination that can be reached only by way of the river of grace is *righteous obedience,* which speaks of a life set apart. Often we try to reach this port through the backwaters of self-will and determination, but we get bogged down and never make it. Only the river of grace can carry us to obedience. That river swells and lifts us above our self-focus. When we are gripped with the truth that God has demonstrated His love for us through the appearing of Christ, we are overwhelmed with gratitude and swept into the safe harbor of obedience. Thus we are motivated, as Titus 2:12 says, to "live sensibly, righteously and godly in the present age."

Titus 2:14 says that Christ "gave Himself for us, that He might redeem us from every lawless deed and *purify for Himself a people* for His own possession, zealous for good deeds." Here is the discipline of God toward holiness. God's grace constrains us because it elicits from us a response that blossoms into holiness of life (see 1 John 4:19). Thus grace is a tool in the hand of the Holy Spirit for our sanctification.

And God is not only gracious, but merciful. These two cannot be separated. We are all sinners. Sometimes we disobey deliberately; at other times we disobey in ignorance, though ignorance is no excuse. But when we are brought to see the destructive nature of our sin and the grave seriousness of our offense toward a holy God, we are filled with fear and remorse. At those times we are made most aware of how utterly we are cast on the grace and mercy of God (see Romans 5:20). Through that influence, our remorse is turned into the godly sorrow that leads to repentance (see 2 Corinthians 7:9–11). Thus says a Puritan of years ago, "The free sovereign mercy of God, when it is apprehended by the sinner, is the true principle of holiness in the heart and life."

Mercy and grace are opposite sides of the same coin. Grace is receiving what we don't deserve; mercy is not receiving what we do deserve. We deserve condemnation and wrath; we deserve hell. But instead we are given forgiveness, reconciliation, and eternal life. In God's grace He has been merciful to us ("In my favour have I had mercy on thee." Isaiah 60:10, KJV), and in mercy He has shown us His grace. "But God, being rich in mercy, because of His great love with which He loved us, even when we were dead in our transgressions, made us alive together with Christ [by grace you have been saved]" (Ephesians 2:4–5; see also Luke 1:78–79).

In 1 John 2:2, Christ is said to be the propitiation for our sins. God sees Christ's sacrifice and says, "That is enough." In the Greek translation of the Old Testament, the Greek word for *propitiation* was used to translate the Hebrew word for *mercy seat*. This adds such richness to our understanding of the Atonement. Christ is *Himself* our mercy seat. Only in Him do we find pardon and peace with God.

Just as we need daily grace, so we need daily mercy. What would become of us if God's mercies were not new every morning (see Lamentations 3:22–23), if we could not find refuge at the mercy seat?

> From every stormy wind that blows,
> From every swelling tide of woes,
> There is a calm, a sure retreat;
> 'Tis found beneath the mercy seat.
> There is a place where Jesus sheds
> The oil of gladness on our heads,
> A place than all beside more sweet;
> It is the blood-bought mercy seat.
> Ah! there on eagle wings we soar,
> And sin and sense molest no more,
> And heav'n comes down our souls to greet,
> While glory crowns the mercy seat.[14]

This we have from God's storehouse of grace, and this is what encourages us to live holy lives. For *Christ appeared* that He might "purify for Himself a people for His own possession, zealous for good deeds" (Titus 2:14).

A Promised Appearing

Titus 2 also speaks of a *future* appearing: "Looking for the blessed hope and the *appearing* of the glory of our great God and Savior, Christ Jesus" (verse 13). Here we see that grace disciplines us to live in the joyful anticipation of a *promised* appearing of Christ. Thus we find a further motivation to "live sensibly, righteously, and godly in the present age," as we look with eagerness and sobriety toward the imminent return of our Lord.

Again in Hebrews 9:28 we read of this promised appearing: "So Christ also, having been offered once to bear the sins of many, shall appear a second time for salvation without reference to sin, to those who eagerly await Him."

First John 3:2–3 sweetly emphasizes how this promised appearing motivates us to holy living: "Beloved, now we are children of God, and it has not appeared as yet what we shall be. We know that, when He *appears,* we shall be like Him, because we shall see Him just as He is. And everyone who has this hope fixed on Him *purifies himself, just as He is pure."* What hope? The blessed hope of the future appearing of Christ (see Acts 1:11; John 14:1–3).

First Peter 1:13 says, "Fix your hope completely on the grace to be brought to you at the revelation of Jesus Christ." So we see that the great hope of this second appearing adds another dimension to God's disciplining us toward holiness. How wonderful! "And now, little children, abide in Him, so that when He *appears,* we may have confidence and not shrink away from *Him* in shame at His coming" (1 John 2:28).

Therefore, "in the present age" we live under a canopy of grace between these two great appearings of Christ: His past appearing in humility for salvation and His future appearing in glory for salvation.

A Present Appearing

But there is yet another appearing of Christ. Hebrews 9 speaks of the *present* appearing of Christ before the Father: "For Christ did not enter a holy place made with hands, a mere copy of the true one, but into heaven itself, *now* to *appear* in the presence of God *for us"* (Hebrews 9:24).

Jesus is our representative before the Father (see 1 John 2:1), our Advocate, pleading our case before God. His blood is our sure defense. Hebrews 7:25 says that He "always lives to make intercession" for us (see also Romans 8:34). How precious is this truth! Christ is continuously appearing before the Father on our behalf, pleading His own blood for God's mercy.

We have indeed, as Peter exclaims, been granted "everything pertaining to life and godliness" (2 Peter 1:3). God has abundantly supplied every necessity and every discipline for our holiness. Shall we not rise to the challenge and do our part?

Through trials, God develops faith and trust; through grace, He develops love. The more we trust God, the more we distrust the world. The more we love God, the more we abhor sin and loathe our own selfishness. Thus the more we walk with God in this intimacy of faith and love, the more holy we become in both heart and life.

CHAPTER THREE

STRIVING

*Pursue…the sanctification without
which no one will see the Lord.*

HEBREWS 12:14

While God has the major part in the development of practical holiness in our lives, we have a part as well. As we saw in Hebrews 12:10, God disciplines us that we might share in His holiness. But, according to verse 14 of that same chapter, we must *pursue* holiness, without which none will see the Lord. This does not mean that we must pay the price of holy living, as though practical holiness earns for us salvation, nor that we must reach a state of *perfect* practical holiness before seeing the Lord.

But it does mean that if there is not at least some striving after holiness, however weak that striving may at times be, we have no claim to positional holiness. We are not in Christ, and we will not see God. Only those who have been made holy in Christ pursue holiness, and only those who pursue holiness will see the Lord.

However, this striving must be generated from the right power source. Unless a new believer is carefully taught and guided after conversion, he will embark upon a journey of self-will and determination to live the Christian life, a journey which will only lead to disillusionment and disappointment. He will live in frustration until he learns that "the flesh profiteth nothing" and that only by walking in the Spirit of God can he hope to avoid fulfilling the desires of the flesh (John 6:63, KJV; see also Galatians 5:16).

Paul said to the Galatians: "Are you so foolish? Having begun by the Spirit, are you now being perfected by the flesh?" (Galatians 3:3). We were not saved by any effort of our own, but by the grace of God. By that grace we were made alive through the quickening power of the Holy Spirit (see Titus 3:5; Ephesians 2:4–5). And it is by His power that we must *walk* as well (see Galatians 5:25).

We cannot conquer our obstinate will with willpower. We must tap into a higher power, the very power that raised Jesus from the dead (see Philippians 3:10), if we would be resurrected out of the quagmire of constant defeat and live holy lives before God.

A PROPER STRIVING

In Psalm 46:10, God gives this command: "'Cease striving and know that I am God.'" To comprehend this intellectually is not difficult. God is God; I am not. But to know how to appropriate this verse for day-to-day Christian living is another matter. First, we must lose confidence in our own efforts, and second, we must believe that God is able where we are not. God *is* "able to do exceeding abundantly beyond all that we ask or think" (Ephesians 3:20).

However, we are an independent lot. It pricks pride to admit that we need God, though we are more needy than we can begin to know. In Matthew 5:3, Christ said: "'Blessed are the poor in spirit, for theirs is the kingdom of heaven.'" In other words, blessed are those who recognize their spiritual poverty, their spiritual neediness, for they will be ruled by God.

We must relinquish control of every aspect of our lives to God. But we will not do so until we come to the end of our self-effort and admit our need for Him. We must not strive in our own strength, depending on our own abilities. We must "cease striving" in this way and put all our confidence in God (see Proverbs 3:26). Yet we cannot sit back and expect God to animate us with His holiness. A striving is required of us, a striving not according to the flesh (self-reliance), but according to the *strength* and *grace* of God.

Paul, speaking of his own strength for ministry, said, "I labor, striving according to His power, which mightily works within me" (Colossians 1:29). This can be applied to every other aspect of holy living as well. The key is *"I labor, striving,"* which is active, not passive; yet "according to *His power,* which mightily works within" (see 2 Corinthians 4:7). What is that power? Paul told the Corinthians: "But by the *grace* of God I am what I am, and His *grace* toward me did not prove vain; but *I labored* even more than all of them, yet not I, but the *grace of God within me"* (1 Corinthians 15:10). Grace is the enabling power of God. Grace undergirds our striving when we rely on God alone.

Martin Luther stressed his awareness that our striving must not be rooted in our own strength or ability with these simple words: "Did we in our own strength confide, / Our striving would be losing."[1]

We must strive after holiness of life, but we must remember on whose strength we rely. We must be careful that our striving proceeds with absolute dependence on God. It is His grace that enables us, not our cunning, cleverness, or personal fortitude.

PRIDE: THE NEGATIVE STRIVING

To strive in the efforts of the flesh is pride. Pride begets pride and puts us in a downward plunge. When temptation comes we resist in the flesh ("I can handle it"), and we either succeed for a time (which puffs us up) or we fail miserably and are crushed by disappointment. We then determine to be stronger the next time, which only sets us up for the next fall. God's Word warns us that "Pride goes before destruction" (Proverbs 16:18) and counsels, "Let him who thinks he stands take heed lest he fall" (1 Corinthians 10:12).

HUMILITY: THE POSITIVE STRIVING

How can we get out of this destructive cycle and begin to live holy lives? Only by humble surrender to God. Until we are humble and truly see our need for Him, we will not surrender, and our striving will reflect our own strength.

The problem is *pride,* the spirit of self-importance and self-sufficiency. James 4:6 and 1 Peter 5:5 tell us that "God is opposed to the proud, but gives grace to the humble." Conversely, humility unlocks and opens the channels in our lives through which grace may flow. Humility, in this case, may be simply described as saying to God, "I need You." Only as we see and acknowledge our need for Him does He give the grace we need to obey.

The clearest illustration of this is in salvation. Ephesians 2:8 tells us that we are saved by grace. But if grace is undeserved, why isn't everyone saved? At least part of the answer is found in 1 Peter 5:5. As long as any man says in his heart, "I can save myself; I don't need God," he cannot be saved because God holds him at arm's length. But when a man is convicted by the Spirit to see God's grace for what it really is, he is humbled in the dust and admits his desperate need. Then God freely gives grace for salvation.

This is paralleled in every act of obedience in the Christian life. If grace does not seem to be flowing in our lives, there must be some element of pride damming up the river. We must ask God to reveal the source of that pride and confess it as sin. Then we must claim the promise that God gives grace to the humble. Grace does not remove temptation, but it does enable the humble to withstand it.

Humility quietly demolishes the dams of pride in our lives, so the river of grace may freely flow. But we need not wait for God to dynamite these obstacles. We can and must accomplish this task ourselves, through humility. If we humble ourselves by simply admitting our need for God, He will respond with an abundance of grace (see James 4:10).

Yet if we refuse to humble ourselves, God will humble us. The grace of God is like a river that flows and never really stops. You can dam it up for a while, but it will cut another path or destroy the dams you've built, because it cannot be resisted for long. Though God resists the proud, He Himself will eventually knock down those walls of pride with His grace, because He is moving us toward the greatest destination of all: *conformity to His holy Son Jesus*. He will not cease until His goal is accomplished (see Romans 8:29, Philippians 1:6). Therefore, it is only wise for us to check often for any element of pride that may be blocking the flow of grace in our lives and quickly confess it to God. It is much less painful to humble ourselves than to be humbled by God.

Biblical Illustrations

Proper striving is pictured in a number of different ways in Scripture. We have referred to Philippians 2:13: "For it is God who is at work in you, both to will and to work for *His* good pleasure"; but we have yet to consider verse 12, which ends with these words: "Work out your salvation with fear and trembling."

Here also is a kind of striving, but it does not mean that we are to work *for* salvation. Rather, we are to work *from* salvation (see Ephesians 2:8–10). We are to work out in practical, everyday living what God is working on the inside. Our work is inspired and energized by His working within. Here again we see two sides to the development of practical holiness: man's striving, energized by the sovereign might of God.

In the first two verses of Hebrews 12, the imagery of a *race* is used to describe the Christian's pilgrimage: "Let us run with endurance the race that is set before us, fixing our eyes on Jesus, the author and perfecter of faith" (Hebrews 12:1–2). In Philippians, Paul uses the same imagery: "One thing I do: forgetting what lies behind and reaching forward to what lies ahead, I press on toward the goal for the prize of the upward call of God in Christ Jesus" (Philippians 3:13–14).

Such striving requires much self-control, but self-control is a fruit of the Spirit (see Galatians 5:22–23). If we will abide in Christ and submit to Him, the Holy Spirit will produce in us the fruit of self-control. He will enable us to subdue our passions and desires, control our tongues and our tempers, reject our sinful inclinations (see Galatians 5:16), and "run with endurance the race that is set before us."

Paul exhorts Timothy to be like a *soldier* in active service, as well as a hard-working *farmer,* a *workman* who does not need to be ashamed, a *vessel* for honor, and the Lord's *bondservant.* All of these are active, responsible roles (see 2 Timothy 2). Here is no call to passivity, but rather an admonition to strive for excellence and perfection.

With these and many other exhortations, the Scriptures admonish us to strive to please God. In contrast to the merry-go-round of the flesh, if our striving is that humble yet resolute determination to please God, which rests solely in the super-abounding grace of God rather than in any inept power of our own, we will mount up on the pinions of His grace.

A PROPER FOCUS

In this chapter we have begun to examine man's part in the pursuit of holiness, *striving according to God's power and grace.* The remainder of this book will consider the different aspects of man's responsibility in that pursuit. Each subject will fall under one of two general headings: knowing God and pleasing God.

However, it is not possible to eliminate overlap between those two, for one important aspect of *pleasing* God is *knowing* God. "I delight in loyalty rather than sacrifice, and in *the knowledge of God* rather than burnt offerings" (Hosea 6:6). In like manner, pleasing God leads to a deeper knowledge of Him. Christ said, "'He who has My commandments and keeps them, he it is who loves Me; and he who loves Me shall be loved by My Father, and I will love him, and will *disclose Myself to him*'" (John 14:21).

Thus *knowing* and *pleasing* God are deeply intertwined in the life of the believer; they are inextricably linked to a deliberate, earnest cultivation of our relationship with God. Let us conclude this chapter with a preliminary discussion of both concepts.

KNOWING GOD

In Jeremiah 31, we read of the New Covenant of which the apostle Paul said he was a servant (see 2 Corinthians 3:6)—a covenant that includes all believers. God declares:

> "I will put My law within them, and on their heart I will write it; and I will be their God, and they shall be My people. And they shall not teach again, each man his neighbor and each man his brother, saying 'Know the Lord,' for they shall all know Me, from the least of them to the greatest of them...for I will forgive their iniquity, and their sin I will remember no more.'" (Jeremiah 31:33–34)

This is a covenant of holiness, of separation: "They shall be My people," a people set apart, each graciously forgiven, each with a heart to obey, each with a personal knowledge of God.

The great atoning work of Christ opened the way for us to know God in this covenant relationship. Christ is the Mediator of this New Covenant, which was enacted through His blood (see Hebrews 12:24; 9; 10). "For Christ also died for sins once for all, the just for the unjust, in order that He might *bring us to God,* having been put to death in the flesh, but made alive in the spirit" (1 Peter 3:18).

Paul told the Corinthians that "God was in Christ *reconciling the world to Himself,* not counting their trespasses against them" (2 Corin-thians 5:19). Here, the word *reconcile* means to make friends again. God did not need to be reconciled to the world, but the world needed to be reconciled to its offended Sovereign! Because God is as just as He is merciful, sin must always be punished. But God does not count our sins against us because He counted them against Christ.

Thus the way is opened for us to know God personally and experientially, and that way is Christ. "For God so loved the world, that He gave His only begotten Son, that whoever believes in Him should not perish, but have eternal life" (John 3:16). Christ defined eternal life as an intimate *knowledge* of both the Father and the Son (see John 17:3).

We do not have to know everything about God to "know" Him. There is a vast difference between knowing *about* God and knowing God. Many people know great truths about God but have no experiential knowledge whatsoever. Yet every babe in Christ has a real relationship with God.

However, each babe must grow and each relationship must be developed. Knowing God is a lifelong pursuit. Even Paul, after years of walking in intimacy with Christ, still demonstrated an all-consuming passion: "That I may *know Him,* and the power of *His* resurrection and the fellowship of His sufferings, being conformed to His death" (Philippians 3:10).

The Cost of Intimacy

To know the power of His resurrection is to have the very life of Christ operating in us. Paul said in Galatians 2:20: "I have been crucified with Christ; and it is no longer I who live, but Christ lives in me." Paul's desire was for every moment of life to be "fed from the perennial fountains of Christ's life."[2]

Paul ushers us into what A. T. Robertson calls the very "Holy of Holies in his relations with Christ."[3] Here is an expression of *passionate longing,* a longing to know Christ in the glorious richness of an intimacy which renders powerless the very *attraction* of sin. And further, a longing so full of love for Christ that even suffering *becomes* an attraction, because it affords an opportunity for *identification* with the one so loved.

To return to Philippians 3:10, Paul exclaims "That I may know Him and the power of His resurrection." Here is no casual "knowing" of Christ! This power attracts us, for power is a provocative thing. But when we see the rest of Paul's desire, we shrink back. We don't know if we want to know Him quite that well!

With Paul it was all or nothing, and so must it be with us. We cannot truly know Christ apart from "the fellowship of His suffering." To suffer with Him *is* to know Him, and Christ is certainly suffering today. He suffers rejection, ridicule, hatred, indifference, neglect, and betrayal; and He is not oblivious to any of this. The closer we get to Christ, the more we will know these hurts. Men may misrepresent us, exclude us, laugh at us, reject us, and hate us, all because of our love for Christ.

This is our holiness. Jesus told the disciples that, because He chose them out of the world, the world would hate them (see John 15:19). Yet even this, though it grieves, does not deter the lover of Christ from his path. If we minister to others we will know the pain of discouragement, disappointment, and frustration. But we will also know a new dimension of the communion that only the saints can understand.

Paul said to the Colossians, "Now I rejoice in my sufferings for your sake, and in my flesh I do my share on behalf of His body [which is the church] in filling up that which is lacking in Christ's afflictions" (Colossians 1:24). Paul is not referring to the *atoning* work of Christ. Christ declared *that* suffering to be finished and complete when He said, "'It is finished!'" (John 19:30). But he does refer to hardships, dangers, persecution, anguish, fears, weariness, and intercessions, all endured in a fellowship with Christ on behalf of His church. Each of us is to have a part in *this* suffering.

The Emblem of Suffering

One of the great secrets of true Christianity is that the cross is its great attraction, not because it represents sacrifice, but because it affords us an expression of love. In Luke 9:23, Jesus said, "'If anyone wishes to come after Me, let him deny *himself,* and take up his cross daily, and follow Me.'"

In our day the popular teaching is that the attraction of Christianity is *personal gain.* People are encouraged to come to Christ for what He can do for them or give them or get them out of, with no thought of repentance toward a holy God or the very real *cost* involved in discipleship. But this is foreign to the teaching of Scripture and to the testimonies of the saints throughout the ages.

Samuel Rutherford said:

It cost Christ and all His followers sharp showers and hot sweats ere they win to the top of the mountain. But still our soft nature would have heaven coming to our bedside when we are sleeping, and lying down with us, that we might go to heaven in warm clothes; but all that came there found wet feet by the way, and sharp storms that did take the hide off their face…and many enemies by the way.[4]

Let us not be among those who must be "carried to the skies on flowery beds of ease."[5] The Cross is the attraction in true Christianity because of Christ. If we would truly know Christ, we must leave our comfort zones and embrace the Cross.

> *Many crowd the Saviour's Kingdom,*
> *Few receive His Cross,*
> *Many seek His consolations,*
> *Few will suffer loss*
> *For the dear sake of the Master,*
> *Counting all but dross.*
> *Many sit at Jesus' table,*
> *Few will fast with Him*
> *When the sorrow-cup of anguish*
> *Trembles to the brim—*[6]

Our love is *tested* and *proven* by our hunger to know God. If we love Him we want to know Him more, no matter what the cost. When we see that God longs for us with a burning love and that though we may grieve Him, we can never cause Him to turn away from us the gaze of that love, then we are filled with longing, with shame, and with *hope* that we might grow to know Him better and love Him more.

PLEASING GOD

The supreme example of a life that is pleasing to God is, of course, the life of our Lord Jesus. Consider His startling declaration in John 8:29: "'And He who sent Me is with Me; He has not left Me alone, for *I always do the things that are pleasing to Him.*'"

These words come with the most heart-piercing conviction. I cannot read them without a sense of both joy and shame: I rejoice in the irresistible beauty of the simple obedience of my Lord, but I am deeply grieved over my own inconsistency.

We do not always do the things that are pleasing to Him; nevertheless, pleasing God ought to be our highest ambition in life. In encouraging the Corinthians to be of good courage in their faith while still in this life, Paul says, "Therefore also we have as our ambition, whether at home or absent, to be *pleasing to Him*" (2 Corinthians 5:9).

During his seminary days, a young man once came to me with a troubled heart. He was very anxious about his future, fearing that he might not be any good in the ministry. His ambition was to be successful, but his concept of success was colored by the world's standards. My advice was to erase the word *success* from his vocabulary and replace it with the word *pleasing,* and I shared with him the verses mentioned above. Today he is a missionary in South America because he set his heart to please God.

The Christian does not have to live by the world's standard of success. What constitutes success in the world's eyes is often in direct conflict with God's definition. To the world, the life and ministry of Christ must have seemed a great failure when He died, deserted even by all His disciples but John. Yet His life and His death were the greatest successes this world has ever known. I believe Paul was thought of as a tragic failure by his family, teachers, and associates, yet they have been forgotten while Paul's life and ministry continue to inspire and instruct the people of God today.

Being

The world is focused on *doing*. To be successful, you must *do* great things better than anyone else. You must order your life to ensure success, whatever that may require. Not to do so would be to fail, and you must not fail.

Competition, keeping up appearances, staying on top—that's the world's purpose for living, and it has deeply entrenched itself in the subconscious motivations of God's own people. If God figures into this success scheme at all, He is seen as a resource to be used for personal gain, as a means toward an end rather than the end itself.

Often, Christians translate this *doing* mentality into service for God, and apply the world's philosophy of success to the building up of the Kingdom. But God is not interested in what we can do for him; He is far more interested in our *being,* and what we must be is pleasing to Him. That is our ambition, and every other goal must be subservient to it.

Now, I do not mean to imply that we are to be inactive, but our activity must be guided by God. This means that our daily schedules must be adjustable. We must leave room for God to intervene. God is molding and shaping us into the kind of people He can use, and we must be pliable in His hands. If we focus our attention on *being* what we ought to be, God will give us plenty to *do*.

Doing

We have established that holiness is first positional, then practical. Holiness is possible because we have been made holy in Christ. Thus in holiness, our doing is based on our being.

Three verses in Scripture speak to the manner of our *doing:*

1. "And whatever you do in word or deed, do all in the name of the Lord Jesus, giving thanks through Him to God the Father" (Colossians 3:17).
2. "Whatever you *do,* do your work heartily, *as for the Lord* rather than for men" (Colossians 3:23).

3. "Whether, then, you eat or drink or whatever you *do,* do all *to the glory of God"* (1 Corinthians 10:31).

If we live according to these three admonitions, we can rest assured that our lives will be a pleasing fragrance to God.

Man Pleasing

We cannot be concerned with pleasing men if we would please God. We should not deliberately provoke others, but we must not be governed by men's opinions or displeasures. That leads to man-*fearing,* which is a disgrace to Christ.

Such cowardice infects much preaching of our day. Many preachers are afraid lest they offend other men. God does not need cowards in the pulpit. He needs men who preach lovingly but uncompromisingly the whole counsel of His Word.

When I was a small boy, the wife of our pastor related how she had once tried diplomatically to smooth over something stern that her husband had said from the pulpit. But what the pastor had said was true and needed to be said, regardless of how it may have stung. The pastor stopped his wife with these words: "I've said it and I'll not take it back." That made a great impression on me.

Being a man-pleaser affects even our faith. We are told in Scripture that without faith, it is impossible to please God (see Hebrews 11:6). Faith requires a focus on God. But if we are concerned with pleasing men, our focus is on men rather than on God.

Thus Christ asked the Jewish leaders who sought to kill Him because they did not believe that He was who He said He was: "'How *can* you believe, when you receive glory from one another, and you do not seek the glory that is from the one and only God?'" (John 5:44). These "leaders" were blinded by their own desires for recognition and praise—what Jesus called "receiving glory from men.'"

Are we concerned with the praise of men? Do we want to be recognized and applauded? If so, even our faith is compromised. We should be far more interested in what God thinks of us than in the opinions of others. We are not to be argumentative or cruel, but we must boldly "speak the truth in love" no matter how unpopular that might be.

Counting the Cost

Certain costs are often involved in pleasing God. For example, a Christian may take a stand on moral issues that will affect his business. That business may fail, for contrary to popular theology, God has not promised any man success in business. But God will take care of His own, not according to what we might prefer at the moment, but according to His kindness and His own good pleasure.

Indeed, down through the centuries, pleasing God has cost many their very lives. If faced with such a prospect, our hope should be that God would grant us the grace to say with Paul: "But I do not consider my life of any account as dear to myself, in order that I may finish my course, and the ministry which I received from the Lord Jesus, to testify solemnly of the gospel of the grace of God" (Acts 20:24).

Again, Christ said:

> "If anyone wishes to come after Me, let him deny *himself*, and take up his cross daily, and follow Me. For whoever wishes to save his life shall lose it, but whoever loses his life for My sake, he is the one who will save it. For what is a man profited if he gains the whole world, and loses or forfeits himself?" (Luke 9:23–25)

Jim Elliot, who lost his life in the pursuit of pleasing God, wrote these stirring words: "He is no fool who gives up what he cannot keep to gain what he cannot lose."[7]

Though we may never die the death of a martyr, we must nevertheless die to self and live to God. It may please God to set us on a high hill for all the world to see or to hide us in obscurity, unnoticed and unappreciated by others. Our lives may be filled with adventure and excitement, or we may live ordinary, seemingly uninteresting lives. But there is nothing ordinary about a life lived to please God. When our lives are lived for the Lord, to the glory of God, and in the name of Christ, *all of life becomes worship.*

"It is inbred in us," says Oswald Chambers, "that we have to do exceptional things for God; but we have not. We have to be exceptional in the ordinary things, to be holy in mean streets, among mean people, and this is not learned in five minutes."[8] Indeed, this must be our practice for a lifetime. Only eternity will show the value of a life lived to please Him.

PART TWO

KNOWING GOD—
FIRST STEPS

"And they shall not teach again,
each man his neighbor and each man his brother,
saying, 'Know the LORD,' for they shall all know Me,
from the least of them to the greatest of them," declares the LORD.

JEREMIAH 31:34

The loftiest pursuit of all, even higher than the pursuit of holiness, is the pursuit of God. If our focus is merely on being holy, we are preoccupied with self and with the measure of our own personal "whiteness," to use Oswald Chambers' word.[1] This again appeals to our pride, and we are either puffed up or disillusioned depending on how we perceive our progress.

But when we focus on God with a heart to know Him, our desires are changed little by little and our lives are brought into conformity to Him. There is no better way to grow in practical holiness than by pursuing personal knowledge of God. There is no greater mark of holiness than knowing and being known by Him.

Meanwhile, Satan will divert us by every craft he commands. He will even entice us into a preoccupation with holiness if that will overshadow our preoccupation with God. Satan's counterfeit for holiness is self-righteousness, which our pride sometimes allows us to mistake for the genuine article.

"'The arrogance of your heart has deceived you,'" said the Lord through the prophet Obadiah (Obadiah 1:3). Hence we are caught up in the pursuit of something that is far less than holiness, and lesser still than communion with God. True holiness of life has nothing to do with self; it comes only through an intimate connection with the Holy One of Israel and His Son, Jesus Christ. Look away to Jesus. This must be our watchword.

Our next focus will be on salvation as the entrance into a relationship with God through Christ. *Salvation* is a broad term. Scripture speaks of three different aspects of salvation. In *justification* we are saved from the *penalty* of sin; in *sanctification* we are being progressively saved from the *power* of sin; in *glorification* we will be saved at the end of our earthly lives from the *presence* of sin.

In chapter 4, however, the word *salvation* will refer to the experience of *conversion,* just as Paul used it in Ephesians 2:8: "For by grace you *have been saved,*" which indicates a moment in time past. In this experience, which is also referred to in Scripture as *regeneration* or the *new birth,* we are enabled to believe the gospel and are thus *justified* before God (see Galatians 2:16). The enmity between us and God is removed. Henceforward, we are established in a personal relationship with Him.

In chapter 5, we will focus on the *security* we can have in that relationship. We cannot go very far on the path of sanctification without some security in our justification. A study of salvation and security reveals and magnifies our first true steps in knowing God, *repentance* and *faith*. And from that point, every step that follows is also a step of repentance and faith. Thus begins the greatest of all journeys, which sets us apart from those who travel the road to destruction: none other than the magnificent adventure of knowing God.

CHAPTER FOUR

SALVATION

"And this is eternal life, that they may know Thee, the only true God, and Jesus Christ whom Thou hast sent."

JOHN 17:3

The way into the adventure of knowing God is an exclusive one. Jesus Christ told His disciples, "'Enter by the narrow gate; for the gate is wide, and the way is broad that leads to destruction, and many are those who enter by it. For the gate is small, and the way is narrow that leads to life, and few are those who find it'" (Matthew 7:13–14).

THE WAY OF SALVATION

There is but one way to God, and that is through the Lord Jesus Christ. He Himself declared: "'I am the way, and the truth, and the life; no one comes to the Father, but through Me'" (John 14:6). We must come to God on His terms or we cannot come at all. This exclusiveness is not some arbitrary means whereby God displays His authority. Rather, it is a necessity because of the severity of our offense to His holiness. It is our sin and the offense thereof that makes the way narrow. No other way would be adequate to deliver us from that sin.

We are all sinners by nature as well as by choice; we inherited the propensity and disposition to sin from Adam, for "in Adam all die" (1 Corinthians 15:22). In addition, each of us has willfully chosen to go his own way rather than God's; "All of us like sheep have gone astray, each of us has turned to his own way" (Isaiah 53:6).

God is a righteous judge who cannot overlook sin, and sin demands an awful price. "The wages of sin is death" (Romans 6:23). What man has earned from sin is not only spiritual and physical death in this life, but an eternity separated from God (see 2 Thessalonians 1:9).

SUBSTITUTION

The Bible reveals that "God was in Christ reconciling the world to Himself, not counting their trespasses against them" (2 Corinthians 5:19). The word *reconcile* means to restore to a right relationship, which here necessitates the removal of sin. God could only do this *in Christ.* The wrath of God toward sin must be born either by the one who earned it or by a substitute. This is the message of the Atonement: Christ has become our Substitute that we might be one with God.

"For Christ also died for sins once for all, *the just for the unjust, in order that He might bring us to God,* having been put to death in the flesh, but made alive in the spirit" (1 Peter 3:18). When we speak of Christ as our substitute, however, we do not mean that He was a stand-in. He did *not* take our place on the cross, as is often expressed in popular gospel songs. That may sound appealing, but it is wrong.

What good would it do for me to be crucified? No death I could experience would satisfy the justice of God. If I were to spend an eternity in hell I could never atone for one sin. Only the sacrifice of the spotless Lamb of God could accomplish so great a task (see John 1:29). Those souls in hell at this very moment are not paying for their sins as a prisoner pays a debt to society; they are suffering the eternal wrath of God because they did not avail themselves of God's atonement.

Romans 5:8 says: "But God demonstrates His own love toward us, in that while we were yet sinners, Christ died for us." In pondering this verse we usually emphasize the word *died,* and what a glorious truth that emphasis expresses. But another equally glorious truth is expressed by emphasizing the word *Christ.* "While we were yet sinners, *Christ* died for us." He was the only one who could. Christ bore a Cross that only He could bear. He did something for us that we could never do for ourselves, because He alone was qualified. To think otherwise is to dishonor Christ and elevate self; it is to make the Cross a great convenience for us rather than an absolute necessity, if the wrath of God would be appeased.

Christ was our substitute in that His death satisfied God's demand for justice, but He was not an equal substitute. He was an infinitely *superior* substitute, by virtue of necessity, because of the awesome holiness of almighty God and the great horror of our sin.

Redemption

Consider the great wisdom of God. Our Redeemer had to be a sinless man to die for the sins of man. But He also had to be divine for His death to have infinite proportions. In addition, He had to be holy, spotless, and pure, that He might be an acceptable sacrifice for sin. Thus the eternal plan of redemption required that the eternal Son should enter the realm of time and space and be born of a virgin, "made in the likeness of men" (Philippians 2:7), retaining His deity yet assuming a sinless human nature—two natures but one person: the God-man.

Christ, the transcendent one, pierced the dark veil of paradox and emptied Himself of the glory of His deity. He took on the form of a bond servant as the tiny Babe of Bethlehem.

This holy child was the fruition of a covenant between God the Father and God the Son, struck in eternity past, to procure our redemption—a covenant which required both the election of the Father and the acceptance of the Son, forged before the worlds began.

The great Puritan, John Flavel, wrote these awe-inspiring words: "Before this world was made, then were His delights in us, while as yet we had no existence, but only in the infinite mind and purpose of God, who had decreed this for us in Christ Jesus."[1]

We were hopeless and helpless until God intervened with His plan, which would both vindicate His justice and secure our recovery—a plan so mysterious, so sacred that its deepest contemplation inspires hushed silence and trembling reverence (see Ephesians 3:9). "He made Him who knew no sin to be sin on our behalf, that we might become the righteousness of God in Him" (2 Corinthians 5:21).

Peter adds: "He Himself bore our sins in His body on the cross, that we might die to sin and live to righteousness; for by His wounds you were healed" (1 Peter 2:24). See to what great extent God went to make a way of salvation: "You were not redeemed with perishable things like silver or gold from your futile way of life inherited from your forefathers, but with *precious blood,* as of a lamb unblemished and spotless, the blood of *Christ"* (1 Peter 1:18–19).

THE TERMS OF SALVATION

Yes, the way of salvation is exclusive, but the terms are exclusive as well. We must not only come God's way, we must come on God's terms.

I often hear a very common appeal given at the end of an evangelistic service or in personal witnessing conversations: "Accept Jesus as your personal Savior." No doubt, this appeal is made by many an earnest Christian. But I believe it to be misleading, however good may be the intentions of those who use it. One problem is the glaring absence of the word *Lord,* the implication being that one can know Christ as Savior without knowing Him as Lord. This cannot be.

The issue of Christ's lordship will be considered in some detail, but first I would like to address a separate problem inherent in the word *accept.* No matter what is intended by the speaker, the implication of this word is that the hearer must decide that Christ and His gospel, that God and His love, are *acceptable* to them. But the question is never, "Is God acceptable to me?" But rather, "Am I acceptable to Him?"

RIGHTEOUSNESS

What, then, makes one acceptable to God? While repentance and faith are necessary for salvation, they are not the basis of our acceptance before God. What God requires is *perfect righteousness.*

Christ said in the Sermon on the Mount, "'Unless your righteousness surpasses that of the scribes and Pharisees, you shall not enter the kingdom of heaven'" (Matthew 5:20). There were none more outwardly righteous than the scribes and Pharisees, yet inwardly they were wicked. And so it is with us. "All our righteous deeds are like a filthy garment" (Isaiah 64:6). Paul wrote, "'THERE IS NONE RIGHTEOUS, NOT EVEN ONE'...for all have sinned and fall short of the glory of God" (Romans 3:10, 23). We have nothing with which to commend ourselves to God. Where righteousness is concerned, we are bankrupt and destitute.

Then surely we are doomed! What can we do to satiate God's holy wrath, to stay His hand of judgment? There is nothing we can do, but there was something God could do, and He has done it. He has satisfied His own demand for righteousness in Christ.

Righteousness is keeping the law from a heart of love. Thus it involves more than right conduct only; it also involves a right heart. Paul knew this very well. He said of himself that, prior to his conversion, he was blameless as regards the righteousness in the law. That is, he could not be accused of transgressing the law based on his conduct before men (see Philippians 3:6). But when he saw, through the commandment "You shall not covet," that covetousness was in his heart, he understood what Jesus had taught in the Sermon on the Mount—that God's expectation for righteousness goes all the way to the desires of the heart (see Romans 7:7–8).

This righteousness must also be perfect because God is perfect, and perfect righteousness requires both perfect conduct and a perfect heart. But none of us rise to this standard. Our only hope is Christ. He said that He did not come to abolish the Law but to fulfill it (see Matthew 5:17). He fulfilled it for us in His life of perfect righteousness and through His death on the cross, for had there been no adequate payment for sin—the blood of the perfectly righteous for the unrighteous—forgiveness would have been not only impossible but immoral (see Hebrews 9:22).

The law of God is divided into three parts: (1) the *moral* law, comprising the Ten Commandments; (2) the *judicial* law, which speaks of God's rule over His people and His judgments concerning them; and (3) the *ceremonial* law, which involves the sacrificial system of the Jews.

Christ fulfilled the *moral* law in His perfect life, culminating in His atoning death. By that death and by His resurrection and ascension, He also fulfilled the *judicial* law, the Cross representing both the judgment of God toward sin and the mercy of God toward sinners. Christ alone could bear God's judgment on sin, for He alone was qualified to be a sacrifice for sin. Finally, as the supreme sacrifice, Christ fulfilled the *ceremonial* law as well.

Thus in Jesus Christ the righteous we have an advocate with the Father. And He is Himself the propitiation for our sins; that is, He satisfies God's demand for righteousness (see 1 John 2:1–2). We are thus acceptable to God only if we are *in Christ* by virtue of His atoning blood, clothed in His glorious righteousness (see Ephesians 1:6).

All of God

But how can we be *in the Beloved?* What must transpire for this blessed position to be secured? Is there not something we must do? Surely, here is where repentance and faith come in.

Yes, but we must be very careful that we do not see these as meritorious in their own right, as though repentance and faith earn for us a place in Christ (see Romans 4:5). It is not by anything that *we* might do, but by God's doing alone that we are in Christ Jesus, "who became to us...*righteousness*" (1 Corinthians 1:30).

Nevertheless, this righteousness does come on the basis of faith, which presupposes repentance. Paul, speaking of himself and his own hope in Christ, desired "that I...may be found in Him, not having a righteousness of my own derived from the Law, but that which is through *faith* in Christ, the righteousness which *comes from God* on the basis of *faith*" (Philippians 3:8–9; see also Romans 9:30–10:4, 10).

Yet, neither Paul nor we can take any credit either for this faith or for the repentance it accompanies, because both are *gifts from God*. We can neither repent nor believe when we choose; these both must be granted us according to God's own good pleasure (see 2 Timothy 2:25; Acts 11:18; Romans 12:3). Otherwise, we could take some credit for our own salvation.

To further illustrate this, Ephesians 2:8–10 yields an easy three-point outline. We are saved by grace, through faith, unto works. We are not saved by works but by *grace;* neither are we saved through works but through faith. Therefore, faith cannot be a work. We also see that works of righteousness, rather than being the means of salvation, are the goal of salvation and the evidence that God has done something supernatural in our hearts, which we could not do for ourselves.

Now, it is clear that God does require repentance and faith for salvation; this was what Paul preached "publicly and from house to house" (see Acts 20:20–21). Yet unless God grants these we are thoroughly without hope. Man is both spiritually dead and fundamentally depraved. Although he is responsible to repent and believe, yet he has no inclination and thus no ability to do so. Man does not have the capacity to choose God apart from God's choosing him. He is in a desperate condition. Not only is he headed for hell, he is powerless to do anything about it. And what's more, he is oblivious to his situation, like a madman who thinks he is sane.

Yet here is the mercy of God: that which He requires, He Himself provides. At an appointed time, according to God's own choice, upon one's hearing the gospel, God the Holy Spirit quickens that which was dead spiritually, immediately effecting genuine conversion or repentance, accompanied by faith in the Lord Jesus Christ. Thereby, God not only enables the sinner to call on the Lord for salvation but guarantees that he *will* call (see John 6:37). It is the mercy of God that those on whom He has set His purpose and His choice are guaranteed salvation by the wondrous saving work of God alone, in which He enables them to do what they cannot do apart from Him: repent and believe.

Salvation is all of God. To Him alone be the glory! He owes no one. If He chooses to save some, it is by His mercy alone (see Romans 9:14–24). Can we then find fault with Him for not saving all? Hell is man's just reward. Hell is what is fair. If God in mercy chooses to rescue some, we can but rejoice that He has saved any (and at what a cost!) and be grateful to be among that number.

What, then, is the need for evangelism? If God guarantees the salvation of the elect, why do we need to preach the gospel? First, because God has told us to, and second, because by it God includes us in what He is doing. The gospel provides the power of God for salvation to those who believe, and God has ordained that it be propagated through preaching (see Romans 10:8–17; 1 Corinthians 1:21). In other words, God has chosen to use men.

In Paul's dramatic conversion on the road to Damascus, Christ said to him:

> "For this purpose I have appeared to you, to appoint you a minister and a witness not only to the things which you have seen, but also to the things in which I will appear to you; delivering you from the Jewish people and from the Gentiles, to whom I am sending you, to open their eyes so that they may turn from darkness to light and from the dominion of Satan to God, in order that they may receive forgiveness of sins and an inheritance among those who have been sanctified by faith in Me." (Acts 26:16–18)

The Lord is not saying that Paul himself is to open their eyes, but that Paul is being sent as a witness so that their eyes might be opened and they might be enabled to turn to the light and believe, and thus be made holy positionally. So Paul asks, "How shall they hear without a preacher?" (Romans 10:14).

God has further ordained that repentance and faith are together the acceptable response to the gospel. This was Paul's message and it is ours too. Evangelism is our responsibility, because it is part of our obedience to Christ's command to go and make disciples (see Matthew 28:19–20). It is also our great joy and privilege, because we have a part in God's program of redemption.

What an honor that God would choose to include you and me in what He is doing to rescue lost souls! Thus we are set free to witness with fervency and not with fear or dread. We witness with a burden, as we are channels for God's own earnestness, but without the crushing sense that we are responsible for another's salvation.

If this takes the incentive out of our witnessing, perhaps an examination of that incentive is in order. Perhaps our motivation is less a desire to please God than a desire for recognition or a personal sense of accomplishment. Too often, witnessing is motivated not by love but by a lust for personal conquest, especially among many of our modern ministers. So many baptisms represent so many notches in our spiritual belts. This is what, in

Jeremiah's day, God called *greed for gain* (see Jeremiah 6:13).

In our day, this greed has caused men to dilute the gospel message to make it more attractive to the world. Thus they heal the brokenness of the people superficially, "'Saying, "Peace, peace," but there is no peace'" (Jeremiah 6:14).

Our message must be clear and it must be true. It must strike deep to the root of the problem, which is man's sin and God's offended holiness. Therefore, it must include a call to real *repentance* and to a genuine *faith* in the Lord Jesus Christ.[2]

REPENTANCE

In the modern church, we treat repentance too lightly if we treat it at all. More often than not, it is completely ignored. The best and the most one usually hears in regard to repentance is, "Turn from your sins and trust Christ."

Now this is good, but is it enough? What does it mean to the average hearer? Does it mean to turn temporarily, just long enough for your sin to be forgiven, and then go back to embracing a sinful lifestyle? Does it mean a promise never to sin again or a commitment to moral reform? Is repentance bargaining with God?

God does not require resolutions or commitments, but a permanent surrender. You cannot go in a new direction without forsaking the old. And if, after forsaking the old, you turn around again, you are not fit for the kingdom of heaven (see Luke 9:62). Indeed, to turn again would disprove the genuineness of the first turning.

True repentance is permanent; it cannot be repented of (see 2 Corinthians 7:10). I am not saying that repentance means we will never sin again, but I am saying that true repentance is a permanent forsaking of a life devoted to self, a permanent choice against the practice of a lifestyle of sin (see 1 John 3:7–9).

There are any number of sinful lifestyles that we could examine: lying, stealing, promiscuity, and pornography, to name just a few. One prime example is homosexuality, which much of our society now views as an "alternative lifestyle," although the Bible undeniably calls it sin (see Romans 1). No one who chooses this lifestyle can legitimately call himself a Christian.

When, however, a homosexual is brought to see the unsearchable riches of God's love, and in repentance and faith surrenders his heart to Christ, God mercifully pours out His grace for salvation. Still, the new convert does not necessarily lose his or her physical attraction to the same sex. In fact, it is rare for this attraction to be extinguished completely and instantly. Yet this person now abhors that attraction, and also the prospect of ever going back to that old, immoral lifestyle. This does not mean that he or she is never tempted to sin in this way again. But if there is a yielding at some point there is also an abhorrence of that yielding, and afterwards a reaffirmation of the moral choice made against that sinful lifestyle.

One who professes love to Christ and then embraces again a lifestyle of sin cannot call himself a Christian, because his repentance is not genuine. Real repentance means permanently forsaking willful sin. Though he may deceive himself into thinking that he can somehow have both Christ and his sin, he cannot. John said in 1 John 3:9, "No one who is born of God practices sin, because His seed abides in him; and he *cannot* sin, because he is born of God."

Imagine someone who has been convicted of sin and its consequences. He sees the gospel as an escape from hell, so he makes a commitment to follow Christ. But his heart is not in it. He trudges along but often looks longingly back over his shoulder toward the world. Indeed, on occasion, he turns and runs toward it. But guilt and fear set in, and he begins again to trudge, with his head hung low, back toward God.

Is this a picture of a Christian? A Christian is one whose heart has surrendered to Christ as Lord. He does not see following Christ as drudgery. Many times he may lose his focus, stumble, and fall; he may find himself entangled in sin. But in that sin he is most miserable. He must forsake it if he is to be free—not from the fear of hell, but from the shame of having offended the God he loves.

If he could make a different choice, repent of his repentance, choose again a lifestyle of sin, and go his own way rather than God's, he would trample underfoot again the Son of God (see Hebrews 10:29). But he cannot. One who does this never was saved in the first place (see 1 John 2:19). For the true believer, the initial act of repentance is permanent. He cannot change his mind. Indeed, he is changed, never to be the same again (see 2 Corinthians 5:17).

It is imperative that we see repentance as more than just a *willingness* to change, but as an *actual* change. True *conversion* is not only a change of mind and direction, but of the heart as well.

The Horror of Sin

Repentance is treated lightly today because sin is treated lightly. We see sin as indiscretion, but God sees it as treason. We see it as a slip, but God sees it as obstinate *rebellion*.

We see sin as merely a moral issue, but God sees it as an *issue of love*. The great rival to God in our lives is self. Sin is loving self rather than loving God. It is more than a moral digression; it is a *forsaking of the Lord our God* (see Deuteronomy 28:20).

If sin is forsaking God, then repentance is forsaking sin: "Let the wicked forsake his way, and the unrighteous man his thoughts." It is also a returning to God: "and let him return to the LORD, and He will have compassion on him; and to our God, for He will abundantly pardon" (Isaiah 55:7).

What would cause a person to forsake sin and turn to God? First, there must be a right estimation of self. We must see ourselves for what we really are: sinners, rebels, enemies of God. Only when we see ourselves in light of God's perfect holiness do we see the horror of our sin.

Sin is horrible because it always means death. Even for the Christian, sin is death: to his influence, his credibility, his sensitivity to both God and men, and to opportunities to minister life to others (see James 1:15). And our sin means death not only for ourselves but also for those we love the most, particularly our children. God told the people of Israel: "I have set before you life and death, the blessing and the curse. So choose life in order that you may live, you *and your descendants*" (Deuteronomy 30:19). And how do we choose life? "By loving the LORD your God, by obeying His voice, and by holding fast to Him; for this is your life and the length of your days" (Deuteronomy 30:20). Sin is choosing death, but repentance is choosing life.

Sin is horrible because it is a rejection of God. The lost are like blind men submerged in their own darkness, unaware that all around them is the glowing brilliance of God's love. We Christians are often not much better, with our petty self-centeredness and our indifference, while God continually lavishes on us His unchanging love. Every time we sin we are rejecting His great love. Does this not prove the horror of sin?

Second, there must be a right estimation of *guilt*. We would so like to blame our sin on someone or something else: our family, our circumstances, our friends, the devil, even God. But God holds us alone responsible for our sin, and we must be honest with Him and ourselves about the guilt of that sin. This is what the word *confession* means.

Confession of Sin

When the Holy Spirit comes with the grace of conviction, and we are made to see our sin in the light of the blazing holiness of God, we despair of self-vindication. Perhaps we had thought we could do our sinning in the shadows and would surely not be caught, but in the light of God's radiant holiness we see more clearly. Reality dawns, and we are put to shame by our self-deception; we have no choice but to confess in humiliation the guilt of our sin. The blessed result is forgiveness.

> How blessed is he whose transgression is forgiven, whose sin is covered! How blessed is the man to whom the LORD does not impute iniquity, and in whose spirit there is no deceit! When I kept silent about my sin, my body wasted away through my groaning all day long. For day and night Thy hand was heavy upon me; My vitality was drained away as with the fever heat of summer. I acknowledged my sin to Thee, and my iniquity I did not hide; I said, "I will confess my transgressions to the LORD"; and Thou didst forgive the guilt of my sin. (Psalm 32:1–5)

Confession is simply coming clean with God and ourselves about our sin. It is owning up to our responsibility to be holy and to our failure in that responsibility. Confession is dragging that sin out into the light and getting real, not only about the sin, but also about ourselves.

For the lost, confession is part of the humbling necessary for the saving, reconciling grace of God to be bestowed. For the Christian, confession is that which restores precious fellowship with God: "If we confess our sins, He is faithful and righteous to forgive us our sins and to cleanse us from all unrighteousness" (1 John 1:9). For both the lost and the saved, confession is part of the process of repentance.

David came to that place of seeing his sin aright: "I know my transgressions, and my sin is ever before me" (Psalm 51:3). He owned his sin before God: "Against Thee, Thee only, I have sinned, and done what is evil in Thy sight." Then look at what he says: "So that Thou art justified when Thou dost speak, and blameless when Thou dost judge" (Psalm 51:4). He does not plead extenuating circumstances; he does not shift the blame or try to justify himself. He simply confesses his sin, owns the guilt, and acknowledges its just reward.

To say that we are somehow justified in a certain sin is to say that God is unjust in condemning it. David extolled the justice of God. Indeed, we see in his words a zeal for that justice. Thomas Watson, in his little book on repentance, said: "In confession we must so charge ourselves as to clear God."[3] This is just what David does; thus confession is acknowledging two facts: I have sinned and God is just.

The Honor of God

True repentance begins with a zeal for the honor of God, which has been besmirched by our sin. This involves turning away, not only from surface sins, but from the very essence of sin, self. We are offended on God's behalf and actually take sides with Him against ourselves. We feel that, at all costs, God's name must be vindicated. Thus we even long for God to inflict some punishment on us that would fit the crime (see 2 Corinthians 7:11).

But just then we realize the ultimate blow to our pride. There is absolutely nothing we can do to pay for our sin; the debt is too great. Yet there is one who has paid that debt for us: Jesus Christ.

Kindness and Sorrow

Here is the *kindness* of God that leads to repentance, a kindness which, when truly apprehended, takes us beyond confession into the realm of genuine change. Just when we expect God to drop a well-deserved anvil on our heads, He kisses us on the cheek and says, "I dropped your anvil on Christ."

It is not the *wrath* of God but the *mercy* of God that breaks our hearts and melts our wills. At Calvary, we see both wrath and mercy working together: wrath toward sin but mercy toward the sinner. As Oswald Chambers so poignantly said: "The cross is the point where God and sinful man merge with a crash and the way of life is opened—but the crash is on the heart of God."[4] Hence the wondrous paradox of the atonement is resolved in Christ's revealing to us this startling kindness: God is both *"just* and *the justifier* of the one who has faith in Jesus" (Romans 3:26).

What is our response when we see with spiritual eyes the great kindness of God? The only possible response is what Paul called *godly sorrow* (see 2 Corinthians 7:9–11). We are caught off guard by God's kindness, overwhelmed, and put to shame. The sorrow this causes produces genuine repentance. Thus godly sorrow is the means whereby the kindness of God leads us to repentance.

Paul makes a distinction, in verse 10 of 2 Corinthians 7, between godly sorrow and worldly sorrow: "For the sorrow that is according to the will of God produces a repentance without regret, leading to salvation; but the sorrow of the world produces death." Worldly sorrow is sorrow that you got caught and must suffer the consequences of your sin, or a remorse over sin without the willingness to forsake it. Godly sorrow is sorrow over having offended a holy and loving God. Worldly sorrow produces a false repentance, a repentance for self. Godly sorrow produces a true repentance, a repentance for God.

Is sorrow always necessary for repentance? Let me answer with another question. How can one who is bathed in the warmth of God's undeserved kindness see the reality of his sin and not have sorrow?

My sins, my sins, my Saviour!
How sad on Thee they fall;
Seen through Thy gentle patience,
I tenfold feel them all;

I know they are forgiven,
But still, their pain to me
Is all the grief and anguish
They laid, my Lord, on Thee.[5]

Not everyone has the same degree of sorrow. "In the new birth" says Watson, "all have pangs, but some have sharper pangs than others."[6] However, in another place, he says, "the more regret and trouble of spirit we have first at our conversion, the less we shall feel afterwards."[7]

"The sacrifices of God are a broken spirit; a broken and a contrite heart, O God, Thou wilt not despise" (Psalm 51:17). The tears of repentance are very precious to God, but they do not earn His acceptance. We cannot help God pay for our sin by being sorry. Nevertheless, there must be some degree of true godly sorrow to allow a genuine turning of the heart toward God. To say otherwise would imply that one could come to God for salvation in indifference to the guilt of personal sin, the offended holiness of God, and the sufferings of Christ. How could this be?

The Fruit of Repentance

The evidence that repentance is real is not a display of emotion at conversion, but works which are appropriate to repentance: restitution for wrongs, all forms of Christian service and ministry, and personal spiritual disciplines (see Acts 26:20). Such works do not precede conversion. In that case, repentance would mean cleaning up your act and turning over a new leaf in order to be saved, which would characterize a works-oriented salvation. Repentance is a deliberate choice, a turning of the heart, a preference for Christ which will be evidenced in how we live our lives. Do our lives display fruit in keeping with repentance (see Luke 3:8)? If not, all we have really experienced is remorse or regret, but not repentance.

Repentance, though effecting a permanent change at conversion, is not just a one-time experience; it is a way of life. If I am not repentant today, what evidence do I have that I have ever repented? What proof do I have that I am not a counterfeit? Paul told the Corinthians to examine themselves to see if they were really in the faith; he put to them this question: "Do you not recognize this about yourselves, that Jesus Christ is in you?" (2 Corinthians 13:5). If we claim to be Christians yet have no current evidence that Christ is in us, how do we know we are not deceiving ourselves? One proof is a life characterized by habitual repentance.

The average professing Christian today, when asked how he knows that he is a Christian, will immediately go back to some experience in the past; a prayer he prayed or a feeling he had. Perhaps that experience was years ago and there has been no evidence of a change in the life since. Can that person truly say that he is saved?

What bearing does our experience of conversion have on our lives today? That is the question. Think of the best Christian you know. If I were to ask you how you know that this person is a Christian, would you recount his or her personal salvation testimony? Probably not— you might not even know those particulars. You would, no doubt, point to the way that person lives his or her life.

And yet, how often I have heard someone say something like this: "Oh yes, he is saved. He made a decision for Christ at junior camp ten years ago and was baptized. Now since then he hasn't been faithful in church and he doesn't live the way a Christian should, but I know he's saved." If there is no repentance in that life today, regardless of what has happened in the past, if one cannot see some evidence in this person of a love for God, then there can be no real confidence in that one's salvation. Real repentance bears fruit, and one fruit it bears is a continual turning from sin to God.

Real repentance is a permanent turning with ongoing results. And real repentance is a turning not only from what we have *done* but from who we *are,* siding with God not only against our *sin* but against *ourselves.* These things set the Christian apart from the world.

Practical holiness is the fruit of true repentance. Or we might say that repentance is the bedrock of practical holiness. We are never more humble than in genuine repentance, never more sensitive to God, never more keenly aware of our sin. Show me a holy man and I will show you a repentant man, one who has turned his back on sin and self and his heart toward God.

FAITH

The second aspect of our responsibility in coming to God is faith. As the writer of Hebrews said: "He who comes to God must believe that He is, and that He is a rewarder of those who seek Him" (Hebrews 11:6). Seeking is a prelude to faith. God commands us to seek Him: "Seek the LORD while He may be found; call upon Him while He is near" (Isaiah 55:6). Yet we cannot seek Him unless He draws us to Himself (see John 3:20–21; 6:44).

Fundamentally, faith is a leap beyond the realm of logic or reason. These can carry us just so far. Faith takes us beyond what can be explained in terms of the tangible alone. Christian faith is more than an intellectual assent to certain propositions. It is looking to a living God. That is why it is so closely linked with repentance. Simply stated, repentance and faith are *turning* and *looking*.

But faith is not a casual glance in God's direction. Rather, it is looking to God as our only hope; it is resting ourselves on Him as our only refuge. By looking to Him as the only master of the will, the only source of salvation, we have life (see Numbers 21:8–9; John 3:14–15). True Christian faith is in the present tense. It is immediate; it cannot just be a memory. If it is not current it is not faith.

Sometimes Christians have doubts about their salvation. They want some experiential assurance that their conversion was real. But the essential question for them is not one of experience, but of faith: "Who am I trusting the whole of my being to right now?" The proof of salvation is not some experience in the past but an ongoing persistence in both repentance and faith. This does not negate the experience of conversion nor does it say it is not vital, but it does say it is not valid if faith does not persevere to the end (see Hebrews 10:39; 1 Peter 1:9).

Faith's Object: The Gospel

Faith is a gift of God, imparted through the proclamation of the gospel (see Romans 12:3). As Paul said, "Faith comes from hearing, and hearing by the word of Christ," or "the word concerning Christ," which is the gospel—the glorious good news of the crucifixion and the resurrection of our Lord (Romans 10:17; see also Galatians 3:2, 5, and Paul's definition of the gospel in 1 Corinthians 15:3–8).

Not all who hear the gospel have this faith; only those who have life by the Spirit (see 2 Corinthians 4:3–4, John 6:63) and are drawn to Christ by the Father (John 6:37, 44, 65). The instrument of the Father's drawing is the gospel (see 2 Thessalonians 2:13–14), which is the absolute, ultimate expression of God's love toward sinners. Thus we may say that the gospel is the grace of God in action. By it, God entices one to trust His love and thus imparts faith. Then, to him to whom faith has been imparted, the gospel is the power of God for salvation (Romans 1:16).

However, one can comprehend even what we have said about the gospel and yet not be saved. But when the Holy Spirit quickens, enabling the sinner to see in the gospel the grace of God, not with the eyes of the intellect, but with *spiritual* eyes (see Acts 26:18), he is overwhelmed, and his heart is conquered. Grace has become irresistible—not like a bulldozer that runs him down and drags him against his will, but like a pool of clear water that is given to a parched and dying man. He is overpowered by the power of love; all he can do is surrender his heart unreservedly. This surrender *is* the faith through which one is saved: "That if you…believe *in your heart*" (Romans 10:9).

Whatever is not of this faith is sin (see Romans 14:23). Thus anything done in self-reliance and self-rule is rebellion, even treason and unbelief; it is rooted in pride. If the knights of King Arthur's court, who were sworn to allegiance, had each rebelled against their sovereign and had gone off to establish kingdoms of their own, their rebellion would have been treason even if they became good kings. Their very goodness would be treasonous. Even so, all of man's goodness is sin if it is the goodness of the flesh apart from God. Even benevolence and philanthropy, which seem admirable, are actually sins themselves if they do not come from simple submission to and dependence on the grace of God.

The gospel alone is "the power of God for salvation," not right teaching on repentance and faith as some seem to imagine. It is important to call men to repentance and faith, and to help them understand the meaning of these terms. But it is neither our presentation of the gospel nor our explanation of a right response which saves, no matter how polished or impressive our approach might be.

Proper teaching, as important as it is, does not open blind eyes. Only God opens those eyes to see "the light of the gospel of the glory of Christ, who is the image of God" (2 Corinthians 4:4). You can shine a light in a blind man's face all day long, but he will not see it no matter how bright it might be. Only God gives the miracle of sight.

This is why our witnessing must be bathed in prayer, and our confidence must be in God alone. We are responsible to shine the clearest, brightest light we can. But neither our clarity nor our cleverness accomplishes salvation for anyone. Neither do the blind heal themselves. Only God gives sight and only through the gospel.

THE BROADER SENSES OF SALVATION

The term *salvation,* in its broader sense, applies not only to justification, but to sanctification and glorification as well. Thus the gospel applies not only to the lost, but to the saved; because it is the power of God *for* salvation, it necessarily includes all aspects of salvation itself.

The Power of God for Justification

By faith we are *justified before God.* That is, by *faith in the gospel* we are declared righteous, the guilt and penalty of our sin is removed in Christ. God promises that if you "believe [have faith] in your heart that God raised Him from the dead [the gospel], you shall be saved [justified]" (Romans 10:9).

In Romans 4:5, Paul said: "But to the one who does not work, but believes in Him who justifies the ungodly, his *faith* is reckoned as *righteousness."* Faith in the finished work of Christ is the only means of justification. "Where then is boasting," said Paul. "It is excluded. By what kind of law? Of works? No, but by a law of faith. For we maintain that a man is *justified by faith* apart from works of the Law" (Romans 3:27–28; see also Galatians 3:21–22).

The power in the gospel is the power of God's love lavished upon the sinner, which elicits from him not only a response of love, but of surrender. This surrender is the expression of true faith, and by this faith alone, the sinner is justified before God.

The Power of God for Sanctification

But the Christian also is empowered by the gospel for sanctification in practical living. "For the word of the cross [the gospel] is to those who are perishing foolishness, but to us who are being saved it is the power of God" (1 Corinthians 1:18). "He Himself bore our sins *in His body on the cross*, that we might *die to sin* and *live to righteousness;* for by His wounds you were healed" (1 Peter 2:24); and again: "He died for all, that they who live should *no longer live for themselves,* but *for Him who died and rose again on their behalf* " (2 Corinthians 5:15).

What is a greater motivation to holy living than the gospel of Jesus Christ? Thus the power of God's love as apprehended in the gospel sets the Christian free from the power of sin to live in righteousness and submit to Christ's lordship.

The Power of God for Glorification

In the same way, the gospel is the power of God for glorification. It is the gripping power of the gospel that holds us and keeps us in a perseverance of faith to the end, to the time of our *future glorification* (see Colossians 1:22–23). Listen to Peter:

> Blessed be the God and Father of our Lord Jesus Christ, who according to His great mercy has caused us to be born again to a living hope through the resurrection of Jesus Christ from the dead [the gospel], to obtain an inheritance which is imperishable and undefiled and will not fade away, reserved in heaven for you, who are protected by the *power* of God through *faith* for a salvation ready to be revealed in the last time...and though you have not seen Him, you *love* Him, and though you do not see Him now, but *believe* in Him, you greatly rejoice with joy inexpressible and full of glory, obtaining as the *outcome* of your *faith* the *salvation* of your souls [future *glorification*]. (1 Peter 1:3–5, 8–9; see also 2 Thessalonians 2:14)

The love of God is the gripping and keeping power of the gospel. True faith is a response of love to this great love. *This* faith perseveres to the end.

Therefore, *every message we preach should be a gospel message,* not just those specifically geared toward evangelism. The gospel applies to the saved as well as to the lost. Thus we must learn to look for the gospel in every text we preach. Wherever the love of God may be seen, the gospel may be seen as well.

In our discussion of faith in the gospel, a word on the resurrection is in order. Scripture places paramount importance on the Resurrection of Christ as an essential for salvation. Indeed, Paul's definitive statement concerning the gospel, 1 Corinthians 15:3–8, is contained within a large passage devoted not to the Crucifixion but to the Resurrection. The Resurrection is so intrinsic to the gospel that both Paul and Peter use it alone to represent the gospel.

In 1 Peter 1:3, we read: "Blessed be the God and Father of our Lord Jesus Christ, who…has caused us to be born again…*through the resurrection* of Jesus Christ from the dead." Here, the Resurrection presupposes the death of Christ. This is reminiscent of Romans 10:9, where the Resurrection presupposes the Crucifixion: "If you confess with your mouth Jesus as Lord, and believe in your heart that God *raised Him from the dead,* you shall be saved." In this verse, belief in the Resurrection is imperative for salvation.

Today, therefore, it is alarming to note that the Resurrection is often slighted, even in many evangelical presentations of the gospel. The great emphasis is on the Crucifixion and, of course, that must be emphasized as the only means of our redemption, but the death of Christ is only half of the gospel message. Without the Resurrection, the Crucifixion would be of no benefit: "and if Christ has not been raised, your faith is worthless; you are still in your sins" (1 Corinthians 15:17). I wonder if this might be a ploy of Satan to distort the gospel message.

LORDSHIP

Another satanic distortion concerning salvation is quite prevalent among evangelicals today: the teaching that Christ's lordship is irrelevant to salvation. Must Jesus be Lord to be Savior? The answer is simply that Jesus *is* Lord. He cannot stop being Lord just to be Savior. If you come to Him for salvation you come to Him as who He is—the Lord Jesus Christ.

Some Fundamental Confusions

One major reason for the controversy regarding lordship and salvation is a confusion in definition. Some falsely believe that the word *lordship* is synonymous with perfect obedience. When they hear the argument that lordship is necessary for salvation, they think they are hearing an argument for a works-oriented salvation; you must be perfectly obedient to be saved. But lordship speaks not of perfect obedience, but of a relationship with a Lord—an Owner and a Ruler.

The natural result of such a relationship is obedience. To disobey puts the lie to that relationship in a practical sense. But obedience does not save. Nor does disobedience cause one to lose salvation, although disobedience does throw things out of kilter, as it is contrary to the lordship of Christ.

Another reason for a view of salvation that excludes the necessity of the lordship of Christ is a watering down of the truth based on a greed for converts. But we do men no favors by diluting the gospel message to make it more palatable. By doing so we exchange the truth for a lie.

Indeed, we have taught (to the point of orthodoxy in many of our evangelical churches) a salvation which costs us nothing, a relationship with God free from any responsibility on our part, either of an ongoing repentance or submission. But the Bible never teaches that we can know Christ as Savior and have the benefits of salvation yet have no sense of God's claim on our lives or our responsibility to obey Him.

Can we be saved and live any old way we choose? No. This thoroughly contradicts the teaching of Scripture. When a person truly comes to God, he comes with a heart for obedience. He does not bring a promise to be perfect; indeed, he admits that without God he is nothing. But he does come in surrender, bowing his will to the will of God, his heart and life in subservience to Christ.

To teach salvation without lordship is to give people false hope and deal treacherously with their deepest need, the need for forgiveness, cleansing, and reconciliation to God. It is to heal the brokenness of the people *superficially,* "'saying, "Peace, peace," but there is no peace'" (Jeremiah 6:14). There is indeed no peace with God until we come to God on His terms, a righteousness based on faith in the *Lord* Jesus

Christ (see Acts 20:21). "For we do not preach ourselves but Christ Jesus *as Lord*" (2 Corinthians 4:5).

By teaching an inadequate view of salvation, we have incurred the judgment of God on our churches, which are filled with "professing" Christians who more resemble the world than Christ. A true Christian is one who has counted the cost of following Christ, the cross of submission (see Luke 9:23). This does not mean that a Christian will never again rebel. But he must inevitably repent of that rebellion because of God's mark of ownership on his life.

That mark is *holiness*. We have been called to holiness, and we must answer that call. Lordship further defines practical holiness: holiness is separation from the world and unto God; lordship is being owned and ruled by no one (not even ourselves) except God. Certainly, we do not begin to know all that our surrender to Christ will mean, but that does not matter. He knows. And just there, we see the nature of true faith: "faith in our *Lord* Jesus Christ" (Acts 20:21).

Some Theological Considerations

In Romans 10:9–10 we see two essentials for salvation: faith in the gospel, which results in *righteousness;* and confession of Jesus as Lord, which results in *salvation.* Some have argued that in these verses, as elsewhere in the New Testament, when the word *Lord* is used to refer to Jesus, it simply means *God.* Thus we must accept Jesus as God in a *conceptual* sense, but not necessarily as our rightful owner and ruler.

However, the word used most often to represent the name Yahweh in the Old Testament (i.e., *Adonai,* which is usually translated as *Lord*) literally means sovereign one, the supreme one, or owner and ruler, because Yahweh *is* the owner and ruler. So to say, then, that Jesus is the same as God (and He clearly is), which is the same as Yahweh, which is the same as Lord, is also to say that Jesus is owner and ruler. Thus the argument against His lordship becomes an argument for it.

New Testament arguments for the sovereign lordship of Christ, as distinct from His Godship, abound (for example, see Acts 2:36 and Romans 14:9). Space does not permit a thorough expostulation here, but one more point must be made. The necessary verbal confession of Jesus as Lord is no more a work to *earn* salvation than is repentance or faith alone. True confession of Jesus as Lord comes only by the enabling of the Holy Spirit (see 1 Corinthians 12:3), who first enables our *sincerity*. Thus salvation is all of God, and to Him be all the glory!

The Heart of the Matter

The lordship of Christ is key to both positional and practical holiness. We are set apart by just this fact: we are not our own; we have been bought with a price (see 1 Corinthians 6:19-20). In addition, we have by the grace of God given ourselves away to Another, and we can no longer live our lives for ourselves. Yet the lordship of Christ speaks not so much of obligation as of privilege; not so much of fear as of love. Paul loved to call himself a bondservant or a love slave of Christ, and such are we.

Lordship speaks of love because lordship speaks of redemption. Redemption is an act of love. Christ paid a purchase price to own us. That price was His own blood, which testifies to an immense, over-powering love. Redemption is an act of rescue—rescuing love, selfless love, love that gives all for the sake of the beloved.

Christ has paid the purchase price for us, not that He might "lord" His authority over us as a dictator, but that we might be free to yield to His embrace (see Hosea 2:16). To confess Him as Lord is to give ourselves to Him in a surrender of love; to see His pierced hands and feet, knowing it was our sin that made those marks, and to say with Thomas the apostle, "'My Lord and my God'" (John 20:28). Our hearts are broken over our own unworthiness. We are overwhelmed. We can but lie back in the ocean waters of His love and be engulfed by them.

Hence our heart is to obey, because true obedience is motivated by love. God's call to holiness is an appeal to love, our love issuing forth as a response to His love for us.

CHAPTER FIVE

SECURITY

*But if anyone loves God, he is
known by Him.*

1 CORINTHIANS 8:3

D oubt is positive if it leads to a discovery of truth. But once
truth is apprehended, faith must be exercised. At this point
doubt is instability and is displeasing to God (see Hebrews
11:6; James 1:6–8). For Christians, doubt or insecurity about their salvation can be devastating.

Security comes with placing our faith in the right object. The
truths regarding the Lord Jesus Christ, His finished work on the cross,
and His glorious Resurrection constitute an adequate object on which
to rest our faith. Furthermore, a clear understanding of the basis of our
acceptance before God bolsters our faith. If we are not grounded in
these truths, we may be plagued with many doubts.

People doubt their salvation for three fundamental reasons:

1. They may be saved but have a poor understanding of the Bible's
   teaching about salvation and security. Thus they fall prey to the
   sometimes paralyzing accusations and lies of the devil.
2. They may be lost, yet because of some false, deceptive teaching,
   they may be deluded and think they are saved. Yet now and
   again they are troubled by doubt. This doubt may be the Holy
   Spirit awakening them to their condition.
3. They may be saved but plagued with guilt over sin in their lives.

Sin often causes Christians to doubt their salvation. Satan tempts them to sin; if they then yield to the temptation, he points an accusing finger. But their distress over sin and the doubts it may cause might actually be an indication of the reality of their Christianity, because sin is so contrary to their new life in Christ.

Paul told the members of the church in Corinth to examine themselves. "Test yourselves to see if you are in the faith; examine yourselves! Or do you not recognize this about yourselves, that Jesus Christ is in you—unless indeed you fail the test?" (2 Corinthians 13:5).

Thus each of us might ask a very direct question: "Am I really a Christian?" Some would say an immediate yes. Some, if honest, would have to say no, even if they appear to others to be Christians. Many others would simply not know. They might express their uncertainty in different ways: "I hope so," or "I'm trying to be," or "I think I'm a Christian." But each of these responses belie the absence of any security. Our security lies only in God and in what He has revealed through His Word.

We cannot approach the subject from every possible angle. We will focus on one: *the lordship of Christ,* which has great bearing on our security. In the gospel of John we find the classic passage on security. Jesus Himself says:

"My sheep hear My voice, and I know them, and they follow Me; and I give eternal life to them, and they shall never perish; and no one shall snatch them out of My hand. My Father, who has given them to Me, is greater than all; and no one is able to snatch them out of the Father's hand. I and the Father are one." (John 10:27–30)

TRIPLE SECURITY

The main point I would like to emphasize is in the first verse. Christ makes a significant statement there: "My sheep hear My voice, and I know them, and they follow Me."

The next statement is a *supportive* statement: "And I give eternal life to them, and they shall never perish." The remainder of the passage is an elaboration on this second statement.

To emphasize the central statement, let us begin with the peripheral and work our way back in. In the latter part of verse 28 through verse 30, Christ describes a *triple security:*

1. We are in His hand. What could be safer or more secure?
2. We are in the Father's hand. Christ uses this as evidence of His own credibility and, therefore, His ability to keep His sheep, which were *given to Him* by the Father who is greater than all. In addition, the Father lends His own power to keep.
3. Christ and the Father are *one.* Thus we are hidden not only within their hands, but within their unity.

Our security rests not in our ability to hold on to Him but in His ability to hold on to us. When I was a student in Dallas, Texas, I attended First Baptist Church, where Dr. W. A. Criswell was pastor. One of the illustrations he used was of a father and his little girl walking down the sidewalk on a busy city street. The father was holding the little girl's hand because the curb was very high and the traffic very heavy. When they came to an intersection, the child saw something shiny in the street and went off the curb after it. But the father, who was holding her hand, simply pulled her back up and sat her down on the sidewalk. If she had been holding on to him, she would have let go and been hurt by the whizzing traffic. But though she fell she was not hurled out into the danger, because *her father was holding her hand.*

SECURITY IN KNOWING CHRIST

The first part of verse 28 contains an emphasis on eternal life: "And I give eternal life to them, and they shall never perish." This is an emphatic statement of fact and promise, with all the power of God behind it.

Christ defined eternal life in the context of an intimate relationship with Himself and with the Father. Addressing the Father, He said: "And *this* is eternal life, that they may *know Thee,* the only true God, *and Jesus Christ* whom Thou hast sent" (John 17:3). Eternal life is more than heaven when we die. For one thing, it begins not when this life is over, but when we are born into God's family.

At that moment an eternal relationship is established. We no longer simply know about God; we know *God*. This is a fulfillment of the New Covenant promise of God: "'And they shall not teach again, each man his neighbor and each man his brother, saying, "Know the LORD," for they shall all know Me, from the least of them to the greatest of them'" (Jeremiah 31:34).

SECURITY IN BEING KNOWN BY CHRIST

In verse 27 of our passage, Christ says: "My sheep hear My voice, and *I know them*, and they follow Me." Now this may at first seem like an awkward statement. The sequence seems not to fit. One might think Christ should have said, "My sheep follow Me when they hear My voice because they know Me." But He specifically stresses a new point: "My sheep hear My voice, and *I know them*, and they follow Me."

This is language of great affection as well as great confidence. *"My sheep,"* He says (indicating that these are very precious sheep), *"hear My voice."* They are attentive to His voice; they know it and can distinguish it from all others.

"And I *know* them." This speaks of intimacy. He knows each one individually. In John 10:3 He says of a good shepherd, "he calls his own sheep by name."

"And they *follow* Me." The word *follow* implies submission. One who is ruled by Christ forsakes all to *follow Him*. Following is ongoing; it is not some event that happened in the past. Following is in the present tense.

The phrase in John 10:27 that will determine the focus of our study is: "And *I know them."* I propose that the foundation of both our salvation and our security rests not in our knowing Him, but in His knowing *us*. For example, 1 Corinthians 8:2–3 says: "If anyone supposes that he knows anything, he has not yet known as he ought to know; but if anyone loves God, *he is known by Him.*" The first verse here is an indictment to our pride—when we look at the omniscience of God, we realize that we don't know anything. Yet if we love God, we are known by Him. The message is clear: *It is better to be known by the One who knows everything than to think we know anything!*

Galatians 4:8–9 says: "However at that time, when you did not know God, you were slaves to those things which by nature are no gods. But now that you have come to know God, *or rather to be known by God,* how is it that you turn back again to the weak and worthless elemental things?" Clearly, being known by God is the more weighty matter in our relationship with *Him.*

Finally, in Matthew 7:21–23, one of the most controversial passages in the Scriptures, Christ emphasizes the imperative nature of His knowing us:

> "Not everyone who says to Me, 'Lord, Lord,' will enter the kingdom of heaven; but he who does the will of My Father who is in heaven. Many will say to Me on that day, 'Lord, Lord, did we not prophesy in Your name, and in Your name cast out demons, and in Your name perform many miracles?' And then I will declare to them, *'I never knew you;* DEPART FROM ME, YOU WHO PRACTICE LAWLESSNESS.'"

In verse 21, note the word *says:* "'Not everyone who *says* to Me, '"Lord, Lord"'"; and again in verse 22: "'Many will *say* to Me on that day, '"Lord, Lord."'" Lip service is never enough. And it might seem that the Lord is advocating a works-oriented salvation, but the next two verses show that this is not the case as He identifies those who would gain heaven on their own merit and calls their works *lawlessness.*

What verse 21 teaches is not a salvation by works, but that a walk of obedience is the true evidence of salvation. No one walks perfectly; we all fall at times. Yet when we fall, we get up, go on in faith, and persevere to the end.

The pronouncement of judgment in verse 23 is startling: "'*Depart from Me,* you who practice lawlessness.'" What a ring of finality! And the reason for this banishment is profound: not "you never knew Me," but "'*I never knew you.'*" On that day of judgment, nothing else will matter but to be known by *Him.*

Note that Christ does not say, "Depart from Me, *I used to know you, but I don't anymore."* He says, "'I *never* knew you.'" We cannot be known by God in this sense one day and not known by Him the next. The idea that one can lose his salvation is completely unbiblical. Sadly, it has arisen partly from an observation of people in the church who claim to be Christians but do not walk accordingly.

What then does it *mean* to be known by *God?* When so much hinges on it, for any real sense of security, we must understand what this means. There is a very simple yet profound answer: to be known by Him is to be known *as His.* Second Timothy 2:19 says, "Nevertheless, the firm foundation of God stands, having this seal, *'The Lord knows those who are his.'"* This may seem too simplistic, but the truly profound is often simple.

SECURITY AND THE LORDSHIP OF CHRIST

Once we have seen that to be known by Him is to be known as His, there is one last question which arises: *His what?* The word *Lord* is a key word, if not *the* key word, in some of the verses that stress the necessity of our being known by Christ; it means *owner* and *ruler.* To find the answer to our question let us consider these words one at a time.

1. If I know Jesus Christ as my owner, He knows me as *His purchased possession.*

First Corinthians 6:19–20 says: "Or do you not know that…you are not your own? For you have been bought with a price." That price is the blood of Christ. First Peter 1:18–19 says: "Knowing that you were not redeemed with perishable things like silver or gold from your futile way of life inherited from your forefathers, but with precious blood, as of a lamb unblemished and spotless, the blood of Christ." Romans 14:7–8 says: "For not one of us lives for himself, and not one dies for himself; for if we live, we live for the Lord, or if we die, we die for the Lord; therefore whether we live or die, *we are the Lord's."* This is *possessive.*

2. If I know Jesus Christ as my ruler, He knows me as His obedi-

ent subject.

In Luke 6:46, Christ asked, "'And why do you call Me, "Lord, Lord," and do not do what I say?'" (see also John 13:13–17). If Jesus Christ is our Lord, we have a responsibility to obey Him.

In 2 Timothy 2:19, we see both aspects of the word *Lord* in one verse. We have only considered the first half of this verse, which clearly speaks of Christ's ownership: "'The Lord knows those who are His.'" But the second half speaks just as clearly of His rulership: "'Let everyone who names the name of the Lord abstain from wickedness.'"

Thus we understand what it means to be known by Christ as His *purchased possession* and His *obedient subject.*

SECURITY IN LOVE

We have defined Christ's lordship as yielding to His embrace of love. Do we really love the Lord? If so, this is the greatest evidence to ourselves that we are His. A sobering scenario, which I first heard proposed by Richard Owen Roberts, throws some light on this question.

"Suppose," said Mr. Roberts, "that you are at home alone in a quiet place and, in the stillness of an instant, God comes to you and says: 'For years now, I have held you suspended by a thread over the jaws of hell. Your life has come to an end. Heaven is full; there is no room for you, and I am about to let you go. Is there any last word that you wish to say to Me?'"

What would you say? You might protest: "But I have done what You require. I have repented and believed." That implies that God owes you salvation and that repentance and faith are meritorious. Not so. A true Christian is aware deep within that he deserves nothing but hell. But there is another awareness inside him, which begins to swell in his breast: He is aware of a love for God, no matter what. This love has been planted there by God and is present in every believer. So, the best answer to the question above is: "If I am about to go to hell, that is only what I deserve. But You, God, deserve all praise. I love You, and I will go down to hell praising You."

Recently, I spoke with a young man in distressing doubt about his salvation, until I shared with him the scenario just mentioned and asked him what his response would be. Without hesitation he answered; "I guess I'd just say, 'I love You.'" In this answer he demonstrated a genuine love for God deep in his heart. I reminded him again that his security lay in being *known by* God, then I took him back to 1 Corinthians 8:3: "But if anyone *loves* God, he *is* known by Him." The love which he knew was in his heart was an evidence that he was indeed known by God. He saw it in a flash, and all the doubts melted away.

When I was a young Christian in my teens, something shook me and caused me to momentarily question what I had unashamedly embraced—that the Lord Jesus Christ was the only Savior from sin. I got alone with the Father, wept, and expressed to Him that if Jesus were not my Savior, I did not want to be saved. I did not want any other Savior but Him, and I still weep when I think back to that day. Where did such a love come from? It was established in me by God Himself. I can say with Rutherford: "Since He looked upon me, my heart is not my own. He hath run away to heaven with it."[1]

ONE FURTHER WORD

Salvation is all of God. Let me add that security is all of God as well. Speaking of Israel as a vineyard, God said, "I, the LORD, am its keeper; I water it every moment. Lest anyone damage it, I guard it night and day" (Isaiah 27:3). Certainly this can be applied to every believer in Christ as well.

"If God is for us, who is against us?" (Romans 8:31). God is the one who saved us; God is the one who keeps us. Salvation and security are not really our steps; they are God's. But they set the stage *for* our steps: *repentance* and *faith*. In these two steps we have our entrance to the path of intimacy with God.

PART THREE

KNOWING GOD—
AN INTIMATE WALK

"So let us know, let us press on to know the LORD.
His going forth is as certain as the dawn; and
He will come to us like the rain,
like the spring rain watering the earth."

HOSEA 6:3

There is a great restraint against using any language of a rapturous nature in reference to God. This may be chalked up to a pervasive sensuality in our thought culture, which relegates any terminology of intimacy to that which is either romantic or inordinate, and perhaps to a fear of being labeled a mystic or a charismatic. Thus we glory in our shame, which is our coolness and our pride; and we are shamed by our glory, which is our personal relationship with God.

The psalmist did not have that problem. Listen to his impassioned prayer: "O GOD, Thou art my God; I shall seek Thee earnestly; my soul thirsts for Thee, my flesh yearns for Thee, in a dry and weary land where there is no water" (Psalm 63:1). Even in our sophistication, we cannot deny that there is a thirst which can be quenched by no other draught than the pure, sweet presence of God. He has made us needy that we might find in Him the fulfillment of our needs.

Yet God does not exist to meet our needs. That is man-centered theology. However, we need God. If we don't have Him, we have nothing. If we have Him, we have everything.

In this regard, the Scripture makes use of an unusual word in reference to God: *portion.* "My flesh and my heart may fail, but God is the strength of my heart and my *portion* forever" (Psalm 73:26). "'The LORD is my *portion,*' says my soul, 'Therefore I have hope in Him'" (Lamentations 3:24; see also Psalm 16:5; 119:57; 142:5). Here is a dear word! The sentiment is that, while others may choose another portion, God is enough for me; He is all I need.

Let me ask you a question. What do you really *have?* Every material possession, every person dear to you could be taken away at any time. The only possession that cannot be taken away is Jesus. Do you have Him?

Again, what do you really *need?* The Christian acknowledges in his heart that, if everything else were stripped away but Jesus remained, He would be enough. The one essential is Jesus.

But let me ask further: What do you really *want?* Here is the unveiling of our hearts. Oh, we want so many things! We are always chasing after something we think will finally satisfy us, only to find that the more we have, the more we want. The truth is that nothing really satisfies but Jesus. Whether we realize it or not, He is all we really want, or ever *could* want.

As the old spiritual says, "You can have all the world, but give me Jesus." Is this shameless sentimentality? No. If it is fleshed out in day-to-day living, it is the essence of true devotion and the wellspring of true holiness.

For the Christian, his entire life is to be an intimate walk with God. But that intimacy is developed one day at a time as he sets aside, each day, some increment of time exclusively for communion with his God. Thus is he fortified to walk with God all through the day. The emphasis in the following chapter will be on our time alone with God. There is no substitute for this time. This is where intimacy begins.

CHAPTER SIX

DEVOTION

*They looked to Him and were radiant, and
their faces shall never be ashamed.*

PSALM 34:5

"Every morning, lean thine arms upon the window sill of heaven
and gaze into the face of thy Lord." So wrote some lover of
Christ long ago, describing what we often call a quiet time of
devotion. For centuries, those who have truly sought to know God
intimately have found it imperative to set aside some time in each day
to focus their attention and affection on Him.

Another shining metaphor for this focus is the word *beholding*,
found in 2 Corinthians 3:18: "But we all, with unveiled face beholding as in a mirror the glory of the Lord, are being transformed into the
same image from glory to glory, just as from the Lord, the Spirit."
This word gives us an overall theme for this chapter. Here we will see
beholding as the essence of *devotion*.

Let us briefly examine this very significant verse, phrase by phrase.

"But we all, with unveiled face..." Here is a contrast between the
veiled face of Moses that represents the veiled glory of a failed
covenant (see 2 Corinthians 3:6–13), and the open-faced liberty of the
New Covenant given us by the Spirit of Christ (see 2 Corinthians
3:17). We also see a contrast between Christians under the New
Covenant and the unbelieving Jews under the Old Covenant, who
Paul said had a veil of unbelief over their very hearts (see 2 Corinthians
3:14–16).

"Beholding as in a mirror..." These words speak of an *intense* focus. In Paul's time there were no clear mirrors such as we have today. To make out your own image you had to look intently at a mirror and focus your vision.

"The glory of the Lord..." Here is the object of our beholding. In devotion, all that is dazzling and glorious about Christ must captivate our thoughts.

As a result of this beholding, we are *"being transformed into the same image from glory to glory..."* We cannot transform ourselves. God transforms us, progressively, into the very image of the Christ we behold.

"...just as from the Lord, the Spirit." The word *Lord,* in reference to the Spirit, is unique to this verse and to the verse which immediately precedes it: "Now the Lord is the Spirit; and where the Spirit of the Lord is, there is liberty" (2 Corinthians 3:17). This speaks of the Holy Spirit as the Spirit of the Lord Jesus.

We will not be transformed by beholding ourselves; we must look away from self to Jesus. Neither are we transformed by looking at the world. That focus leads only to restlessness and dissatisfaction. But when Christ is our heart's focus, nothing else matters but Him. Even in the worst of circumstances, we have an inner contentment and joy. As John Newton wrote long ago:

> Content with beholding His face
> My all to His pleasure resigned,
> No changes of season or place
> Would make any change in my mind;
> While blest with a sense of His love,
> A palace a toy would appear,
> And prisons would palaces prove,
> If Jesus would dwell with me there.[1]

By this beholding, Paul could say, "For to me, to live is Christ" (Philippians 1:21), and "When Christ, who is our life, is revealed" (Colossians 3:4). Christ must not be just one *part* of our lives; He must *be* our life. Are our lives *defined* by devotion to Him? Is intimacy with Him our hunger, our passion, our flame? If so, then God the Holy Spirit is free to do His work of transformation in our lives.

This intimacy, of necessity, involves time alone with God. We cannot get to know anyone if we do not spend time with him. So it is in our relationship with God.

MOTIVATION FOR TIME ALONE WITH GOD

When we speak of a "quiet time," so often the major emphasis is on the *how* rather than the *why*. Substandard and inadequate motivation only leads to frustration, inconsistency, indifference, and failure. Therefore, we will first consider the *why* of devotion, with the hope that it will be an incentive to true intimacy.

WHY: A MATTER OF LOVE

Let us briefly consider three very pointed questions pertinent to the development of an intimate walk with God.

Does a Christian want to sin? We may immediately say no. And yet, when faced with temptation, we are often "carried away and enticed" by our own lust (James 1:14). In that moment of temptation, we do want to sin. Were this not so, temptation would be like dropping a match in water. For us, it is often more like dropping a match in gasoline. Nevertheless, if we yield to temptation, afterward we regret it and reaffirm in our hearts that sin is not what we really want. The true heart of the Christian is to please God (see Philippians 2:13). *The Christian does not want to sin.*

Does a Christian have to sin? Romans 6:7 says that we have been crucified with Christ and that "he who has died is freed from sin." This means that we are freed from *bondage* to sin, from the *dominance* of sin (see Romans 6:6–14). The lost man is enslaved to sin; he does not have a choice—he *has to sin*. But the Christian has been given the ability to choose not to sin.

First Corinthians 10:13 says: "No temptation has overtaken you but such as is common to man; and God is faithful, who will not allow you to be tempted beyond what you are able, but with the temptation will provide the way of escape also, that you may be able to endure it." In addition, we are told in 2 Peter that we have been granted "everything pertaining to life and godliness" (2 Peter 1:3). In other words, we have been given everything we need to live a godly life. That includes the indwelling of the Holy Spirit, the enabling grace of God, and the "precious and magnificent promises" of God's Word (2 Peter 1:4). *The Christian does not have to sin.*

Why do we sin? If we don't *want* to sin and don't *have* to sin, then why *do* we? The answer is simple but painful: We sin because we *don't love God.*

Now that statement may cause many to protest, "But I do love God!" Yes, but do you love Him *enough* to obey?

Listen to the words of our Lord to His disciples: *"If you love Me, you will keep My commandments"* (John 14:15). Thus our *obedience* is in direct proportion to our *love*.

The Dilemma of Lovelessness

Love is not a warm, fuzzy feeling. We ought to feel deeply about God, but if that is all there is, it is mere sentimentality. We think love—even love for God—must gratify the senses. So we look for a stimulant to make us feel love. But this is more an indication of self-love than love for God. One may be sentimental about God or proclaim a deeply felt devotion and yet live in perpetual disobedience. This is not love. Love is *obedience*. Obedience is both the expression and the evidence of genuine love toward God.

A lack of love for Christ is at the root of all that is wrong with the church today. Where there is not a total disregard for true obedience (accompanied by a self-indulgent fascination with every self-help technique we can slap a "Christian" label on), there is a "good deeds" mentality that has at its root not love, but greed—a desire to win by our good works the approval of God or men.

There may also be a sense of obligation rooted in guilt. Sad to say, this is often fostered by pastors who put the cart before the horse, emphasizing obedience to the commandments without establishing the proper motivation. They simply fail to teach people to love Jesus and to obey as an expression of that love. This fosters a loveless righteousness which is not true righteousness at all. This quickly degenerates into a form of legalism, at best a commitment to a program. Thus people are inadvertently encouraged to substitute busy-ness and activity for intimacy with Christ.

Any motivation for obedience, other than love for Jesus, is substandard and will sooner or later lose its punch. However, if we focus on loving Jesus, we *will* keep His commandments as an expression of that love.

The Absence of Intimacy

Why, then, don't we love Him? Simply because we *don't know Him.* We believe so many lies from Satan about God: God is a disapproving dictator who is impossible to please; God is aloof and indifferent to our individual needs, and so on. But one who truly knows God sees through the lies of Satan and loves God spontaneously; he cannot help himself, because he sees how truly lovable and loving God actually is.

What, then, is the primary thing we have to know about God in order to love Him? Simply this: that *He loves us.* First John 4:19 says, "We love, *because* He first loved us." It is His love that motivates us to love in return. When we first fell in love with God, it was because He loved us first. It follows that *the more we see of His love, the more we grow in our love for Him.*

The supreme expression of God's love is the Cross. That is why the great Charles Spurgeon urged other preachers to "make much of the cross." That is why Paul said, "I determined to know nothing among you except Jesus Christ, and Him crucified" (1 Corinthians 2:2). Our love for God will grow as we appreciate His love for us expressed through the Cross. If we will focus on *knowing God,* who sacrificed His own Son for us, we will grow in our love for Him and thus in our obedience.

The Shame of Neglect

But *why do we not know God any better than we do?* Surely, it is because *we spend so little time with Him.* Here is where the quiet time comes in. We cannot expect to know another person without spending time with him, and so it is with God. We must spend time with Him—time enough for real communication—if we ever expect to really know Him.

We cannot, however, get to know God just by being in His presence. We must talk to Him and listen to what He has to say to us. We speak to God in prayer, and He speaks to us primarily through His Word. Thus as we spend time in prayer and in meditation on the Word, God begins to reveal Himself to us, little by little. Then we really begin to know Him.

The Tragedy of Indifference

Then *why do we spend so little time with God?* The obvious answer is really twofold: first, a *lack of desire,* and second, a *lack of a sense of need.* We may see time alone with God as a benefit, but do we see it as a *necessity?* In truth, it is our lifeline. How do we expect to do anything but sin if we don't spend time with God?

We may profess that we need that time, but if we let other things take its place, we contradict our words with our actions. After all, we always find time to do the things we really want to do. Every time we go out of the house without having spent time with God we are saying that we don't really need Him.

The Pride of Our Hearts

Why don't we see the need? The bottom line is *pride.* At least one aspect of pride is an independent spirit. It is saying to God, whether consciously or subconsciously, "I don't need You."

Pride is the *taproot of all sin.* Every sin can ultimately be traced back to pride. Selfishness, or an inordinate self-love, is the *essence* of sin. It is easy to see how any particular sin can be traced back to selfishness, because selfishness says, "I want." But selfishness can be traced back to pride, because pride says, "I have a right to what I want; I am what matters; I am the center of the universe!" Every manifestation of pride is a form of either loving self above God, which is spiritual adultery, or worshiping self in place of God, which is idolatry. However, when we humble ourselves before Him, we see our sin for what it is, and thus, we see our great need for God. Humility, to a great extent, is simply saying to God, "I need You."

Acknowledgment of Our Need

When we first come to God, we readily admit our need. We are so humbled by our sin and by the grace of God. But later we tend to revert to our independent ways. Even if we are quite dependent on other people, we like to be very independent from God.

The truth is that we are dependent on Him for everything, whether we realize it or not. God has built into our everyday lives constant reminders of our need for Him. Within every twenty-four-hour period we must stop periodically to eat, and we must sleep to renew our strength for the next day. This should remind us that we are weak and needy, and that all good things come from God. Every breath we take, the delicate balance of our health, our abilities and talents—all these are gifts from God.

Childlike Humility

A young couple once asked me what I thought was the most important thing they could teach their children. I reminded them that, from the time children enter the world, we do everything we can to teach them to be independent from us—to walk and talk on their own, to feed and dress themselves, and so on. As they grow, we give them the tools they need to think and do for themselves.

This is all good, but we also need to teach them two things. First, their total dependence on *God*—that the air they breathe and the food they eat, as well as health and sunshine and butterflies and puppy dogs and all good things, come from God—and second, that they are to *depend* on God and thus to consult God about everything. God is worthy of their trust, and they often know that better than we do.

God's role as Father never changes. Though we reach different levels of maturity as Christians (see Philippians 3:15–18), we never cease being little children in our dependence on God. We began as children and we must continue as children. Christ said, "'Truly I say to you, whoever does not receive the kingdom of God like a child shall not enter it at all'" (Mark 10:15); and, "'Whoever then humbles himself as this child, he is the greatest in the kingdom of heaven'" (Matthew 18:4).

The famous missionary Hudson Taylor, who had tremendous "grown-up" responsibilities as the founder and head of the China Inland Mission during the 1800s, loved this little, anonymous prayer:

> Make me humble and mild,
> Just a very little child…
> To be used, dear Lord, by Thee.[2]

Enabling Grace

If we will humble ourselves before God as little children and admit our need for Him, God will give us the grace we need to spend time with Him. And we do need grace even for this. Have you ever felt a certain resistance to just *opening the Bible?* Why? It is because of pride. Just the simple act of opening the Bible is an admission of our need for God, and we are often too proud to admit that need.

What must we have to open the Bible? Will power? No. We need *grace.* "GOD IS OPPOSED TO THE PROUD, BUT GIVES GRACE TO THE HUMBLE" (1 Peter 5:5). Therefore, if we will humble ourselves by admitting our need, God will give us grace to open the Bible.

Hunger for the Word

One of Satan's great lies is that the Bible is as boring as dry toast— nourishing perhaps, but *flavorless.* This lie seems to be born out in the experiences of many people. But this is because they have rarely, if ever, had a real *taste* of the Word of God.

David said of the precepts of God, "They are more desirable than gold, yes, than much fine gold; sweeter also than honey and the drippings of the honeycomb" (Psalm 19:10). The prophet Jeremiah said: "Thy words were found and I ate them, and Thy words became for me a joy and the delight of my heart; for I have been called by Thy name, O LORD God of hosts" (Jeremiah 15:16). David and Jeremiah knew what it was to taste the Word of God. They hungered for it. If we taste the Word often enough, we begin to develop a hunger for it as well.

But what does it really mean to taste the Word? It means more than just reading it, though reading is essential to tasting; it means more than just meditation or memorization, although these are vital as well. Truly to taste the Word of God is to have that Word applied by the Holy Spirit to some need in our lives: a question answered, a promise given, a wound healed. When the Word of God meets the need of our hearts, it tastes good; and if we taste it often enough, we develop a hunger.

There are three basic approaches to reading the Bible, all of which should be part of our lives. The first approach is *study,* which is very essential if we would please God and be people of the Word. Paul admonished Timothy: "Be diligent to present yourself approved to God as a workman who does not need to be ashamed, handling accurately the word of truth" (2 Timothy 2:15). In study, we primarily seek to know *the Bible.* This is the proper time to pull commentaries and study helps off the shelf.

The second approach is what I call *leisure reading.* This heading includes the through-the-Bible reading programs and reading large sections of Scripture at a time for personal enjoyment, which is extremely helpful for gaining a sense of continuity.

The third approach is *devotional reading,* or reading to *know God.* As we spend devotional time in the Word and in prayer, God is pleased to commune with us and to reveal more of who He is, little by little. As He does, our relationship with Him naturally deepens, and we appreciate His love to greater degrees. Our response is a keener love for Him, resulting in a life characterized more by obedience and holiness than by sin.

What is the result of *obedience?* Jesus says: "He who has My commandments and keeps them, he it is who loves Me; and he who loves Me shall be loved by My Father, and I will love him, and will *disclose Myself to him"* (John 14:21). According to this verse, the result of obedience is a deeper personal communion with the Father and the Son, in which Christ reveals more of Himself to us so that we may know Him even better.

Thus a wondrous circle is established. As we spend time with God, we grow to know Him, and thus to love Him and to obey Him. When we obey Him, He lets us know Him better, and thus we love Him more, and thus obey Him more, and thus He reveals more of Himself to us—and so the circle continues.

Why should we spend time with God? Let us return to the first question we asked: *Does a Christian want to sin?* If the answer is no, then time alone with God is more than a good idea; it is a necessity.

WHY: A MATTER OF TRUST

Another result of not knowing God is not *trusting* Him. How can we truly trust Him if we do not know Him? And how can we know Him if we do not spend time with Him? As we spend time in devotion, beholding His glory, God allows us to know Him little by little and thus to trust Him, because we see just how trustworthy He is.

What, then, must we know about God in order to *trust* Him? There are three basic truths which answer that question:

1. God wants only what is best for us.
2. Only God can give us what is best.
3. Only God knows what is best.

The first truth is based on God's love. If God loves us, surely He wants only what is best for us. The second is based on God's omnipotence. God is all-powerful; therefore, He alone is equipped to give us what is best.

The third (and here is where our faith so often fails) is based on God's omniscience. He knows everything, including what is best for us. Sometimes we think that we know better than God does, but we are mistaken. God sees the future and knows what is coming around the next corner, while we can't see beyond our noses. It just makes sense to trust a God like that. But we will trust Him only if we really know Him well enough to believe that these three things are true.

Trusting God begets trusting God. The better we know Him (not know *about* Him, but know *him*), the more we see His faithfulness, and thus the easier it is to trust Him. It is not our faith that is great but His faithfulness. God always comes through. It doesn't take a great amount of faith to trust a God like that.

Trusting God manifests itself in *submission* and *dependence*. If we trust God, it is easy to submit and to depend. This is true humility, and God gives grace to the humble—even for obedience.

The Sin of Not Loving and Not Trusting

We see, in our lack of knowledge about God, a *reason* or an *explanation* for our lack of love and trust in Him, but not an *excuse*.

Not to love and not to trust God are very great sins. Not to *love* God is to break the first and foremost commandment: "'"YOU SHALL LOVE THE LORD YOUR GOD WITH ALL YOUR HEART, AND WITH ALL YOUR SOUL, AND WITH ALL YOUR MIND"'" (Matthew 22:37). Not to *trust* God is unbelief, and unbelief is the basis of man's condemnation: "'He who does not believe has been judged already, because he has not believed in the name of the only begotten Son of God'" (John 3:18; see also John 12:44–48; Hebrews 11:6).

Any sin we could name is actually a manifestation of either lovelessness or unbelief or both. These sins before all others *must* be confessed to God. Horatio Bonar expresses this poignantly:

> Ah! mine iniquity
> Crimson hath been,
> Infinite, infinite
> Sin upon sin:
> Sin of not loving Thee,
> Sin of not trusting Thee,
> Infinite sin.

The simple way to gain victory over these and all other sins is simply to spend time with God. Nothing sets the Christian apart from the world more than daily, loving communion with God, and nothing is more holy than obedience as an expression of love and trust. This kind of obedience is the manifestation of practical holiness.

A METHOD FOR TIME ALONE WITH GOD

Next, we will consider the *how* of time alone with God. There are many approaches, all of which have merit. The following suggestions can be particularly helpful in getting the most out of that time.

PRELIMINARY GOALS

First, we must know what our goals are. We need both an *overall goal,* which should be one that exceeds our grasp, and a *daily goal* that we can actually attain.

Our overall goal, and the highest goal possible, is simply *knowing God*. That may seem too simplistic, but this is a goal toward which we will be striving throughout eternity. Every other goal is substandard. There is a difference between knowing the *Bible* and knowing the *God* of the Bible. Again, there is a difference between knowing things *about* God and knowing *God*. Our supreme goal in our devotional time is just to *know Him,* and nothing less will do.

However, we must also have a realistic daily goal. That goal is simply *to spend time with God*. When we contemplate what that really means, we begin to see the loftiness of such a goal. Yet it is attainable on a daily basis.

There are substandard goals here, too. Some people are naturally self-disciplined; thus they may tend to have a quiet time just because they have been told they should. But having this as their only motivation is little more than checking off another discipline. Some may observe a quiet time to appease their consciences and make them feel good about themselves, but that also falls short of a focus on God.

Often, the goal is to learn new truth, but even that goal is less than the best. What about those times when it seems we are not learning anything? If learning new truth is our highest goal, we will be discouraged and quit. God has purposes for times of silence. Sometimes He is silent to test our faith and perseverance. At other times His silence is necessary for our spiritual development.

We go through growth spurts spiritually, then we experience a time of God's silence, and this can cause distress. It might be due to sin in our lives. But it might have nothing to do with sin. It might simply be a time for God to use our circumstances to test and solidify us.

Sometimes we get impatient with this process, as I did as a young Christian. An old, saintly woman said to me once: "Son, God is growing you up as fast as He can without killing you!" How true!

If we set a daily goal to truly *spend time with God,* without ever settling for anything less, then even if God is silent, we will have lifted ourselves up to the holiest privilege any single day could possibly hold.

What, then, does it really mean to spend time with God? We

sometimes think it is a matter of "conjuring up God" through having everything ordered just so. We must have the right frame of mind, the right emotion, the right place, the right time—even the right Bible, the right notebook, and the right pen! Does this not sound like a ploy of the devil to keep us from even trying to spend time alone with God?

We cannot conjure up God. Instead, we learn to be aware of His *presence,* not by a feeling but by *faith.* There will be days when God seems very near, and others when He seems quite distant. But we know He is with us even at those times, because of our *faith* in the witness of His Word:

> Where can I go from Thy Spirit? Or where can I flee from Thy presence? If I ascend to heaven, Thou art there; If I make my bed in Sheol, behold, Thou art there. If I take the wings of the dawn, if I dwell in the remotest part of the sea, even there Thy hand will lead me, and Thy right hand will lay hold of me. (Psalm 139:7–10)

As we are faithful in our everyday goal to spend time with God, little by little God will help us realize our overall goal: to know Him. It is necessary to set aside a certain amount of time to spend alone with God. I think that everyone needs at least thirty minutes to cover Bible reading, prayer, and worship. It may not be long before we want to add more time, but thirty minutes is a good beginning.

HOW: BIBLE READING

Let me suggest a method for reading devotionally, which consists of two preparations and a three-step process.

The Right Approach: Preparing Our Hearts

Before reading the Scripture, we must approach it correctly. Our approach should include *prayer, faith,* and *patience.* This is simple enough, but each element is important and must not be left out.

Prayer

Every morning, before we begin to read, we must pray, humbly asking God to speak to us through His Word *if He wants to*. This last phrase is very important. We are not demanding, but requesting, and if God chooses not to speak specifically to us on a given morning, that is His prerogative. We must not worry. Our daily goal is simply to spend time with God. If we follow these steps we can go away from our quiet time knowing that we have done just that, even if we have not heard a specific word from Him. God may be silent to test our faith, which is the next preparation.

Faith

We have asked God to speak; now we must believe that He will if He so chooses. Often we ask God for something but never believe that He will give it. We must approach our quiet time not with insistence, but with expectancy, believing that God can and will communicate with us as He chooses.

Patience

The third aspect of our approach is *patience*. We must put the urgent demands of the day out of our minds and guard this time as essential and sacred, doing all we can to quiet our souls. We are waiting before a holy God. We have an audience with the King of kings, and thus should not be in a hurry to rush away from this time of privilege.

The Right Posture: Praying through Scripture

As we have approached Scripture with prayer, faith, and patience, so we must read in the same posture.

Prayer

As we read, we must talk to God about what we are reading, asking questions, claiming promises, obeying commands, and confessing sins that may come to light. We must also listen and silently contemplate what we think God might be saying to us through what we have read.

However, this is not the time to run to the shelf for a commentary and start studying the passage in that way. There is a time for study, but our quiet time is not that time. In quiet time, we read to know God. The Bible is the meeting place where we come face to face with God and behold His glory.

Faith

Next, we must read the Scripture with *faith,* believing specifically that God is present. We do not know His presence by feelings, which come and go, but by faith. Faith is what pleases Him (see Hebrews 11:6). Do we believe that God is present with us? We can believe it simply because He says so (see Psalm 139).

Patience

We must never be in a hurry to finish a verse or a chapter. Our daily quiet time goal is just to spend time with God, keeping in view our overall goal to *know* Him.

In these moments alone with God we must patiently listen and allow Him, if He so chooses, to guide us through what we are reading. When God is speaking through a passage, a phrase, a verse, or even a single word, we must not be in a hurry to go further. We should "camp out" in that place until God ceases to speak and then quietly move on. When our time is up we should stop right where we are, even if it is in the middle of a verse, and pick up right there the next morning.

Why should we be in a hurry? God is in no hurry. We must give Him complete freedom to take us where *He* wants us to go. It is usually best to pick out one book of the Bible and finish that before going on to another. Pray for God's guidance as to which book to read. All of which leads to a wonderful sense that we have been through that book with God, at His pace, under His leadership—great incentive to continue on!

HOW: PRAYER

There are a number of approaches to *prayer* during quiet time. I have found it helpful to write my prayers out in a notebook. It is always encouraging to go back and read those entries and see how God has answered past petitions and prayers of intercession.

Our prayer time should include certain elements, such as confession of sin, praise, thanksgiving, personal requests, and intercession. The order is not so important; we should let God lead in that. One of the best prayers we can pray for ourselves is that God would put us on the hearts of some others who will lift us up to Him. Then we can focus more on intercession.

It is good to have a list of people for whom we are praying, but lists can become so cumbersome that we end up just calling out names before God. It may be best to divide the list by the days of the week. There may be some we want to pray for every day, but others can be given to specific days of the week. Even at that, it is best to look at the list for each day and ask God to point out one or two people for whom to pray very specific prayers on that day. God will burden our hearts if we are sensitive to Him. A list is a tool and a guide, not a law. As God directs, we will eventually pray quality prayers for everyone on our list.

The Reason We Pray

Why do we pray? Do we pray to get God's attention? No. We *have* God's attention. Matthew 10:29–31 says: "'Are not two sparrows sold for a cent? And yet not one of them will fall to the ground apart from your Father. But the very hairs of your head are all numbered. Therefore do not fear; you are of more value than many sparrows.'"

Do we pray to inform God? No. God already knows everything. Matthew 6:8 says, "'Your Father knows what you need, before you ask Him.'" Nevertheless, it pleases Him for us to ask for what we need, because, by asking, we confess our dependence on Him.

What's more, by coming to Him with our requests, we keep the lines of communication open. This speaks of the real reason we pray, which is to glorify God by getting to *know* Him. As we get to know Him, we become *reflections of His glory.*

Prayer is not manipulating God or bringing Him around to our way of thinking. We cannot through prayer use God for our own purposes. True prayer originates with God, not with us, whether it is prayer for ourselves or for others.

Prayer for ourselves begins with the providence of God in our circumstances and relationships. By that providence *He* shows us our need for *Him,* and with the Word *He* shows us our own hearts (see Hebrews 4:12).

True prayer for others—real intercession, which can accomplish much—begins with a burden from God, and with *His* revealing to us, in moments of stillness, how *He* would have us pray. Then we in turn release that burden back to Him. It does not begin with our sympathy for others, nor with explaining what we think they need. Therefore, an essential part of intercession is listening as God reveals *His* best will for them. Then we pray accordingly.

Some see intercession as a way to impose their own will on another indirectly. For example, parents of teenagers may pray for their children, not necessarily according to the guidelines of Scripture, but according to what they think is best, without really considering that God's best might be very different from their own. They may pray very earnest prayers, thinking they can get God on their side, and thus have their own way. Yet as much as those parents love their children, God loves them more, and He alone knows what is best for them. The best prayer any of us can pray for those under our care is for God to have *His* way.

Prayer is not about *our* will; it is about the will of *God.* The basis of answered prayer is not our desire, earnestness, or faith, but the will of God. Consider two more fundamental truths in this regard.

First, God's will in regard to everything, great or small, in any part of time, was established in eternity past independent of the limits of time. In other words, *God already knows what He intends to do.*

However, *God has chosen to do what He intends to do in answer to prayer.* Thus He includes us in His providential will by burdening us to pray, so that in answer to our prayers, He may do what He fully intended to do in the first place. What a tremendous honor this is for us! When we pray with a God-given burden, it is because He has chosen to use us as an integral part of carrying out His will. God will add to our prayers whatever He must, including supernatural miracles that alter the natural laws of cause and effect. But He will have His way.

Intercession reaches across all boundaries of space and time, because God is eternal and omnipotent. When we raise our thoughts, our hearts, and our faith to a true harmony with the will of God toward another, our prayer touches that life regardless of all boundaries. Even when those we love are many miles away, there is a common ground of fellowship with them in prayer.

> There is a place where spirits blend,
> Where friend holds fellowship with friend:
> Tho' sundered far, by faith they meet
> Around one common mercy seat.[3]

The Way We Pray

We are instructed to pray *in Jesus' name* (see John 16:24). This means to pray according to what *Christ* wants, not what we want. His name represents *His* interests, *His* will, and everything that *He* is.

If you were sent to France as an ambassador of the United States, when speaking to the officials of that government or to the French people, you would represent the foreign policy of the president of the United States. Likewise, when we pray in Jesus' name we are representing *His* desires. We would do well to know what those desires are. Many are revealed in Scripture, but He also reveals His will in times of prayer.

Prayer in Jesus' name is a serious matter, one of great responsibility. It must be approached with humility and a sobering realization of our fallibility. Yet, so often, we very lightly tag "in Jesus' name" on the end of our prayers. Some treat the words like a talisman, and they treat faith in His name like a magic wand or a bag of fairy dust that they can sprinkle on their prayers to ensure that they will get whatever they want.

This is the name-it-and-claim-it mentality of our day, which too often sees prayer as a means for personal gain, faith as a secret formula for success, and God as an errand boy who jumps if we push the right button or use the right formula. If you say the right things and have enough faith, God will give you whatever you want. This is misplaced faith—faith in *faith* rather than faith in *God*.

Faith is, of course, an essential component of an effective prayer life, but the *amount* of faith is not nearly as important as the *object* of faith. Faith must have an adequate object, and only God is an adequate object for faith.

Faith is the *confidence* of things *not seen* (see Hebrews 11:1). The only way to pray with real confidence is to pray *according to the will of God.* First John 5:14–15 says: "And this is the confidence which we have before Him, that, if we ask anything *according to His will,* He hears us. And if we know that He hears us in whatever we ask, we know that we have the requests which we have asked from Him."

Only when we get past our selfishness and sympathies, into the heart and will of God, can we know that our prayers will be heard and answered. Praying, "Thy will be done" is seen by some as a cop-out for lack of faith. However, a true heart for God's will to be accomplished, rather than for one's own selfish ends to be served, is the perfect companion for any amount of faith and a true expression of trust in God.

At the same time, if we have a burden for someone and cannot discern how God would have us pray for them, our main work of intercession is to hold them before God and ask the Holy Spirit to intercede through us for them (see Romans 8:26–27). This is part of what the Bible calls standing in the gap (see Ezekiel 22:30).

To be an intercessor is an awesome responsibility. It is also hard work; it requires selflessness, perseverance, and above all, true intimacy with God.

HOW: WORSHIP

Worship is simply a *humble preoccupation with God.* All but the one object that captivates our attention flies away and is gone. Truly to worship God is to be so focused on *Him* and so fascinated with *Him* that we forget about ourselves, "lost in wonder, love, and praise."[4]

Worship is not merely a preoccupation of the mind, but also of the *heart.* Each day, in our quiet time, we must worship God by *fixing our hearts on Him.* It is frighteningly true that we can spend time in the Word and in prayer and yet never do this one essential thing. Fixing our hearts on God involves a deliberate stirring of our *affections* toward Him. We do this by reminding ourselves of who God is and what He has done.

We can accomplish this by simple meditation on one of His divine attributes, or on one of the names of God, or perhaps on some evidence of His great love. Here is where hymns and poetry are most helpful. It is good to have a hymnal available during quiet time.

What good is a quiet time if our hearts are not thus fixed on God? We would be left to face the day with roving hearts and unmet longings. "'They have forsaken Me, the fountain of living waters, to hew for themselves cisterns, broken cisterns, that can hold no water'" (Jeremiah 2:13).

Now, there are days when all of this seems easy and natural, but other days when our hearts seem cold. Even our quiet time seems like walking through molasses. But that is when we must *deliberately* remind ourselves of God, disregarding our negative feelings.

Sing a hymn about the precious blood of Jesus, or God's amazing grace, or His great faithfulness. It won't be long before your feelings will come "whimpering along behind" and catch up with your obedience and faith.

If we do not fix our hearts on God in the morning, they will fix on the next thing that comes along. When temptation comes, our hearts will fix on that, and we will sin (see 2 Chronicles 12:14). Or when an opportunity comes along that may not be God's will, our hearts will fix on that opportunity. Then if we go to God at all, we will go not for *guidance,* but for *permission,* and there is a vast difference between the two.

Practicing the Presence of God

Practicing God's presence simply means practicing *an awareness of God by faith.* Hebrews 4:13 says, "And there is no creature hidden from His sight, but all things are open and laid bare to the eyes of Him with whom we have to do."

When I was in high school, students were not allowed to smoke on campus. But some of the boys would smoke in the bathrooms at recess. My mother found out and told me not to go in that bathroom and smoke. Then she said a curious thing: She would not always see everything I did, but God would. That has stuck with me all these years. We can never hide from God. He is always there.

By deliberately practicing this awareness, we can learn to be conscious of God even in our busiest moments, even when circumstances and relationships threaten to hinder that consciousness. Indeed, these are the two things which tend to make us feel most separate from God.

For example, imagine that you have just had a wonderful time of meditation and prayer in the presence of God. You come out of your house ready to face the day, but just as you are about to get into your car, you discover that one of your tires is flat. You might react with frustration and anger, or you might react with take-charge ingenuity and totally focus on fixing the problem. After you get on the road and calm down a bit, you remember the sweet time of fellowship with God just fifteen minutes earlier, but now He seems quite distant. What happened? You let the circumstance point you *away from* God rather than *to* God.

Instead, learn to *see God in those circumstances.* Nothing happens that a sovereign God does not allow for His own purposes and our ultimate good. If we see this, the circumstances of life point us *to* God rather than *away,* and our awareness of His presence is never hindered.

The same is true in relationships. Perhaps there is a person at work or at school or even in your family who rubs you the wrong way. Or perhaps there is someone you would like to impress. Interaction with these people causes you to lose your sense of the presence of God. Why? Because you don't see *God* in those relationships. Therefore, they are distractions that point you *away from* Him rather than *to* Him. But relationships fall under the providence of God as well.

Add to the mix of circumstances and relationships the constant bombardment of satanic enticements and our own natural bent toward sinning, and we have what constitutes the *stuff of life.* God sets us down in the midst of all this stuff and challenges us to keep our focus on Him.

So we must renew our awareness of God by faith. Before long, the presence of God becomes the very air we breathe. Nothing is so sweet as this rarefied atmosphere. We are not so quick to sin because nothing is worth losing our enjoyment of the presence of God. Hence we learn to walk with God in true fellowship and communion.[5]

This is what Paul meant when he said, "Pray without ceasing"

(1 Thessalonians 5:17). We are to live in a posture of prayer. Prayer is more than just words spoken to God; prayer is also having our thought life open to God and our hearts turned toward God. Yet prayer is also a deep sensitivity to the inward promptings of the Spirit of God and an acknowledgment that the source of our power lies beyond this world (see Romans 8:14). When we walk in this kind of intimacy with God, every day becomes an expression of worship.

THE MARK OF INTIMACY WITH GOD

Intimacy with God is the essence of holy living. It was the prayer of Christ that His followers would walk in intimate union with Him and with His Father (see John 17:21–23). Intimacy speaks of personal fellowship, of *secrets* shared. Do you have any secrets with God? Every Christian should have at least three:

> "But when you *give alms*, do not let your left hand know what your right hand is doing that your alms may be in *secret.*" (Matthew 6:3–4)

> "And when you *pray,* you are not to be as the hypocrites; for they love to stand and pray in the synagogues and on the street corners, in order to be seen by men…. But you, when you pray, go into your inner room, and when you have shut your door, pray to your Father who is in *secret.*" (Matthew 6:5–6)

> "And whenever you *fast*…anoint your head, and wash your face so that you may not be seen fasting by men, but by your Father who is in *secret.*" (Matthew 6:16–18)

At the end of each of these passages, the Lord also adds these words: "And your Father *who sees in secret* will repay you" (Matthew 6:4, 6, 18).

In your times alone with God, do you share things that are only between Him and you? Is God doing some hidden work in your life that no one else knows about? Perhaps God has taken you somewhere you have never been and shown you things you've never seen. Often, this happens in conjunction with some form of suffering, that we may be humbled rather than puffed up (see 2 Corinthians 12:7).

"He that dwelleth in the secret place of the most High shall abide under the shadow of the Almighty" (Psalm 91:1, KJV). There is a secret place where Jesus is everything; where the very atmosphere is Jesus, a place of peace, safety, forgiveness, love, and joy. Only in the secret place can we find a true perspective and an ordered focus.

Hear the voice of the Lord calling you to the secret place of His presence and love: "'O my dove, in the clefts of the rock, in the secret place of the steep pathway, let me see your form, let me hear your voice; for your voice is sweet, and your form is lovely'" (Song of Solomon 2:14). Do you have burdens that weigh you down, heartache too deep to bear? Come away with Jesus to the secret place and find fulfillment for all your needs.

This is the hidden life with Christ in God about which Paul wrote, and this is life indeed: a life of intimacy and union with God, a life of private devotion and secret communion, a life of inwardly gazing upon God even in the midst of the hustle and bustle of everyday responsibilities (see Colossians 3:3).

As A. W. Tozer said: "The Triune God will be our dwelling place even while our feet walk the low road of simple duty here among men."[6] These thoughts are beautifully captured in the last stanza of a lovely old hymn by Gerhard Tersteegen:

Keep my heart still faithful to Thee,
That my earthly life may be
But a shadow of that glory
Of my hidden life in Thee.

CHAPTER SEVEN

CONSECRATION

"You shall consecrate yourselves therefore and be holy,
for I am the LORD your God. And you shall keep My statutes
and practice them; I am the LORD who sanctifies you."

LEVITICUS 20:7–8

Consecration is our response to God's work of sanctification. In sanctification, God sets us apart from the world and unto Himself. In consecration, we set ourselves apart; we give ourselves to God for His purposes. Thus in Leviticus 20:7–8, we are instructed to *consecrate ourselves,* and this instruction comes from the God who sanctifies us. The English words *consecrate* and *sanctifies* in this verse are really translations of the same Hebrew word. The difference is in who is doing the action.

We used the word *beholding* to represent a devotional focus on Christ. But where beholding in devotion is a focus of the *heart,* beholding in consecration is a focus of the *life.* This focus begins at conversion when we surrender to Jesus as Lord of our lives. We consecrate ourselves to Him. But consecration does not end there. Within each of us lie uncharted mountains of self-reliance and rebellion, unclaimed territory to be subdued and transformed.

Consecration is an ongoing process. We must daily look to God with our hearts and consecrate our lives to Him. In Romans 6:13, Paul said: "And do not go on presenting the members of your body to sin as instruments of unrighteousness; but *present yourselves* to God as those alive from the dead, and your members as instruments of righ-teousness to God." Here, Paul is instructing Christians *continually* to set themselves apart from sin and unto God.

Hence consecration is a fundamental part of our daily striving toward practical holiness. Ongoing consecration is *our* responsibility, and it corresponds to God's ongoing work of sanctification. As the Holy Spirit performs this sanctifying work, drawing us away from worldly pleasure, revealing the beauties of Christ to us, we respond by giving ourselves more and more to Him.

The Cross is the one inescapable attraction that ultimately compels this response in us (see Galatians 6:14). When we behold the self-oblivious sacrifice of our Lord Jesus Christ, our hearts are stirred to give ourselves to Him.

> When I survey the wondrous cross
> On which the Prince of glory died,
> My richest gain, I count but loss,
> And pour contempt on all my pride.
> Were the whole realm of nature mine,
> That were a present far too small.
> Love so amazing, so divine,
> Demands my soul, my life, my all.[1]

THE SIGNIFICANCE OF EXPERIENCE

There are differing views on the significance of experience with respect to consecration. Some men of God whom I greatly admire, such as Oswald Chambers, R. A. Torrey, and D. L. Moody, have taken one unusually deep or dramatic experience of consecration in their own personal lives, which apparently loomed larger to them than any other, and have interpreted it as a second great work of God, treating it with such significance as to make it seem almost comparable to conversion.

Hence we hear terms such as *full sanctification, absolute surrender,* the *second blessing,* and the *baptism of the Holy Spirit.* While I would not argue with the genuineness of those believers' experiences, I would argue with some of the ways they are interpreted and with any attempt to insist that every Christian pilgrimage should include a similar experience.

In my own life I have had more than one experience which I would call an unusually significant encounter with God, each of which has left me changed to one degree or another. Yet none were comparable to conversion. As I look back I see that my journey has been punctuated with precious moments. I want to share one of those moments with you, but with an understanding that my experience is just "my experience."

I have what I call a "prayer loop," a thirty-minute drive out in the country that I usually take at night to pray over certain things. On one particular night I had come to a certain spiritual crisis and was on my loop beseeching God for illumination. I had a sense of being drawn by God to a deeper level of consecration, and yet something in me was resisting. I neither knew what it was nor how to deal with it. I also felt, with a sense of urgency, that this was a critical moment, but I was at a loss. I had done all the praying and all the yielding I knew how to do.

I cried out, "Father, You will have to do something. I can't; and I fear that if You don't do something truly supernatural right now, the very foundations of my faith will be shaken." I waited. Then again, I began to pray the things I had been praying for quite some time: "Father, I want You to have Your way with me. I want to have nothing between my heart and Yours; I want…."

Then it seemed the Lord quietly said, "Why don't you ask Me what *I* want?"

I was startled; then I gushed, "Oh yes, Father, what do *You* want?"

Then came the simple, quiet answer: "I want *you.*" Somehow, in the hearing of those words directly from Him, all resistance faded away. I had given my life to God long before this, but now He was, with these words, effecting in me a deeper separation from the world, sin, and self. My heart was somehow changed, and I knew that God had done the supernatural something I had been longing for.

The next night I went out again on my prayer loop, but this time with great enthusiasm. Like a child with a new toy, I asked: "Father, what do *You* want?"

And again the sweet answer came: "I want you." But this time, the emphasis was on the word *want.*

I was overwhelmed, caught completely off guard. How could He love me so? Though I had been a Christian for many years, I had never felt anything like this joy of really feeling wanted by God. I was enveloped in the warmth of an unexpected love.

Now, although you might not have had such an experience, you are loved and wanted by the God of the universe in the very same way. God does not need any of us, but He does *want* us. What a blessed thought! What God wants *from* you and me is the one thing that we all can give: ourselves.

Christ told the church members of Laodicea, who had become complacent thinking they had "arrived" spiritually, that they were in need of a certain transaction with Him:

> "Because you say, 'I am rich, and have become wealthy, and have need of nothing,' and you do not know that you are wretched and miserable and poor and blind and naked, *I advise you* to *buy* from Me *gold* refined by fire, that you may become rich, and *white garments,* that you may clothe yourself, and that the shame of your nakedness may not be revealed; and *eyesalve* to anoint your eyes, that you may see." (Revelation 3:17–18)

This admonition applies to us as much as to the Laodiceans. In these verses gold might represent wisdom from God, white garments might represent the righteousness of Christ, and eye salve might represent the gift of discernment, the ability to see things the way God sees them. Christ is saying that He is the source of these commodities, and they must be acquired from Him. But what currency do we have for such treasure?

The Lord said through Isaiah, "You who have no money come, buy and eat" (Isaiah 55:1). Again, the one thing we have, shabby as it may be, is the one thing He wants:

> But drops of grief can ne'er repay
> The debt of love I owe;
> Here Lord, I give myself away,
> 'Tis all that I can do.[2]

DRAWING LINES WITH GOD

One practical aspect involved in presenting ourselves to God is the very definite, deliberate decision to draw no more "lines" with God, and to erase all previous lines as they are revealed to us by the Holy Spirit. What I mean by drawing lines is simply saying to God: "This far and no further."

Drawing lines with God is reserving the right to make the final decision and putting stipulations on our obedience. It is a manifestation of pride, rebellion, and unbelief. The progressive aspect of consecration could well be seen as the process of discovering lines we have previously drawn and erasing them, one at a time.

When we are in the early stages of knowing and trusting God, there is a resistance to this sort of abandonment to His will. When we begin to discover just what God really does require of us, we may find that our desires are in direct conflict with His. Yet along with that resistance is another growing desire deep within, which we might call the "want to want." This reveals the conflict between the lower, base desires of self and the higher desires generated by the Holy Spirit through His indwelling (see Philippians 2:13).

At first the selfish desires are overwhelming. At times like these we need only pray this simple, little prayer: "Father, I want to want to please You above all others." As we persist we discover that, though we still must contend with self on a daily basis, our true heart's desire *is* to please God. We find a settled willingness in us to go anywhere and do anything the will of God requires.

THE CONSECRATION OF THE BODY

In Romans 12:1, Paul refers to a very specific form of consecration: presenting the body to God. He says, "I urge you therefore, brethren, by the mercies of God, to present your bodies a living and holy sacrifice, acceptable to God, which is your spiritual service of worship."

This is not a mystical experience so much as an act of the will. Yet it is an act of a will that has been changed by God (see Philippians 2:13). John Philips, in his commentary on this verse, says that this presenting of the body is "the most strategic thing we can do as Christians."[3] It is (and note this keenly) the crucial link between positional holiness and practical holiness. Hence the day-to-day living out of our lives in holiness hinges on this transaction between ourselves and God.

At conversion we do not begin to know all that our surrender may mean. It is, therefore, a significant day when we realize with spiritual understanding that our bodies were and are included in our consecration. Paul wrote to the Corinthians:

> Or do you not know that your body is a temple of the Holy Spirit who is in you, whom you have from God, and that you are not your own? For you have been bought with a price: therefore glorify God in your body. (1 Corinthians 6:19–20)

In Romans 12:1, Paul urges believers to deliberately and consciously consecrate their bodies to God, if they would live in a way that pleases God. Whatever life we live, it will be lived out in the body. Only as we are conscious that our bodies are God's and are to be dealt with as consecrated vessels, can the life of Christ be manifested in our mortal flesh (see 2 Corinthians 4:10–11).

Let us carefully consider the different components of Romans 12:1. First, the body is to be consecrated as an object for *sacrifice*. Indeed, the body is to be seen as a vessel "devoted to destruction," set apart to the Lord only for sacrifice and thus "most holy to the LORD" (Leviticus 27:28). Yet this sacrifice is not to be destroyed; it is not to be a dead sacrifice, but a *living and perpetual* one. This sacrifice, Paul says, is a reasonable response to the great mercy of God. By practicing consecration, the living out of each day becomes a form of worship and praise.

Often young Christians, after dealing for a while with the lusts of the flesh, become frustrated with their bodies. They see them as hopeless drags on their spiritual life and wonder why God has left them with a corrupt "ball and chain" by which they are doomed to failure.

But God's plan of redemption includes the body (see Romans 8:11). He intends for us to live holy lives within these vessels, and He intends one day to transform them into an incorruptible testimony to His grace (see 1 Corinthians 15:53; 2 Corinthians 5:1–4).

Meanwhile, we live holy lives by continually presenting these bodies to God, putting to death the deeds of the body by the power of the indwelling Spirit (see Romans 8:13).

PRESENTING OUR MEMBERS TO GOD

Even more specific is Paul's admonition in Romans 6:13 concerning the members of our bodies, which will either be instruments of sin or instruments of righteousness depending on whom we continually present them to (see Romans 6:16–22; Colossians 3:5).

For example, as James put it, the tongue is a small part of the body and yet, if not consecrated to God, it "is a fire, the very world of iniquity" (James 3:6). "From the same mouth come both blessing and cursing" (James 3:10). The tongue must be presented to God continually as an instrument of righteousness, and that presentation must be sealed with the prayer of David: "Set a guard, O LORD, over my mouth; keep watch over the door of my lips" (Psalm 141:3).

Our eyes must know the same consecration. Job consecrated his eyes as a safeguard against sexual lust: "I have made a covenant with my eyes; how then could I gaze at a virgin?" (Job 31:1). Consider the admonition in Proverbs 4:25–27: "Let your eyes look directly ahead, and let your gaze be fixed straight in front of you. Watch the path of your feet, and all your ways will be established. Do not turn to the right nor to the left; turn your foot from evil." Here is preventive maintenance that yields great benefits.

We see in Proverbs 6:16–19 the seriousness of a lack of consecration concerning our members:

> There are six things which the LORD hates, yes, seven which are an abomination to Him: haughty eyes, a lying tongue, and hands that shed innocent blood, a heart that devises wicked plans, feet that run rapidly to evil, a false witness who utters lies, and one who spreads strife among brothers.

The tendency, especially among ministers, is to consecrate gifts, talents, and abilities to God, such as preaching or teaching, without consecrating the body and each of its members. This has several devastating results. One is seeking "spot" anointing.

We want God's anointing on our preaching, but do we want His anointing on our lives? Are we consecrated while gearing up for some spiritual assignment, entreating God for His blessing on one hour of preaching or teaching, only to afterwards return to an unconsecrated lifestyle? After preaching the unfathomable riches of Christ, do we then go to restaurants with our cronies and engage in gossip and innuendo (with a pious face, of course) to make us feel bigger than we are? Do we then use those same mouths for overeating, an obvious overindulgence of the flesh? Or do we go home and "relax" while we take in through our eyes and ears all kinds of filth on the television?

Have we the notion that our *time* is our own? We call leisure time our "free" time, and that is fine as long as we do not seek freedom from God. We don't take breaks from God. Leisure time is time for relaxation, but if we see it as a time to put our consecration on hold, it will have a devastating effect on the way we use the members of our bodies.

I once counseled a single pastor who lived alone in the parsonage of his church. One Sunday night, after the evening service, a young woman with whom he was acquainted came to the parsonage, and he very foolishly invited her in. He explained to me that he had had a long, full day of preaching, and his "guard was down." In other words, he put his consecration on hold, perhaps even thinking he deserved this break as a reward for faithful service. He and the young woman ended up having sex that night, and the results were quite devastating.

Sadly, this sin is not reserved only for the young and impetuous. Many preachers of our day, young and old, have fallen to immorality. At least part of the cause is an incomplete consecration and a careless handling of leisure time and the body.

When asked what he felt was the greatest need of his congregation, Robert Murray McCheyne, beloved Scottish pastor of the 1800s, replied, "The holiness of their pastor."[4] Such holiness requires a continuous consecration. But the danger of a careless handling of consecration extends to the layman as well: We are all more susceptible to any form of temptation when we have failed in consecration. Ongoing consecration is preventive medicine and a great deterrent to sin.

We often see this partial or temporary consecration when we are in trouble and need God to bail us out or when we really want something such as a new car, a new house, or a new job. We consecrate our lips for prayer, perhaps even our eyes for tears. But after our dilemma is over or after we get what we want, we go back to using those same members as we choose.

Do we think that we are fooling God? He may allow this for a time, but eventually He must discipline us into a deeper level of consecration. We would do well to take to heart the words of F. R. Havergal's wonderful hymn:

> Take my life, and let it be
> Consecrated, Lord, to Thee.
> Take myself, and I will be
> Ever, only, all for Thee.[5]

MORTIFICATION OF THE FLESH

How then do we keep our bodies consecrated to God? Romans 8:13 says: "For if ye live after the flesh, ye shall die: but if ye through the Spirit do *mortify* the deeds of the body, ye shall live" (KJV).

To understand this verse, we must understand the scriptural use of two main words: *mortification* and *flesh*. In this context, *mortification* means to put to death, to have done with, to subdue.

Flesh means the physical body and its members. But additionally it means the sensuous or that by which we have experience through our five senses. The word *flesh* also at times represents a hunger for worldly pleasures, and therefore a resistance to the Spirit of holiness (see Galatians 5:17). Thus in these cases, it signifies our depravity. The flesh is a war zone for sin. "But I see a different law in the members of my body, waging war against the law of my mind, and making me a prisoner of the law of sin which is in my members," said Paul (Romans 7:23).

Now, the body is not evil in itself, but it is the vehicle through which evil, present in each of us, is expressed in our conduct. Paul wrote, "I find then the principle that evil is present in me, the one who wishes to do good. For I joyfully concur with the law of God in the inner man, but I see a different law in the members of my body" (Romans 7:21–23).

The flesh is manifested in any evil deeds which are carried out in the body. Thus it is imperative that we *mortify* the flesh, that we *subdue* the flesh by putting to death the deeds of the body. How do we do this?

1. We must submit to the Holy Spirit. It is by the Spirit that we put to death the deeds of the body (see Romans 8:13). The Holy Spirit produces the fruit of self-control and thus enables us to mortify the flesh (see Galatians 5:24).

2. We must recognize that there is *no good thing* in our flesh (see Romans 7:18). We are by nature full of sin and desperately in need of God.

3. We must "put *no confidence* in the flesh" but only in God (Philippians 3:3).

4. We must be careful to "make *no provision* for the flesh in regard to its lusts" (Romans 13:14). That is, we must try to avoid any circumstance, companion, place, or thing that might provoke the passions of the flesh within us.

5. We must abstain from all appearance of evil (see 1 Thessalonians 5:22). We must not give anyone cause to accuse us of wrongdoing. Our lives are not our own; all that we do in the body is a reflection on our Master and either honors or dishonors Him.

6. We must deliberately, by the power of the Holy Spirit alone, *restrain* the flesh. Paul said, "I buffet my body and make it my slave, lest possibly, after I have preached to others, I myself should be disqualified" (1 Corinthians 9:27). Christ used even stronger figurative language when He said to pluck out the eye and cut off the hand if they cause you to sin (see Matthew 5:29–30).

7. We must recognize that the consecration of the body is an essential part of God's design for holy living. We must see our bodies as separate from the world, self, and sin, and as belonging to God. They are ours, yet they are not ours to use as we choose. They are sacred vessels, set apart for God's own purposes. They are, indeed, the temples of the Holy Spirit (see 1 Corinthians 6:19).

THE EXAMPLE OF CHRIST

We have an impeccable pattern to follow in the Lord Jesus Christ. His heart was to do the Father's will, but to do that, He had to *have a body*. The writer of Hebrews attributes these words to Christ:

> Therefore, when He comes into the world, He says, "SACRIFICE AND OFFERING THOU HAST NOT DESIRED, BUT *A BODY THOU HAST PREPARED FOR ME;* IN WHOLE BURNT OFFERINGS AND sacrifices FOR SIN THOU HAST TAKEN NO PLEASURE. THEN I SAID, 'BEHOLD, I HAVE COME *TO DO THY WILL*, O GOD.'" (Hebrews 10:5–7)

Christ's body was a consecrated vessel, a sacred instrument for the Father's use. Only the bodily sacrifice of the spotless Lamb of God could satisfy the holiness of God. Only Christ could carry out the Father's holy will.

That will is the driving force behind our sanctification, and Christ's submission to that will is the means thereof. We were made holy positionally through the voluntary presenting of Christ's body (see Hebrews 10:10). And we are being made holy *practically* only by the submission of Christ to the Father's will through the voluntary presentation of His body (see 1 Peter 2:24).

HIS INCARNATION

Thus the absolute necessity of the Incarnation is apparent. Apart from this blessed event there is no redemption, justification, or sanctification, and there will be no glorification. But Paul declares, "When the fullness of the time came, God sent forth His Son, born of a woman, born under the Law, in order that He might redeem those who were under the Law, that we might receive the adoption as sons" (Galatians 4:4–5).

Had there been no babe in Bethlehem's manger, there could have been no sacrifice on Calvary's cross. The Crucifixion looms as the quintessential apex of God's dealing with man. It is the essential fulfillment of the divine plan of redemption. But as marvelous as that event is to the redeemed, it is a consequence of one still greater. The

Incarnation is the most cataclysmic event in all the history of the universe. Every other historical fact pales in comparison to this incomprehensible wonder: God has come in the flesh! (See 1 Timothy 3:16; 1 John 4:2–3; 2 John 1:7.)

We speak of the Bible as being filled with paradox: seeming contradictions that find their resolution in God. Here is the greatest of all paradoxes—that the Redeemer must be both God and man—reconciled in a tiny baby.

> A Babe on the breast of a maiden He lies
> Yet sits with His Father on high in the skies.
> Before Him their faces the seraphim hide,
> While Joseph stands waiting, unscared by His side.
> O wonder of wonders, which none can unfold:
> The Ancient of Days is an hour or two old.
> The Maker of all things is made of the earth;
> Man is worshiped by angels, and God comes to birth.[6]

"In the beginning was the Word, and the Word was with God, and the Word was God. He was in the beginning with God" (John 1:1–2). Here the Holy Spirit takes us back to the place of Genesis 1:1—"In the beginning God created the heavens and the earth"—where everything besides God and the angels began.

In that verse the Holy Spirit points us forward into the stream of human history. But in John 1:1 He points us back into eternity past: "In the beginning *was the Word.*" When the Creation began, the Word already was, *pre-existent* and *eternal.*

The next phrase in John 1:1, "And the Word was *with* God," shows the *co-existence* of the Word with God. The next, "And the Word *was* God," shows the *co-equality* of the Word with God.

Then, in verse 2, the personal pronoun *He* is used in reference to the Word: "*He* was in the beginning with God," making it quite clear that this is a reference not to the inanimate thoughts of God, but to a person distinct from God the Father.

Finally, in verse 14, John proclaims: "And the Word became flesh, and dwelt among us, and we beheld His glory, glory as of the only begotten from the Father, full of grace and truth." Obviously, all this refers to the Lord Jesus Christ. The divine person—the pre-incarnate Word—assumed a human nature to become one person with two natures, truly God and truly man.

Before the voluntary presenting of His body as a sacrifice for sin, there had to be this voluntary taking on of a body. This is the eternal, pre-existent *God the Son* manifesting Himself as the *Son of Man* (see John 1:18).

> Who, although He existed in the form of God, did not regard equality with God a thing to be grasped, but emptied Himself, taking the form of a bond-servant, and being made in the likeness of men. (Philippians 2:6–7)

Paul said to the Corinthians: "For you know the grace of our Lord Jesus Christ, that though He was rich, yet for your sake He became poor, that you through His poverty might become rich" (2 Corinthians 8:9). Yet the Son of God became the Son of Man, not to side with men against the Father, but to side visibly with the Father against sin.

Therefore, Jesus emptied Himself, not of His deity, but of the *glory* of His deity, the outshining, outward, visible manifestation of the inward reality (see Colossians 1:19). Though He is God, yet He took on "the form of a bond-servant," was "made in the likeness of men," and "found in appearance as a man" (Philippians 2:7–8). Isaiah said of Him, "He has no stately form or majesty that we should look upon Him, nor appearance that we should be attracted to Him" (Isaiah 53:2). Jesus looked just like an ordinary man. Yet He was the Son of God.

In addition, He emptied Himself, not of the attributes of His deity (otherwise, He would not have remained God), but of the *constant use* of those attributes. Yet, in the Gospels we see Him taking them up again when He so chooses. Jesus, the omnipotent Christ, exhibits His infinite power (yet always in union with the Father and in harmony with His will), to heal the sick, calm the storm, and raise the dead.

Yet again, He does nothing independently from the Father. The purpose of His works before men is to demonstrate that He and the

Father are one and that He was sent from the Father; that He came in *submission* to the Father. In John 5:36, Jesus said: "'For the works which the Father has given Me to accomplish, the very works that I do, bear witness of Me, that the Father has sent Me.'"

Addressing the Jews who were seeking to kill Him, Jesus said: "If I do not do the works of My Father, do not believe Me; but if I do them, though you do not believe Me, believe the works, that you may know and understand that the Father is in Me, and I in the Father" (John 10:37–38).

Later, in the upper room discourse with the disciples, Jesus said to Philip:

> "Do you not believe that I am in the Father, and the Father is in Me? The words that I say to you I do not speak on my own initiative, but the Father abiding in Me does His works. Believe Me that I am in the Father, and the Father in Me; otherwise believe on account of the works themselves." (John 14:10–11)

Still, there are other subtle, almost hidden instances of Christ taking up some attribute of deity to give us a hint of that sublime union that He and the Father shared.

When Peter asked Jesus for the money to pay taxes, Jesus sent him to the sea and told him that he would catch a fish in whose mouth would be enough money to pay them in full (see Matthew 17:27). Was that omniscience, omnipotence, or both?

It would be fascinating to know how many times Jesus took up His omnipotence, His omnipresence, and His omniscience without anyone seeing or recording anything about it. John, in the closing verse of his Gospel, said: "And there are also many other things which Jesus did, which if they were written in detail, I suppose that even the world itself would not contain the books which were written" (John 21:25).

Yet, for the most part, we see Jesus limiting Himself. In His incarnation He did not come as a full-grown man, but as a helpless infant who had to learn how to walk and talk, how to read and write. As a boy and a young man He studied and memorized the Scriptures, of which He is Himself the author. He studied by the light of an oil lamp, though He is Himself the creator of electricity (see John 1:3; Colossians 1:16–17).

He, who in His deity is omniscient, limited Himself to learning from others and from experience. Yet He did not learn as we do. He didn't have to unlearn anything. He didn't have to learn anything twice or "the hard way." He was perfectly attentive, perfectly teachable, and perfectly submissive.

In His sacred, unhindered relationship with the Father, He walked in total dependence. And on a moment-by-moment basis, He sought direction as to what He should both do and say (see John 5:10–20; 7:16; 12:49–50).

His Self-Consecration

Did Jesus know from infancy who He was and what He had come to do? This is not the impression one gets from reading the New Testament. In Luke 2, for example, we see a definite progression. Verse 40 says that "the Child continued to grow and become strong, increasing in wisdom; and the grace of God was upon Him." In the temple, at age twelve, He was clearly seeking to learn, as we see in verse 46: "And it came about that after three days they found Him in the temple, sitting in the midst of the teachers, both listening to them, and asking them questions."

In verse 49, His surprised response to Mary's concern over His being lost from her and Joseph shows a growing sense of responsibility to the Father: "'Why is it that you were looking for Me? Did you not know that I had to be in My Father's house?'" Then in verse 52, we read, "And Jesus kept increasing in wisdom and stature, and in favor with God and men."

Our very lives should be characterized by a constant pursuit of the loftiest view of Christ possible. But to recognize a progression in the development of His human nature need not be a deflection from the grandeur of His divine nature. We must acknowledge the twofold nature of Christ. As William G. Blaikie says in *The Inner Life of Christ,* "It cannot be right for the higher to conceal the lower."[7] Blaikie further comments:

The qualities that made Him "fairer than the children of men" reached their maturity by degrees, as the oak attains its strength, or the peach its flavor. Year by year the human nature unfolded itself, and its beauty increased, reaching its climax...when the voice burst from the sky, "This is my beloved Son, in whom I am well pleased."[8]

Blaikie goes on to speak of the deliberate consecration of Jesus to the Father's will. He describes three stages:

The First—that announced in the Temple—when, as a Child, He gave Himself, simply and frankly, to His Father's business.... A further stage...would be reached when, in view of the work and office of the prophets, He gave Himself, like them, to the public service of His Father.... Lastly, the self-dedication of Jesus would be completed when He gave Himself to the office of Messiah. But here we come into contact with elements which we are unable fully to comprehend. At what period of His life did Jesus deliberately and consciously give Himself to this office?[9]

Yet it is clear that Jesus was profoundly submissive to the Father's will. He speaks of His own will as distinct from the Father's. In John 5:30, for instance, we see two wills at play: "I do not seek My own will, but the will of Him who sent Me." And again in John 6:38: "For I have come down from heaven, not to do My own will, but the will of Him who sent Me."

Yet Christ's emphasis on this distinction is always within the context of free, joyous submission, as in John 15:10–11, when He told the disciples: "'If you keep My commandments, you will abide in My love; just as *I have kept My Father's commandments,* and abide in His love. These things I have spoken to you, that *My joy* may be in you, and that your joy may be made full'" (see also John 4:34).

Jesus' stellar devotion to the Father's will was an expression of that mutual love He shared with the Father. Jesus could not dream of anything but submission to the Father's blessed will, no matter where that submission would lead. Hence those agonized words uttered in

Gethsemane: "'Not My will, but Thine be done'" (Luke 22:42).

In the submission of Christ we see the humility of Christ. Indeed, Christ used these terms Himself in describing His own character: "'I am gentle and humble in heart'" (Matthew 11:29). Philippians 2:8 shows to what length both the humility and the submission of Christ extend: "And being found in appearance as a man, He *humbled* Himself by becoming obedient to the point of death, *even death on a cross.*"

In John 10:17–18, Jesus said, "'For this reason the Father loves Me, because I lay down My life that I may take it again. No one has taken it away from Me, but I lay it down on My own initiative.'" This is the *one thing* that Jesus does on His own initiative! In John 5:30, speaking of His day-to-day ministry, He said, "'I can do nothing on My own initiative'" (see also John 8:28). In John 12:49, He said, "'For I did not speak on My own initiative'" (see also John 14:10). Further, in John 8:42, He said, "'I have not even come on My own initiative.'"

Yet Jesus speaks of laying down His physical body as a sacrifice for sin, as an act of His own free will. Yet even this He does in obedience to the Father's command: "I have authority to lay it down, and I have authority to take it up again. *This commandment I received from My Father*" (John 10:18).

In this *obedience* we see His love for the Father; in this self-sacrificial *initiative,* we see His love for man. Thus the great condescension of Christ is motivated by love.

Love is what causes the Christian to "go low," to humble himself and serve. If the Christian elevates himself in pride, he displays only his emptiness. But what is he empty of? *Love.* Pride is being empty of love.

When the Christian humbles himself, he is following the blessed example of Christ's condescension. Madam Guyon added, "Oh! What a weight is love, since it caused so astonishing a fall, from heaven to earth—from God to man!"[10]

HIS EXALTATION

Because of Christ's obedience to the Father's will:

> God highly exalted Him, and bestowed on Him the name
> which is above every name, that at the name of Jesus *every*

knee should bow, of those who are in heaven, and on earth, and under the earth, and that every tongue should confess that Jesus Christ is Lord, to the glory of God the Father. (Philippians 2:9–11)

This exaltation began when God raised Christ from the dead. That same body with which He clothed Himself as a babe in Bethlehem's manger, the same body in which He bore our sins on Calvary's tree, was raised on the third day in glorious triumph over death and the grave.

This exaltation continued when He ascended on high and took His place at the right hand of the throne of God (see Hebrews 10:12). We believe He dwells, even now, in bodily form in the presence of the Father.

This exaltation culminates in the promised return and future reign of Christ (see Acts 1:11; Hebrews 10:12–13) leading to that event in eternity future when He shall present to the Father the completed kingdom (see 1 Corinthians 15:24). We believe in the *bodily* return and rule of our Lord and that "of his kingdom there shall be no end" (Luke 1:33 KJV; see also Daniel 7:14, 27; 2 Peter 1:11; Revelation 11:15).

These truths are of great comfort to us. It is especially comforting that Christ dwells in a body even to this day, as a pledge that we will have a similar bodily resurrection (see 1 Corinthians 15:21–22). By way of His death and resurrection, Christ took away forever the sting of death, which is sin (see Hebrews 2:14; Romans 6:9). Thus "Death is swallowed up in victory" (1 Corinthians 15:54). There is no more fear of death for the Christian.

The only thing uncomfortable about the contemplation of death is the prospect of being without a body. We don't know what that is like. Hence we cherish the great promise of the Resurrection: "But when this perishable will have put on the imperishable, and this mortal will have put on immortality, then will come about the saying that is written, "Death is swallowed up in victory." (1 Corinthians 15:54; 2 Corinthians 5:1–4). Those saints who die before the Resurrection are with Jesus, for to be absent from the body is to be present with the Lord (see 2 Corinthians 5:6–8).

God did not create man to live an out-of-body existence. The body is a vital part of all that God created man to be. Likewise, the body of Jesus was essential to His incarnation, His crucifixion, and His resurrection.

> Since then the children share in flesh and blood, He Himself likewise also partook of the same, that through death He might render powerless him who had the power of death, that is, the devil; and might deliver those who through fear of death were subject to slavery all their lives. (Hebrews 2:14–15)

His Identification with Man

Jesus became flesh and blood and dwelt among us because men are flesh and blood. Jesus identified with us, not to understand or to sympathize with us, but to redeem us and to give us an eternity with Him.

The Greek word in John 1:14 for *dwelt* is *skene,* from which we get the English word *skin,* and this Greek word is a translation of the Hebrew word which means *tabernacle.* In the Old Testament the tabernacle was a temporary dwelling place for God, a tent made of animal skins, which could be broken down and carried as the children of Israel wandered. In this tent, God dwelt among His people.

This is a wonderful picture of the human body of our Lord. He took on Himself a skin—a temporary dwelling place for God—and tabernacled among us. Yet, although the tabernacle of His flesh was a temporary dwelling place, He has condescended to dwell in it to this very day.

In Revelation 20–21, John recorded a vision of things yet to come—among others, the great white throne (20:11) and the new Jerusalem coming down out of heaven from God (21:2). "And I heard a loud voice from the throne, saying, 'Behold, the *tabernacle* of God is among men, and *He* shall dwell among them, and they shall be *His* people'" (Revelation 21:3). Could this be a reference to the resurrection body of our Lord? Could it be that *for our comfort* He has chosen to live for all eternity in a body that can be both seen and touched—a tabernacle?

John also wrote these words: "Beloved, now we are children of

God, and it has not appeared as yet what we shall be. We know that, when He appears, we *shall* be like Him, because we shall *see* Him *just as He is*" (1 John 3:2). This truth should elevate our view of the body and motivate us to present our bodies to God as living and holy sacrifices! This is consecration.

CHAPTER EIGHT

THE RENEWING OF
YOUR MIND

Do not be conformed to this world, but
be transformed by the renewing of your mind.

ROMANS 12:2

T ransformation is God's work alone, yet it hinges on something that we must do. We must *behold*—or *focus
intently*—on all that is glorious about Christ. In response,
God performs His supernatural work of transforming our very lives.

We have discussed Romans 12:1: "I urge you…brethren…to present your bodies a living and holy sacrifice." Now, let us consider the
following verse: "And do not be conformed to this world, but be transformed by the renewing of your mind, that you may prove what the
will of God is, that which is good and acceptable and perfect"
(Romans 12:2).

In the first verse, Paul emphasizes the concept of presenting our
bodies to God, which is consecration. The word *living* speaks of the
life lived in the body, a holy and sacrificial life. In the second verse he
continues the holiness theme, but with the emphasis on renewing our
minds: "And do not be conformed to this world."

Because of the emphasis on living, I believe Paul is saying, "Don't
let the world determine the way you live." Rather, live with an
awareness that you are not your own, that your body belongs to God
(see 1 Corinthians 6:19–20). Thus the transformation of which Paul

speaks is not merely that of the mind, but of the life.

"As [a man] thinketh in his heart, so is he," said Solomon (Proverbs 23:7, KJV). What we think affects *who we are*. It is crucial that we bring our minds into conformity to God's mind. Although God has said that His thoughts are infinitely higher than ours, we are encouraged by Paul to have in us the mind or attitude of Christ—a mind which so clearly dictated the sacrificial life He lived (see Isaiah 55:8–9; Philippians 2:5–8).

What, then is the *reason* or *purpose* for this transformation that comes through a renewal of the mind? Romans 12:2 gives us the answer: "that you may *prove* what *the will of God is,* that which is *good and acceptable and perfect.*" Or, more pointedly: "that you might actually *be the proof* of what God wants a man or woman, a boy or girl, to be."

Paul does not say, "Don't conform *yourselves* to the world," but rather, "Don't *be* conformed." It is so easy to be like the world; it requires no effort on our part whatsoever. We have to fight to *keep from* being conformed.

"'The flesh is weak,'" Jesus said (Matthew 26:41). It requires no coaxing to yield to temptation; one rolls over into sin with great ease. Yet Jesus also said that the *spirit* is *willing*. The Christian does not want to sin. But not to allow ourselves to be conformed to the world requires some effort.

However, we cannot transform ourselves; transformation is the work of God accomplished through the renewing of our minds. And here is where our effort begins.

We are responsible to *focus* our minds, to give God our attention. *Beholding* is not only a focus of the heart and life, but of the mind as well. We are to focus our thoughts and meditations on what is impressive and wonderful about Christ. This is part of beholding the *glory* of the Lord.

The Christian's mind must be in a process of renewal, daily. Although he has been fundamentally renewed in repentance and regeneration by the Holy Spirit (see Titus 3:5), he has lost neither his depravity, nor his memory. Thus evil thoughts still plague him; memories come back to haunt him. Old habits, of action as well as thought, are often still entrenched. New habits must be learned to replace the old.

The Christian does not instantly receive all new knowledge. He must progress in his understanding, both intellectually and spiritually. This renewing of the mind is a lifelong process and a major part of God's sanctification in our lives. But it can also be seen as a part of our consecration.

We do not mean turning over our minds to God in some hyper-spiritual sense and thus being controlled by Him, as in a trance. Nor are we to turn off or close our minds to creative and expansive thinking. This is not God's desire. Instead, He wants us to use and develop our minds to their highest potential. Thus Christ included the word *mind* in the greatest commandment: "'YOU SHALL LOVE THE LORD YOUR GOD WITH ALL YOUR…*MIND*'" (Matthew 22:37). We love God with our minds by consecrating them to Him and by guarding them against any wrong thoughts that might displease Him.

THE INSTRUMENT OF RENEWAL: THE WORD OF GOD

The primary instrument for renewing the mind is God's Word. Our part is to love, to study, and to obey His Word; His part is to illumine that Word to our minds, endear it to our hearts, and apply it to our lives.

MEDITATION

"Thy words were found and I ate them, and Thy words became for me a joy and the delight of my heart; for I have been called by Thy name, O LORD God of hosts" (Jeremiah 15:16). This verse speaks of the much neglected practice of Christian *meditation*, which has a wonderful Judeo-Christian heritage.

Unfortunately, the word *meditation* has been blighted by its use in the religions of the East. Meditation, in that context, is seen as an *emptying* of the mind through the repetition of a *mantra*—a single word that may or may not have some meaning to the user. In contrast, Christian meditation is a *filling* of the mind, a concentration on the Word of God; a discipline which, if practiced faithfully, results in a transformed, holy life. Consider the testimony of the psalmist:

How blessed is the man who does not walk in the counsel of the wicked, nor stand in the path of sinners, nor sit in the seat of scoffers! But his delight is in the law of the LORD, and in His law he *meditates* day and night. And he will be like a tree firmly planted by streams of water...and in whatever he does, he prospers. (Psalm 1:1–3)

In meditation we focus our thoughts on a passage with attention to each word and phrase, contemplating various shades of meaning, and are rewarded with rich insights. Insights from the Word, like nuggets of gold, are available to anyone who is willing to mine for them. This takes time, effort, and above all, *thought*. In our instant, convenient society, we have forgotten how to really think! Thinking that goes into the realm of study and meditation is hard work, and we grow impatient with it, deeming it a drudgery rather than a delight. What a tragedy!

Not only do we miss treasures directly from the Word, but also from the meditations of others who have gone before us. I love good Christian poetry—not sentimental fluff, but meaty, inspirational verse based on contemplation of biblical themes and passages. A poet can give expression, in concise yet startlingly beautiful couplings, to what we perhaps have in our hearts but have no words to convey. Although it may take effort to understand some poetry, the benefits are extraordinary.

I also love old hymns based on God's Word, because they are poetry of the profoundest nature; they really have something to say! They make us think of truths that stretch our minds toward God and call us to a deeper consecration of heart and life.

MEMORIZATION

"Thy word have I hid in mine heart, that I might not sin against thee" (Psalm 119:11, KJV). Here is a most practical deterrent to sin. But the Word of God cannot be hidden in our hearts until it has first been hidden in our minds.

Scripture memorization is a key element in renewing the mind because it gives the Holy Spirit something to work with toward our sanctification. Jesus told His disciples that, after His departure, the Holy Spirit would bring to their remembrance the things He had said to them (see John 14:26). And so He does with us today, but only if there is something *in* our minds to *bring* to our remembrance.

I know of nothing better that a person can do for himself than to memorize Scripture. Besides the personal benefits, memorization gives us a humble confidence when sharing with others and teaching the Word, partly because it gives us a sense of the unity of Scripture. No matter where we read in the Word, we are reminded of verses that we have memorized from other parts of Scripture that enhance what we are reading then. Thus our teaching is transformed from a flat surface into a three-dimensional image, from black-and-white to Technicolor (see Appendix B).

THE ESSENCE OF RENEWAL: A NEW MINDSET

As we give our attention to the Word, God uses it as an instrument to renew our minds. The essence of that renewal is simply the development of a *new mind-set,* or a new way of thinking, resulting in a new way of living.

In Colossians 3:5 we are instructed to *consider* the members of our bodies as dead to sin (see also Romans 6:11). The word *consider* speaks of a new way of looking at things, as when James said, *"Consider* it all *joy,* my brethren, when you encounter various *trials"* (James 1:2).

This new mindset results in *action,* as we see in some of the verses that follow Colossians 3:5. For example, verse 8 says, "But now…*put them all aside:* anger, wrath, malice, slander, and abusive speech from your mouth." This putting aside speaks of *action* that results from this new mindset.

In verses 9 and 10, Paul points to the reason for this action: *"Since* you *laid aside* the old self with its evil practices, and *have put on* the new self who is being *renewed to a true knowledge* according to the image of the One who created him" (Colossians 3:9–10; see also Romans 6:6).

In Ephesians, a parallel passage complements Colossians 3: "That, in reference to your former manner of life, you *lay aside* the old self, which is *being corrupted…*and that you *be renewed* in the spirit of your *mind,* and *put on* the new self, which in the likeness of God has been created in righteousness and holiness of the truth" (Ephesians 4:22–24).

The *old* self represents the former *unregenerate state.* The *new* self represents the *regenerate state* of the new creature, the spiritual man. So the new mindset is not merely the reflection of some moral reform but the result of a changed state of being, a moving from death to life. Primarily, our actions speak not of outward conduct but of inward holiness, which is our fundamental separation from the world. The result of this inward holiness is a new way of living.

PREVENTIVE MAINTENANCE: GUARDING THE MIND

We must constantly guard and protect our minds from unworthy and evil thoughts. The old adage about sin is certainly true: The battle is either won or lost *in the mind.* This is why, in the context of spiritual warfare, Paul said: "And we are taking *every thought captive to the obedience of Christ"* (2 Corinthians 10:5; see also verses 3–4). But how do we take our thoughts captive? One practical method is simply to replace one thought with another.

One of the most practical verses in all of Scripture is Philippians 4:8: "Finally, brethren, whatever is true, whatever is honorable, whatever is right, whatever is pure, whatever is lovely, whatever is of good repute, if there is any excellence and if anything worthy of praise, let your mind dwell on these things."

This practice is particularly helpful in dealing with sinful thoughts, which we are admonished to replace deliberately with thoughts that are wholesome and good. Those replacement thoughts might be about a hobby, or the memory of a good experience, or thoughts about doing something good for someone else. These are higher thoughts that elevate our thinking and discipline our minds to leave base and vulgar thoughts behind.

But thoughts that are higher still are those that come from meditation on the Word of God, perhaps on verses we have memorized or passages which speak to us of the attributes of God or the different names of God. Still higher thoughts are just thoughts about Jesus.

How beautifully Philippians 4:8 describes Christ: true, honorable, right, pure, lovely, of good repute, excellent, and worthy of praise!

An area of thought life that is seldom addressed is that of our *leisure* thoughts. Yet, these thoughts are crucially important to the health and well-being of our spiritual lives, and just as any others, they must be brought into conformity to the mind of Christ. Francis Paget, in his book from the late 1800s, *The Spirit of Discipline,* says of undisciplined habits in our leisure thoughts:

> There is the tremendous power of habit; the constant, silent growth with which it creeps and twines about the soul, until its branches clutch and grip like iron that which seemed so securely stronger than their little tentative beginning. So the mind spoils its servants, till they become its masters; *and the leisure time of life may be either a man's garden or his prison....*There is, perhaps, nothing on which the health and happiness and worth of life more largely turn than this—that the habitual drift, the natural tendency of our unclaimed thought, should be towards high and pure and gladdening things.[1]

Habitual sin betrays a mind undisciplined with leisure thoughts that has thus gravitated to base things, indulging the desires of the flesh to the point of mental distraction. A little deliberate focus on higher things is like breathing in fresh, clean air. Yet if we continue in an undisciplined thought life, it will tell in how we live.

We may think that our inner, personal thoughts will remain private and will never make themselves evident in what we say or in how we act. But Jesus said, "'For the mouth speaks out of that which fills the heart'" (Matthew 12:34; see also Matthew 10:26, 1 Corinthians 4:5, and 2 Corinthians 4:2).

Quoting Bishop Steere from his day, Paget goes on: "Do not think that what your thoughts dwell upon is of no matter. *Your thoughts are making you.* We are two men...what is seen, and what is not seen. *But the unseen is the maker of the other.*"[2]

It is imperative for the sake of *hearing from God* and of *being usable to God* that we develop this self-mastery in regard to our leisure thoughts. Here is one last passage from Paget's beautiful little book:

> For it is in pure and bright and kindly lives that the grace of
> God most surely takes root downward, and bears fruit
> upwardHe works unhindered and untroubled in the soul...
> trained to think in all its leisure times of true and high and
> gentle thoughts. He enters in and stays there, not as a wayfar-
> ing man, but as a willing, welcome Guest in a house that has
> been prepared and decked and furnished as He loves to see it.
> There the surpassing brightness of His presence issues forth
> unchecked, and there the will of His great love is freely
> wrought. Yes, and there too the Voice of God is clearly heard.
> There is no knowing whither God might call us.... He may
> have for any one of us a task, a trust, higher by far than we can
> ask or think; some work for His love's sake amidst the suffer-
> ings of this world; some special opportunity of witnessing...of
> ministering to others, of winning to Him those who know
> Him not. And on the drift and tone which our minds are now
> acquiring it may depend whether, when the time comes, we
> recognize our work or not; whether we press forward with the
> host of God, or dully fall away, it may be, into the misery of a
> listless, aimless life.[3]

Through the desire to love God with our minds and to please Him
with our thoughts, we learn techniques in the art of taking every
thought captive to the obedience of Christ. Thus our minds are
renewed day by day. This is *beholding:* It is a focus of the mind. God
uses this focus to bring us little by little into conformity to Christ.
Thus we are transformed into the image of the One we behold by the
renewing of our minds.

Chapter Nine

Imitation: Part One

*Therefore be imitators of God,
as beloved children.*

Ephesians 5:1

A newborn baby comes into the world bearing the image of its parents, but another dimension is added as the child grows. Through imitation the child begins to take on mannerisms, characteristics, and even the values of its parents.

When we were born again into God's family, we were given life by the Spirit (see John 6:63; Titus 3:5), newly created in Christ (see 2 Corinthians 5:17), and stamped with the likeness of God. Through persistent, loving imitation, this likeness grows more distinct as the years go by.

Yet how is one to imitate God? By imitating Christ. Jesus said, "'He who has seen Me has seen the Father'" (John 14:9). By imitating Him, we imitate the Father.

Now the word *imitation* does not mean *counterfeit.* It means adopting the ways of another. This is done consciously through careful observation and unconsciously through loving association. The result is a growing likeness to Christ.

Some see imitation as primarily a Catholic doctrine, which makes the Christian life solely an effort of man. But this idea is refuted by Christ's own admonitions for us to follow His example. Imitation is not all there is to living the Christian life, but it is a significant part.

We must carefully study the life of Christ if we would truly be like Him. This is why we must never stray too far from the Gospels in our devotional lives, for they most clearly present to us the man Christ Jesus. Through carefully beholding, observing, and studying Him in His earthly life, specifically in how He related to the Father and to men, we discover more clearly how to be like Him. This discovery produces imitation, a *response of love*.

Imitation is part of what Paul meant by "perfecting *holiness* in the *fear* of God" (2 Corinthians 7:1). Of this fear, J. C. Ryle said:

> A holy man will follow after the fear of God. I do not mean the fear of a slave, who only works because he is afraid of punishment and would be idle if he did not dread discovery. I mean rather the fear of a child, who wishes to live and move as if he was always before his father's face, because he loves him.[1]

In this childlike love holiness is being perfected, the natural expression of which is imitation: "Be imitators of God, as beloved children" (Ephesians 5:1).

Christ demonstrated what practical holiness is in human form. As we grow in Christlikeness, we grow in holiness. A life lived in conformity to the image of Christ is a holy life, because Christ is holy. The holiness, which is inherently ours in Christ, begins to be ours in actual, day-to-day living.

Is this not at least part of what Paul meant when he said: "But we all, with unveiled face beholding as in a mirror the glory of the Lord, are being transformed into the *same image from glory to glory*" (2 Corin-thians 3:18)? By imitation we begin to conform to Christ's image in holiness.

IMITATING CHRIST:
HIS RELATIONSHIP TO THE FATHER

Love and *trust* are the essential elements in a walk of intimacy with God. In Christ we see the perfect pattern for this walk: His love for the Father was flawless, and He always exhibited an indefatigable trust.

IN LOVE

In the upper room discourse, on the night of His arrest, Jesus proclaimed clearly His love for the Father: "'But that the world may know that I love the Father, and as the Father gave Me commandment, even so I do'" (John 14:31). This is the only time He refers emphatically to His love for the Father, but that love is proclaimed throughout His life in His joyous devotion and righteous obedience to the Father's will.

Christ is the quintessential illustration here. His obedience is never compromised or coerced. Rather, He finds His very sustenance in carrying out the Father's will: "'My food is to do the will of Him who sent Me, and to accomplish His work'" (John 4:34).

Christ speaks with great confidence of the Father's love for Him, as in His intercession to the Father for His followers in John 17: "'as Thou didst love Me'" (verse 23); "'for Thou didst love Me before the foundation of the world'" (verse 24); "'that the love wherewith Thou didst love Me may be in them'" (verse 26).

Jesus had an abiding sense of the Father's love, not a taste of it now and then. He lived, He dwelt, He was at home in that love, as He had been for all eternity. As William G. Blaikie says, "His soul was bathed in it, as a water plant is bathed in the water of its pool."[2] And what a source of joy this was to His heart!

Christ told His followers to abide in *Him*. We are to abide in His love and to respond to that love more and more by loving Him in return. Our love is then expressed in obedience, as was His love for the Father. "We love, because He first loved us" (1 John 4:19).

This abiding in His love is thus a major part of our imitation of Christ; the result is that we have the same joy of obedience. Please take careful note—joy is not the result of obedience, it is *itself* obedience—*loving* obedience. We find true joy in pleasing the God we love. As Malcolm Muggeridge, one of the great Christian thinkers of the twentieth century, said: "There is only one great joy—'Thy will be done.'"

IN TRUST

In the Gospels we see quite forcefully the explicit trust that Christ had in the Father. The Christian life is a walk of trust, and our pacesetter is Christ Himself. Trust is evidenced in two things: *submission* and *dependence.* These are never more clearly seen than in the life of Christ. Hence they constitute a great portion of our imitation of Him.

The Easy Yoke

"'Come to Me, all who are weary and heavy-laden, and I will give you rest. Take My yoke upon you, and learn from Me, for I am gentle and humble in heart; and YOU SHALL FIND REST FOR YOUR SOULS. For My yoke is easy, and My load is light'" (Matthew 11:28–30). I used to read this and wonder at the Lord's words. It seemed that the yoke of Christ was anything but easy, until I learned that it is a yoke of submission and dependence.[2]

The imagery of the yoke was very familiar to those to whom Christ spoke these words. They knew well that if a farmer wanted to train a young ox to do a certain task, he would yoke him to an older ox seasoned in that task. At first the young animal might pull against the yoke. But the older ox, being bigger and stronger, would pull him back in line. If he resisted, the yoke was hard. But when he submitted, the yoke was not so difficult.

The yoke of Christ in our lives is His lordship. We were permanently yoked to Him when we gave Him our hearts. But each day we must submit afresh to Him and walk in humble dependence. Being yoked to Christ speaks of a relationship in which we learn to walk in the way He walked with the Father.

Jesus said, "Learn of Me." How then do we learn? By *observation.* And what do we learn? Christ answers: "'For I am *gentle* [meek] and *humble* in heart.'"

Here is a rare glimpse into Christ's own character. In these two concepts, meekness and humility, we have valuable insight into how He related to the Father, for they speak of *submission* and *dependence.*

Meekness and Submission

In the word *meekness* we have the idea of strength brought under control. Often it is said of a tamed horse that he is as meek or gentle as a lamb. The horse is still a powerful animal, but his strength has been so harnessed that a child could walk up and pet him. This pictures *submission.*

Christ had a submissive spirit, not because He was weak but because He was strong enough in His own sense of who He was that He did not have to prove anything through self-assertiveness or self-promotion, and strong enough in His confidence in the Father's love that He gladly deferred to the Father's desires.

In Matthew 8:5–10, we find an encounter in the life of Christ which sheds some light on submission:

> And when He had entered Capernaum, a centurion came to Him, entreating Him, and saying, "Lord, my servant is lying paralyzed at home, suffering great pain." And He said to him, "I will come and heal him." But the centurion answered and said, "Lord, I am not worthy for You to come under my roof, but just say the word, and my servant will be healed. For I, too, am a man under authority, with soldiers under me; and I say to this one, 'Go!' and he goes, and to another, 'Come!' and he comes, and to my slave, 'Do this!' and he does it." Now when Jesus heard this, He marveled, and said to those who were following, "Truly I say to you, I have not found such great faith with anyone in Israel."

What was so extraordinary about this centurion's faith? Simply that he saw and believed that Jesus was *from God*. No one in all of Israel had fully realized this yet. He had observed that Jesus had authority in His teaching and authority over disease (see Matthew 7:29; Matthew 8:2–3). Perhaps the centurion had also observed His authority over demons, sin, and even death. The centurion also had authority over a large group of soldiers, but only because he was himself in submission to a higher authority. Thus he concluded that Jesus must be in submission to a higher authority as well. Based on what Jesus had authority over, he concluded that Jesus must be under the authority of God.

Humility and Dependence

In the word *lowly* or *humble* we see a childlike *dependence;* Christ walked in a constant sense of His need for the Father and thus in constant dependence on Him. In John 5:19–20, He said:

> "Truly, truly, I say to you, the Son can do nothing of Himself,
> unless it is something He sees the Father doing; for whatever
> the Father does, these things the Son also does in like manner.
> For the Father loves the Son, and shows Him all things that He
> Himself is doing."

This dependence of Christ speaks of His having been sent from
God for a purpose—to carry out the Father's plan—and that purpose
could be realized only in full dependence on the Father.

Voluntary Subordination

It is vitally important that we see Christ's submission and dependence
as *voluntary*. On a first reading of the Gospels, one might conclude
from the Lord's words and actions that He was somehow less God
than the Father. One could also suppose the Holy Spirit to be third in
rank and even less God than the Father or the Son.

However, the Holy Spirit's acquiescence to the Son and to the
Father is of His own free will, as is the Son's to the Father. Hence this
voluntary submission does not diminish the deity of either the Spirit
or the Son. In the Gospels we see Christ willingly, joyfully subordinate
Himself to the Father, although He is Himself every bit as much God.

Sent from God

Jesus repeatedly used the word *sent* in reference to Himself in the
Gospel of John—thirty-three times. He used the word *send* seven
times, five of which are in His high priestly prayer in John 17, where
He repeatedly used the phrase, "'Thou didst send Me'" (John 17:8,
18, 21, 23, 25).

In John 3:17 the Lord said, "'For God did not send the Son into
the world to judge the world, but that the world should be *saved
through Him.*'" Here, He declares His *purpose for being sent*. This
speaks of the great plan of redemption enacted in eternity past, when
God the Father agreed to be the sender and God the Son agreed to be
the sent.

John the Baptist picked up the same theme: "'For He whom God has *sent* speaks the words of God'" (John 3:34). John was saying, "Listen to Him!" Throughout John's Gospel this theme is echoed in Christ's public and private teaching. He stressed in every way possible that He was sent from God.

In John 8:33–59 we see a heated confrontation between Christ and the Jews. Christ, though bold and confrontational, remained in complete control and never once lost His composure. He boldly informed these Jews, who first boasted of Abraham and then of God as their father, that they were actually children of the *devil!* He said this as a contrast to the fact that He had been *sent* from God, who was indeed His Father. This so outraged them that they even accused Christ of having a demon.

The conflict reached its climax when Christ declared: "'Truly, truly, I say to you, before Abraham was born, *I am*'" (John 8:58). By this the Jews were driven to hysteria, and "they picked up stones to throw at Him" (v. 59). But Christ eluded their grasp.

Sadly, because of their pride, the Jews had failed to understand Christ's simple message—that He *was* sent from God. But without missing a beat, He turned to the disciples and immediately found a way to burn into their minds the same message. He used a "visual aid" in the form of a blind man (see John 9:1–3).

Now Christ could have healed this man just by speaking a word or touching His eyes, but instead, He did a curious thing: "He spat on the ground, and made clay of the spittle, and applied the clay to [the blind man's] eyes, and said to him, 'Go, wash in the pool of Siloam' [which is translated, *Sent*]. And so he went away and washed, and came back seeing" (John 9:6–7).

Did you catch that? *Siloam,* the name of the pool in which the blind man washed, means *Sent!* The pool of Siloam represents the *Savior sent from God,* who alone is able to open blind eyes to see the light.

In Submission

Christ came in *submission* to the Father. In John 8:42, Jesus said clearly, "'I have not even come on My own initiative, but He *sent* Me.'" One cannot be sent unless he first submits. Thus we see clearly that the Father was the initiator and Christ the responder. He responded by always submitting to the Father's will.

In John 6:38, Jesus declared, "'For I have come down from Heaven, not to do My own will, but the will of Him who *sent* Me.'" To this course He was true to the end (see John 4:34; 5:30; 6:57; 8:28–29).

The climax of His submission to the Father's will was reached in the Garden of Gethsemane, where Christ prayed, "'My Father, if it is possible, let this cup pass from Me; *yet not as I will, but as Thou wilt*'" (Matthew 26:39).

We are told in Hebrews 5:8–9 that, "Although He was a Son, He learned obedience from the things which He suffered. And having been made perfect, He became to all those who obey Him the source of eternal salvation." Christ learned from the experience of obedience, which was also accompanied by suffering. Obedience, though often accompanied by joy, always costs; saying yes to God always involves saying no to self on some level.

In the Garden, Jesus said yes to God. This marked, as Robert Law said, "The uttermost triumph over self, the point beyond which self-surrender absolutely cannot go—only so could…His victory become potential victory for every man."[3]

In Dependence

Again, Christ came in *dependence* on the Father. We specifically see this in verses like John 7:16: "'My teaching is not Mine, but His who sent Me'"; and John 12:49, which concludes His last public discourse: "'For I did not speak on My own initiative, but the Father Himself who sent Me has given Me commandment, what to say, and what to speak.'"

Jesus was dependent on the Father for the truths He taught and for the very words He said (John 14:10, 24). If we would be like Christ we must depend on the Father, even for the words we say. Peter thus admonishes us: "Whoever speaks, let him speak, as it were, the utterances of God" (1 Peter 4:11; see also Matthew 10:19–20).

The Crux of the Matter

In chapters 13–17 of John's Gospel, which detail for us the last admonitions of Christ to His disciples before His crucifixion, He stresses again the great truths that (1) He was sent from God and (2) He came in a posture of submission and dependence (see John 13:16, 20; 14:24; 15:21; 16:5; 17:3, 8, 18, 21, 23, 25). But now, He begins to apply these truths to His followers.

In John 13, after the foot-washing scene, Jesus says to the disciples: "'Truly, truly, I say to you, a slave is not greater than his master; neither is one who is *sent* greater than the one who *sent* him'" (verse 16). He adds, "'Truly, truly, I say to you, he who receives whomever I *send* receives Me; and he who receives Me receives Him who *sent* Me'" (verse 20).

The upper room discourse in John 17 culminates in Christ's earnest intercession for the disciples, in which He pours out His heart before the Father. In this prayer the same message is still burning in His heart. In verse 3 He prays, "And this is eternal life, that they may know Thee, the only true God, and Jesus Christ whom Thou hast sent.'"

Here, He further applies the word *sent* to His followers; and not only to the twelve, but to all who would believe through them (see John 17:20). That includes us. Christ prays in verse 18: "'As Thou didst *send* Me into the world, I also have *sent* them into the world.'" We are on a *mission;* we are not here on our own initiative; we have been *sent.*

And, we have a commission from the Lord. We are to do what He does, go where He sends, and say what He gives us to say. When we preach, teach, or share one-on-one, the words we speak are not to be our words, but the words of Him who *sent* us. We are to do nothing independently of Christ and the Father, but only what we see Them doing (see John 5:19–24). As Henry Blackaby says, "God reveals to us His work in the lives of others around us…that we might adjust our lives to join Him in that work."[4]

In addition (and please hear this carefully), we are to carry out our mission *in communion with Him.* Christ earnestly prayed for this intimate union with these words: "'That they may all be one;

even as Thou, Father, art in Me, and I in Thee, that they also may be *in Us.*'" Why? "'That the world may believe that *Thou didst send Me'*" (John 17:21).

Here is the heart of *lifestyle evangelism.* The entire gospel is contained in these words: *"Thou didst send Me."* If a person really comes to believe that Jesus was sent from God, he must also conclude that He truly must be the only way to God: "'I am the way, and the truth, and the life; no one comes to the Father, but through Me'" (John 14:6). He truly must be the sacrifice for sin: "'I am the good shepherd; the good shepherd lays down His life for the sheep'" (John 10:11). He truly must be the source of eternal salvation: "'I am the resurrection and the life; he who believes in Me shall live even if he dies'" (John 11:25). In just these three "I am" statements, we see the *gospel.*

But how is one to know the truth of the gospel? Jesus points here to *the life we live before men.* By walking together in union with Christ, and in imitating Christ in His own walk with the Father, our very lives give credibility to our message before those who observe us. They look at our lives and conclude that what we *say* about Christ must really be true: He really was sent from God! Here is God's plan of evangelism, a message that is illustrated and legitimized, to those who observe, by a life.

After His resurrection the Lord appeared to His disciples and used the word *sent* one last time: "'As the Father has *sent* Me, I also *send* you'" (John 20:21). These blessed words certainly apply to all of Christ's followers.

IMITATING CHRIST: THE PRAYER LIFE OF JESUS

Christ communicated with the Father as every other man does, through simple prayer. When He prayed, He was not performing some pious exercise; He prayed because He *needed* to. Though He was Himself God and, therefore, all-sufficient, He was also man and, therefore, full of need for God.

Here is one of the mysteries of God manifested in the flesh. Jesus needed to pray to the Father, not for forgiveness, but for physical strength, for mental clarity, and for wisdom.

Prayer is not a one-way street, not just our *talking to* God; it is also our *hearing from* God. He communicates with us in times of prayer through insights from His Word and through impressions of His will on our minds and hearts. So it was with Christ. Jesus prayed because He needed to *hear from the Father*.

However, we must be careful to approach hearing from God with *humility*. We must wait with fear and trembling, lest when God speaks, we misunderstand. Christ is, by His very nature, humble. He often spent long periods of time in solitude from men but in intimate communion with His Father, waiting and listening before Him.

In one-on-one conversations, such as with Nicodemus and the Samaritan woman at the well, Christ's oneness with the Father shines through. He always knew just what to say to communicate the mind of the Father. As a result He always received eternally significant responses, whether positive or negative, from those to whom He spoke.

This ability was a spontaneous overflow from His communion with the Father in solitary prayer and also from His moment-by-moment communion with Him even as He was interacting with men. Jesus possessed a keen sensitivity to the hearts of men and the heart of the Father.

In decision making, Christ always sought direction from the Father, as when He chose the twelve disciples: "And it was at this time that He went off to the mountain to pray, and He spent the whole night in prayer to God. And when day came, He called His disciples to Him; and chose twelve of them" (Luke 6:12–13).

Jesus prayed because He needed the Father's *companionship*. There was no one on earth to whom Jesus could turn for understanding. Not even His family or His closest disciples understood Him fully. Our Lord knew better than any other man what true *aloneness* was. Yet He could say with the sweet peace of true acceptance, "And He who sent Me is with Me; He has not left Me alone" (John 8:29).

Again, shortly before His arrest, Jesus said to His disciples, "Behold, an hour is coming, and has already come, for you to be scattered, each to his own home, and to leave Me alone; and yet I am not alone, because the Father is with Me" (John 16:32). Not until that terrible moment on Calvary was this intimate companionship broken, and only then for love's sake.

Jesus prayed because He *enjoyed* praying. It was a blessing and a refreshment to bring His petitions before the Father's throne. Prayer was a joy because He had explicit trust in the Father. He knew that the Father heard and would answer (see John 11:42).

Sometimes He also gave Himself to all-night seasons of secret prayer. There is a delight in the nearness of God that naturally fosters an expansion of prayer. As Blaikie says:

> Topic suggests topic, intercession genders intercession, till the whole field of the kingdom is embraced.... Men often ridicule long prayers, and when prayers are made long on the pretext of sanctity they deserve the ridicule; but prayers prolonged in secret because the oil is multiplying and the assurance is given of a blessing that there is not room enough to contain—that, doubtless, is like Christ's all-night prayer; it is prayer without the sense of weariness; it is prayer that brings down the very elixir of life, the very abundance of heaven.[5]

To be like Christ, we must imitate Him in His prayer life. Our prayers must be born of a sense of need. We must give time to pray with joyful confidence in God.

Jesus' prayers were direct. His address was simply "Father," which suggests an audible continuance of a ceaseless inner prayer. Thus He did not have to approach with formality or petition for hearing. He prayed with familiarity; "'*Father*, I thank Thee that Thou heardest Me. And I knew that Thou hearest Me always; but because of the people standing around I said it, that they may believe that Thou didst send Me'" (John 11:41–42); or, "'*Father*, forgive them; for they do not know what they are doing'" (Luke 23:34).

We need not pray complicated prayers full of pretense. We can pray simple, direct prayers as a continuum of prayer in our inner life, as we humbly practice by faith His continuous presence. In this we imitate our Lord.

But there is another dimension to the prayer life of Jesus. Throughout, there is *the sensitivity of a broken heart*—a heart broken over sin, over the tragedy of unbelief and unrequited love. Although He was in full sympathy with the purposes of the Father, how keenly He must have felt the tragic loss of what might have been, had other men only believed and responded to the divine love! Thus we see Him weeping over the fate of the city of Jerusalem.

All around Him was the constant evidence of pride, rebellion, and self-gratification. How His pure heart must have recoiled from the defilement of this fallen world! Jesus was the only truly innocent man—sinless, guiltless.

Yet beyond His innocence was His holiness. Not only had He never done anything wrong, He was fundamentally *other than* wrong. Evil was foreign to His very nature. How loathsome, how heartrending must have been the prospect of bearing sin in His own body on the cross, of *becoming* sin and, therefore, of being forsaken by the Father (see 2 Corinthians 5:21).

In the garden, with His soul "'deeply grieved to the point of death,'" Jesus prayed: "Abba! Father! All things are possible for Thee; remove this cup from Me; yet not what I will, but what Thou wilt" (Mark 14:34, 36). At this crucial moment of agony and dread, though His human nature seemed to recoil from the approaching hour, His deeper purpose was to do the Father's will.

How the Father must have suffered with Him and yet rejoiced over His obedience. He was heard, but—and here is the depth of desolation—He was not saved from death. He could not be saved if He would be the source of eternal salvation (see Hebrews 5:9). Jesus took the cup. He went all the way to the Cross and was obedient to the point of death (see Philippians 2:8).

How do we apply to ourselves this deep, mysterious aspect of the prayer life of Jesus? First, we may imitate Him in His absolute surrender to the Father. But second, we must recognize that our obedience will surely cost us. Indeed, it may cost us our very lives, as it has so many martyrs through the ages. God heard *their* prayers (see Revelation 5:8) but did not deliver *them* from death. Yet from their sacrifices have sprung many rivers of revival, and the purposes of God for eternal salvation have been realized. Like Christ, we must be willing to suffer whatever the will of God requires.

Hast thou no scar?
No hidden scar on foot, or side, or hand?
I hear thee sung as mighty in the land,
I hear them hail thy bright ascendant star,
Hast thou no scar?
No wound? no scar?
Yet, as the Master shall the servant be,
And pierced are the feet that follow Me;
But thine are whole: Can he have followed far
who has no wound nor scar?[6]

We may not suppose that, if we follow in the steps of our Master, it will cost us nothing. But as God conforms our hearts to His own heart through prayer, we will embrace whatever His purposes demand.

CHAPTER TEN

IMITATION: PART TWO

"For I gave you an example that you also
should do as I did to you."

JOHN 13:15

There was never a man like Jesus: "holy, innocent, undefiled, separated from sinners" (Hebrews 7:26). His thoughts were infinitely higher, His motives infinitely purer, His purposes infinitely more noble than those of any other man. He amazed everyone with whom He came in contact. Many rejected Him, but none could be indifferent; here was a man who in every respect was set apart from others.

Yet He was, indeed, a man, and He could identify with men and call them to identify with Him. We will now consider how He related to and communicated with men and what bearing that has on our imitation of Him.

IMITATING CHRIST:
HIS COMMUNICATION WITH MEN

Without dispute, Jesus Christ was the greatest communicator this world has ever known. For evidence we need only consider two things: the validity and import of what He communicated, and the effect this had—and continues to have—on men.

Quite simply, He communicated the *truth*. Pontius Pilate asked, "What is truth?" Jesus Christ embodied the answer. Christ said to the

Father, "'Thy word is truth'" (John 17:17), and He *is* that Word incarnate (see John 1:14). Indeed, He declared to the disciples, *"I am* the way, and the *truth,* and the life'" (John 14:6).

Christ had an astounding impact on those who believed the truth He preached. More than a commitment to a philosophy or a creed, He engendered a relinquishing of all to Himself. And so it is today among the millions who know Him as Lord.

Christ's favorite designation for Himself was "Son of Man." He communicated with men as not only a man, but also as the God-man. He communicated in a number of other ways as well: as prophet, priest, and king.

But above all else He communicated with men in two very significant ways, as a *teacher* and as a *servant.*

AS A TEACHER

Jesus was the master teacher. He revolutionized the concept of teaching through His unique form of *discipleship.*

Before Jesus began His ministry, discipleship was an established method of instruction. The Pharisees, the Sadducees, and John the Baptist all had disciples (see Mark 2:18). But these disciples, or students, saw their teachers primarily as resources. When one resource ran dry, they simply moved on to another, as seen in the apparent ease with which some of the disciples of John the Baptist moved on to Jesus (see John 1:35–40).

However, with Jesus, although the content of His teaching was extraordinary, the more profound thing He communicated was *Himself.* To be His disciple was to have a relationship with Him in which one sought to be like Him (see Matthew 10:24–25).

This discipleship also meant a *cost:* "'Whoever does not carry his own cross and come after Me cannot be My disciple,'" Jesus said (Luke 14:27; see also Matthew 16:24). This dictum applies to us today.

Although Jesus was the Master Teacher, He used simple methods, such as:

- *Repetition,* as in His use of the word *sent;*
- *Mind pictures,* given through stories or parables;
- *Visual aids,* such as the blind man, the fig tree, the loaves and fishes;
- *Object lessons,* such as washing the disciples' feet;

- *Illustrations*—the moon, the stars, the seasons, a child, and so on;
- *Probing questions,* as when He repeatedly asked Peter, "Do you love Me?" (John 21:15–17);
- *Experiences* from His personal walk with the Father (see Luke 9:58; 10:18; John 6:38; 8:38; 10:25; 11:15; 12:49–50; 15:18; 16:28).

Christ taught with unparalleled authority (see Matthew 7:29). The scribes and Pharisees said of Him in wonder, "'Never did a man speak the way this man speaks'" (John 7:46). He taught by example, and He Himself was the perfect illustration of all that He taught His followers to be and do. He taught with a heart of compassion (see Mark 6:34). No one ever loved as Jesus loved.

Although He was private and wisely cautious (see Mark 7:24; John 2:24), He was not afraid to be open and transparent when necessary. He openly shared His personal feelings, at times letting His followers see His very heart (see Luke 10:18, 21; Mark 6:34; 8:2, 12; 9:19; 10:14; 14:33–34). Sometimes He was direct, sometimes subtle. He knew people and took them from where they were to where He wanted them to be.

As a teacher He showed extraordinary patience and infinite wisdom, as when He waited for the disciples to ask before He taught them how to pray. They had observed His prayer life and marveled. One of them asked: "'Lord, teach us to pray just as John also taught his disciples'" (Luke 11:1). Jesus was ready with what we call The Lord's Prayer, an answer *more* than adequate (see Luke 11:2–4). In this short prayer He taught them not only what to pray, but what the attitude of their hearts must be.

First, each one had to have a heart for *intimacy:* "'Father, hallowed be Thy name'" (Luke 11:2). The word *Father* speaks of a unique, intimate relationship. We must hallow the name *Father* in our hearts and in our lives and cultivate a heart for intimacy.

Second, a heart of *submission:* "'Thy kingdom come'" (v. 2). Where there is a kingdom, there must be a king who *rules.* Thus we may say that the kingdom of God is the *rule of God;* we must also have a heart to see His rule in our own lives on a daily basis, and in the lives of others as well.

Third, a heart of *dependence:* "'Give us this day our daily bread'"

(v. 3). This speaks of dependence for our daily sustenance—not only bread, but every necessity of life. God is the giver of all good gifts (see James 1:17). We must look to Him with faith and anticipation.

Fourth, a heart of *forgiveness:* "'And forgive us our sins'" (v. 4). And further: "*'For we ourselves also forgive everyone who is indebted to us.'*" Jesus is instructing each of us not only to ask *for* forgiveness, but to ask *with a heart* of forgiveness. He wants us to pray with a heart like His own heart. If we will not forgive, we show that we do not see our own wretchedness.

Fifth, a heart for *obedience:* "'And lead us not into temptation'" (v. 4). With this, Jesus teaches that one must have a heart for obedience, a hunger and thirst for *righteousness.* "Father, please guard my path. I don't want to sin, so lead me not into temptation."

With these five short requests, Christ reveals to us the posture of heart from which every prayer must flow. But His instruction to the disciples is not over quite yet.

> "Suppose one of you shall have a friend, and shall go to him at midnight, and say to him, 'Friend, lend me three loaves; for a friend of mine has come to me from a journey, and I have nothing to set before him'; and from inside he shall answer and say, 'Do not bother me; the door has already been shut and my children and I are in bed; I cannot get up and give you anything.' I tell you, even though he will not get up and give him anything because he is his friend, yet because of his persistence he will get up and give him as much as he needs." (Luke 11:5–8)

Is Christ painting a picture of God the Father? No. He is drawing a contrast: If a man will finally leave his comfort zone to help a friend, not because of friendship, but because he is nagged into it, how much more will God, who is inclined to hear and answer, give us what we need? Jesus is not condemning persistence, He *is* saying that we do not have to nag God. Nagging comes from fear, doubt, unbelief, and a sense that we know better than God does what we need. Faithful persistence comes from submission to the will of God and a sense that we are praying according to that will; it is the expression of consistent dependence on God.

Then the contrast is fully stated: "'And I say to you, ask, and it shall be given to you; seek, and you shall find; knock, and it shall be opened to you. For everyone who asks, receives; and he who seeks, finds; and to him who knocks, it shall be opened'" (Luke 11:9–10).

But how is this statement of our Lord reconciled with James 4:3: "You ask and do not receive, because you ask with wrong motives, so that you may spend it on your pleasures"? The answer is found in the five postures of heart which we saw in Jesus' model prayer. If we have the right heart, then we may ask and *receive,* we may seek and *find,* we may knock and the door be *opened.* Christ then brings the lesson back full circle to the word *father:*

> "Now suppose one of you fathers is asked by his son for a fish; he will not give him a snake instead of a fish, will he? Or if he is asked for an egg, he will not give him a scorpion, will he? If you then, being evil, know how to give good gifts to your children, how much more shall your heavenly Father give the Holy Spirit to those who ask Him?" (Luke 11:11–13)

God always meets the needs of His children—not only their physical and material needs, but also their spiritual needs. And He will meet our greatest need: communion with Him through the Holy Spirit.

Some say that Christ was just a great teacher, but this goes beyond what a mere man, no matter how wise, could articulate. All His words are pregnant with eternal significance and have the ring of truth, because He *is* the truth.

Each of us is a teacher in some respect. If you are a parent or grandparent, a sister or brother, a friend or companion, then you are a teacher. And the principles that characterize the teaching of Jesus can be part of how you communicate, as well.

As a Servant

Jesus Christ epitomized the grace of servanthood. In His incarnation He took "the form of a bond-servant" (Philippians 2:7), and throughout His earthly ministry He served others. Jesus said of Himself,

"'The Son of Man did not come to be served, but to *serve,* and to give His life a ransom for many'" (Matthew 20:28).

Christ made it very clear that servanthood is the standard of greatness in His kingdom: "'Whoever wishes to become great among you shall be your servant, and whoever wishes to be first among you shall be your slave'" (Matthew 20:26–27; see also Matthew 23:11; Mark 9:35; 10:44; Luke 22:26).

Servanthood is more than just acts of service. It finds its roots in the *attitude of the heart.* Perhaps the most challenging verse in all of Scripture is Philippians 2:3, which says: "Do nothing from selfishness or empty conceit, but with *humility of mind* let each of you regard one another as *more important than himself.*"

This is a tall order! It goes so against the grain of our pride and self-absorption! How can we "do nothing from selfishness"? Our natural instinct is to take care that we always come out on top. How then can we honestly think of others as "more important" than ourselves?

We can do this only by looking to Christ and following His supreme example. Thus Philippians 2:5 says: "Have this attitude in yourselves which was also in Christ Jesus." Then follows that wonderful passage that speaks of Christ's self-emptying on our behalf. Clearly, He thought of us as more important than Himself.

Selfishness is the essence of sin. Every sin is an expression of selfishness. But what does Paul mean by *"empty conceit"*? Conceit is a very unattractive trait even in those who might seem to have some basis for it. But there is nothing more distasteful than an ugly person who thinks he or she is attractive or a person with no talent who has delusions of grandeur. This is *empty* conceit.

Yet at times we all think of ourselves more highly than we ought. We may camouflage our pride with false humility and even deceive ourselves into thinking we are humble, but in reality we have conceit in our hearts, and that conceit is quite empty. So often, we glory in our shame like frogs impressed with their warts.

Philippians 2:3 says, "But with humility of mind let each of you regard one another as more important than himself." Humility is not morbid self-debasement. It is simply self-oblivion. When we forget about ourselves we are free to focus on the needs of others, to see their needs as more important than our own.

We are not commanded to think of others as qualitatively *better* than ourselves, but as *more important*. This raises the issue of *self-worth*. What is it that gives us worth?

Self-Worth

Often people are puffed up about some personal feature they deem valuable, such as looks or intellect. They have, perhaps unknowingly, entered the realm of empty conceit. These people would never dream of actually serving others, for that would be beneath them.

They have great self-confidence but it is misplaced. Proverbs 3:26 says, "The LORD will be your confidence, and will keep your foot from being caught." Second Corinthians 3:5 says, "Not that we are adequate in ourselves to consider anything as coming from ourselves, but our adequacy is from God."

Others have poor self-images and are constantly looking for something to give them a sense of worth. They feel that, if others value them, they must have some worth. So they work hard at being impressive, with little success. These people would never dream of serving others unless it were to gain approval. Otherwise, to serve another would be to admit that someone else is better than they are.

Both of these types of people are bound in chains. They do not have the freedom to serve. The first is caught up in delusion; the second in fear. The startling reality is that neither type has any innate self-worth.

Many have a fear of never really being loved the way they long to be loved, in an unconditional way. Behind this fear is a deeper fear that they are not worthy to be loved. That is why they are constantly trying to prove their worth, not realizing that no one else but God *can* love them in a purely selfless way. It is very liberating for them to finally realize that what they have feared is really true. They have no worth in themselves, but neither does anyone else. It is God's love alone that gives us worth.

God has not loved us because of our inherent worthiness. If we were worth loving, grace would not be grace. Christ did not die for us because we were worth dying for, yet each of us has infinite worth because Christ *did* die for us.

The lost must come to the end of their delusions about personal merit before God if they would be saved: "Nothing in my hand I bring; Simply to Thy cross, I cling."[1] Even so, *we* must come to the end of our delusions about merit in order to *serve*.

We are not better than anyone else, and no one is better than we are. In truth we are all *equally nothing* apart from Christ. But in Christ, we are all of *infinite* worth. Seeing this sets us free; we can humbly serve in silent joy with no explanation, because God knows and that is all that matters.

This runs contrary to the teaching of the world, which says that we somehow *deserve* to have whatever we want because we are worth it—"it" being whatever self-indulgence suits us at the moment. What we really deserve is hell, but God in His great mercy has freed us from that horrible fate. We are now free to *serve*.

This is part of the freedom for which we were set free in Christ (see Galatians 5:1). Thus Paul said, "For you were called to freedom, brethren; only do not turn your freedom into an opportunity for the flesh, but through love serve one another" (Galatians 5:13).

Identity

In John 13 we have the account of Jesus washing the disciples' feet:

> Jesus, knowing that the Father had given all things into His hands, and that He had come forth from God, and was going back to God, rose from supper, and laid aside His garments; and taking a towel, He girded Himself about. Then He poured water into the basin, and began to wash the disciples' feet, and to wipe them with the towel with which He was girded. (John 13:3–5)

This is the most striking object lesson recorded in the life of Jesus. Foot washing was a lowly task, reserved for the least important servant, yet Jesus did it with no hesitation. It shocked the disciples. Peter protested—perhaps his pride was offended. He was certainly put to shame by the great humility of his Lord.

In verse 3 is a parenthetical phrase which, at first glance, does not seem to fit: "knowing that the Father had given all things into His hands, and that He had come forth from God, and was going back to God…." Why was this included?

Well, nothing is in the Scripture by accident. This phrase gives us insight into the person of Christ and how He saw Himself. It shows us that He had complete confidence in His relationship with the Father (see Matthew 11:27) and that He knew clearly both His origin and His destiny. Jesus did not have an identity crisis; He felt no compulsion to prove who He was to anyone.

Jesus didn't explain His freedom to serve; He just served. Then, after washing the disciples' feet, He asked:

> "Do you know what I have done to you? You call Me Teacher and Lord; and you are right, for so I am. If I then, the Lord and the Teacher, washed your feet, you also ought to wash one another's feet. For I gave you an example that you also should do as I did to you." (John 13:12–15)

If we will imitate Jesus we will find in Him our true identity. Each of us will develop the same quiet heart and servant spirit that characterized Jesus' earthly life.

IMITATING CHRIST: HOW HE RELATED TO MEN

Christ related to men in a way that caused them to relate to Him. They saw in Him all that they at least secretly held as an ideal: perfect freedom and ease, candor, approachability; His winsome nature and charisma, wisdom, boldness, and tenderness. Many despised Him from sheer envy. Many saw Him as a threat, and almost all eventually rejected Him. But none could deny His appeal.

IN TRUTH

He related to men in *truth*. There was no hypocrisy in Him, no deception, no fraud. He used discretion, not always entrusting Himself to men because He knew their hearts (see John 2:24). But He was unpretentious, honest, and piercingly real.

When the soldiers who came to arrest Him in the garden were confronted with this quintessential reality, they were overcome. Jesus asked them, "'Whom do you seek?'" They replied, "'Jesus the Nazarene.'" When Christ said "'I am He,'" they instantly fell backwards to the ground! (John 18:4–6). Perhaps, in that instant, they caught a glimpse of who Jesus really was.

We are by nature pretentious and deceptive. David said, "The wicked are estranged from the womb: they go astray as soon as they be born" (Psalm 58:3, KJV). We never have a completely pure motive in anything, though we may deceive ourselves into thinking otherwise. We manipulate circumstances and people to suit our own ends. We have hidden agendas, ulterior motives, and when confronted over sin, extenuating circumstances. We are pretenders, thinking we are holy when we are merely self-righteous.

To be like Christ, we must stop pretending to be more spiritual, mature, and holy than we actually are. We must stop trying to impress others and just be real with God and with men. Our prayers should be real, even if they sound childish. Our conversation should be real, even if what we have to say exposes us to ridicule and rejection (see Colossians 4:6). Every facet of our lives should reflect the reality of God's holiness and the grace and mercy from which we benefit each day.

IN RIGHTEOUSNESS

Christ was the only one who ever lived a life of perfect righteousness. He *always* did what pleased the Father, and His motive was *always* a heart of perfect love. He loved the Father supremely, and He loved His neighbor as Himself. Thus the life He lived before men reflected that love.

His teaching in the Sermon on the Mount and other like passages was geared toward this loving righteousness, which went beyond conduct to the motive of the heart (see Matthew 5:20). But Christ did more than teach this love; He modeled it. Jesus loved immensely; He loved selflessly; He loved indiscriminately.

Christ did not show partiality (see Acts 10:34–35). He loved the poor, the rejected, the sinful, and the sick as well as the prestigious, the healthy, and the self-sufficient. If we would be like Him we must love like this as well, not showing partiality, not promoting the rich over the poor, not governed by any discriminations (see James 1:9–11; 2:1–13).

Christ loved with more than words; He also loved with deeds of kindness and generosity. He was not afraid to touch people. So often, what people need is not a theological discourse, but a loving touch. Jesus healed the sick, fed the hungry, and forgave the sinful, and we must do the same.

IN MEEKNESS AND HUMILITY

Christ was also meek and humble before men, as in His example of servanthood. There were times when, of necessity, He was confrontational, but always with restraint and self-control. Yet when He was reviled, "He did not revile in return; while suffering, He uttered no threats" (1 Peter 2:23). In the final days of His earthly ministry, while hatred mounted against Him, Christ stayed His course and was meek even before His accusers. "Like a lamb that is led to slaughter...like a sheep that is silent before its shearers, so He did not open His mouth" (Isaiah 53:7).

In His meekness before men, we see Christ going in a direction that is unfamiliar to most of us. We are not so sure we want to follow. Neither meekness nor humility fit what men have come to believe is the norm for masculinity, and thus we hold Christ at arm's length. Without realizing it, we are bound in chains to a false image of what a real man is.

Christ was not weak. He displayed a strength that this world knows little of: the strength to be gentle and kind in the face of hatred and rejection; the strength to turn the other cheek and think of others as more important than Himself; the strength to confront evil but with no hint of cruelty or self-aggrandizement; the strength to cry, to be vulnerable; the strength to face calmly and humbly all that the forces of evil might hurl and yet never revile in return.

If we want to see what a real man is we must look to Jesus. He alone is the perfect example. To be like Christ requires going against the drift of society. As the old saying goes, "Any old dead fish can float downstream." It takes real strength of character and a stout heart to fight the current and go against the flow. But that is God's way.

Women in our society are no better off than men. Rather than rejoicing in those things that make them distinctly *different* from men, they seem to be doing everything they can to be *like* men. And often, the qualities they try to imitate are the worst ones, which is nearly as evident in the church as in the world. Peter encouraged women to put eternal things above temporal things and to be more concerned with inner beauty than with outward appearance. He defined this inner beauty in terms of meekness and humility:

> And let not your adornment be merely external—braiding the hair, and wearing gold jewelry, or putting on dresses; but let it be the *hidden* person of the heart, with the imperishable quality of a *gentle* and *quiet* spirit. (1 Peter 3:3–4)

Even the instructions in Scripture for women to submit to their husbands speak more to their relationships with God than with their husbands (see Ephesians 5:22; 1 Peter 3:5). If wives cannot submit to their own husbands, how can they submit to God? Christian women must realize the glorious truth that, in their submission, they are given an added opportunity to be like Jesus. When men are instructed to love their wives as Christ loved the church (see Ephesians 5:25), they are given a unique opportunity to do likewise.

What is a real man or a real woman? One who reflects in all aspects the meekness and humility of Jesus Christ. But Satan does all he can to make Christ seem unattractive, and both the world and the church have played into his hands. The he-man, macho image of masculinity and the aggressive, hard-nosed image of contemporary feminism—both are perversions of what is truly admirable in either gender. These are well-devised schemes of the devil, designed to keep people from knowing and being like Christ.

To our shame we Christians have often bought the devil's lie. We actually fit the mold of the world more than the image of Christ. We like to hear about the boldness and courage of Christ, His zeal, His command, His authority, but we look with consternation at His tenderness and transparency.

Satan incites us to be impressed with the smug, the arrogant, the clever, and the fashionable of this world. When we then emulate such negative qualities, the world pats us on the back while Satan smiles. We are like those frogs again, impressed with their own warts. We go on blindly in our deceived state, not knowing the shame we bring on ourselves and on Christ.

Finishing with Self

Meekness is *finishing with self*; coming to the end of self-assertion, self-promotion, and self-reliance. Jesus did not have to finish with self; He was never self-seeking but always self-adjuring. Although He was zealous for the Father's honor, the Father's house, and the integrity of the Holy Spirit, He was as gentle as a lamb in regard to Himself.

We also must finish with self if we would be like Him. S. D. Gordon, in *Quiet Talks on Power,* gives a compelling four-part definition of what we must finish with:

1. Self is the thing in us which *covets praise.* Even if we are not overt in our pursuit of praise, we do at least enjoy having our egos stroked, and we tend to pout when we are not appreciated.
2. Self is the thing in us which *shrinks from criticism.* We do not like to be criticized, even if the criticism is constructive. Inside we tend to be defensive.
3. Self is the thing in us that *is assertive,* or pushy and aggressive. Self always wants its own way; sometimes, it demands its own way.
4. Self is the thing in us which *has an insatiable appetite.*[2] The more we indulge self, the more ravenous it becomes. Self always wants more.

As Christians, let's apply this definition of self in a very practical way to meekness:

1. If self covets praise, then meekness is finishing with self-confidence, self-promotion, self-glorification, and self-conceit.

2. If self shrinks from criticism, then meekness is finishing with self-defense.
3. If self has to have its own way, then meekness is finishing with self-assertiveness, self-insistence, self-sufficiency, and self-reliance.
4. If self has an insatiable appetite, then meekness is finishing with self-indulgence.

Forgetting about Self

If meekness is finishing with self, then humility is *forgetting about* self. Humility is not a sense of inferiority; rather, humility is being oblivious to any personal significance in view of the contrasting wonder of God. The way to forget about self is simply to remember God and all His glory. Andrew Murray says, "Humility is the disappearance of self in the awareness that God is all."[3]

Here is real Christianity and real Christlikeness, plain and simple. I know many believers, but I know very few Christians in this sense of the word. When these truths of meekness and humility are apprehended, we have at least a start in actually knowing how to be like Christ. Thus we lose every reason for not being like Him but one: *desire.* Do we really *want* to be like Him enough to pay a price?

Oh, we may profess that we want to be conformed to His image, but when we see that this involves finishing with self, do our hearts fail, like that of the rich young ruler? Do we go away sad because we have "much riches" in self (see Luke 18:23)? If we love Christ we see in Him the *beauty* of meekness and humility, and we are drawn to be meek and humble likewise, no matter what the cost.

Quieting Self

But what of times when we are mistreated or ill-used? Are we expected to have a meek and humble disposition even then? This is where the *price* comes in, where the reality of our Christlikeness is really tested and proved. In 1 Peter 2, we find a passage little spoken of today:

For this finds favor, if for the sake of conscience toward God a man bears up under sorrows when suffering *unjustly.* For what credit is there if, when you sin and are harshly treated, you endure it with patience? But if when you do what is *right* and suffer for it you patiently *endure* it, this finds favor with God. (1 Peter 2:19–20)

These verses teach us that God is pleased when we refuse to defend ourselves, even when we are wronged, misrepresented, or misunderstood. This is hard on our pride. When we "suffer unjustly," everything in us wants to rebel. We want to protest, to complain. Our first reaction is to justify, to vindicate ourselves, even to retaliate. But if we look to Christ we are silenced. Peter points us to the supreme example of meekness and humility in verses 21–23:

For you have been called for this purpose, since Christ also suffered for you, leaving you an example for you to follow in His steps, WHO COMMITTED NO SIN, NOR WAS ANY DECEIT FOUND IN HIS MOUTH; and while being reviled, He did not revile in return; while suffering, He uttered no threats, but kept entrusting Himself to Him who judges righteously.

We have this promise then, that if we refuse to exalt ourselves but instead humble ourselves before Him, God will Himself exalt us at the proper time (see 1 Peter 5:6). Hence we have another key to Christ's endurance and to ours.

Rather than revile or threaten, Christ "kept *entrusting* Himself to Him who judges righteously." We must do this as well; we must submit to God and trust that, in His time, He will set aright all that is wrong. As long as our consciences are clear before Him, and in meekness and humility we accept whatever comes from His hand to shape and mold, we can have peace in our hearts.

Psalm 16:5 declares, "Lord, You have assigned me my portion and my cup; you have made my lot secure" (NIV). Elisabeth Elliot bears witness to this: "I know of no greater *simplifier* for all of life. Whatever happens is *assigned....* As I *accept* the given portion other options are canceled. Decisions become much easier, direction clearer, and hence my heart becomes inexpressibly quieter."[4]

Does this mean then that we are to let others take advantage of us? Sometimes (see Matthew 5:38–42). Nevertheless, this does not negate our responsibility to bring everyone we can along to a higher level of maturity, for the sake of the kingdom. We are not to indulge the selfishness of others. That is not having their best interests at heart. But we are to be humble in our approach to everyone, forgetting about ourselves as we remember the love of Christ.

With the Standard of the Cross

The world's standard measure is *fairness*. We have been conditioned all our lives to judge everything accordingly. If we feel we have been treated unfairly we become anxious, restless, indignant. This is a far cry from having a quiet heart.

When my brother and I were growing up, everything had to be *even* between us; everything had to be *fair*. Our chores were evenly divided. If I mowed the backyard, he mowed the front; if he washed the dishes, I dried. If anything was ever out of balance we protested its great unfairness. In our society the whole judicial system is based on this standard of measure. And well it should be—if not, we would have social chaos.

But Christianity recognizes a higher standard of measure. That standard is the *cross of Jesus Christ*. The Cross represents selflessness and sacrifice. There was nothing right or fair about the crucifixion of Jesus. It was the most ludicrous mockery of human justice ever performed. Yet it was the express will of God, the gavel-strike of God's justice in His judgment on sin.

If it pleased the Father to crush His Son so that He might be a guilt offering (see Isaiah 53:10), does it not stand to reason that He will at times be pleased to crush us, as well? This does not sound very appealing until we see that the Cross also represents God's great love toward us. The true attraction of real Christianity is the Cross.

"No," you may say, "*forgiveness* is the attraction." Indeed, how wonderful is the gift of forgiveness! But an even more beautiful attraction is what it cost God to provide for us that forgiveness. The Cross represents *death;* thus God's invitation to those who would imitate Christ is not "Come and *live*" but rather, "Come and *die.*"

But what of Christ's declaration that He came to give life, and life abundant (see John 10:10)? True, but this abundant life is not an enhancement of our self-life; it is a resurrection life, which requires that there must first be a death (see Romans 6:1–13; Galatians 2:20; Colossians 3:1–3).

Some may romanticize death to self from a distance, as one would romanticize martyrdom. But there is nothing romantic about the reality of death. Yet when we love Christ, we are drawn to follow Him in death. This death is a daily, deliberate finishing with and forgetting about self. When one dies there is no more pain, and on the other side, *resurrection* (see Luke 9:23–25).

The Cross is the standard that we must hold up to the world. But today, in our society, most of us who profess to know Christ would never dream of offering the Cross to the world. This is because we are not attracted to it ourselves.

Thus there is a constant attempt in the church to attract the world with the world. We offer entertainment, facilities, personalities—but not the Cross. Yet Jesus said, "'If I be lifted up from the earth, will draw all men to Myself'" (John 12:32).

What then is the gauge of our likeness to Christ? Is it an anointing on our teaching or preaching? Is it charisma? Is it our ability to persuade? No. It is death to self; it is the Cross. We must take no thought for ourselves but put the needs of others above our own; and in this mindset daily exhibit to them the fruits of love, joy, peace, patience, kindness, goodness, faithfulness, gentleness, and self-control (see Galatians 5:22–23), the characteristics of the resurrection life, empowered by the Holy Spirit.

In the Fruit of the Spirit

The character traits listed above are what Paul called the "fruit of the Spirit." It is interesting to note the close connection between these different elements. In a sense, each one helps define the others.

This is very clear in the life of Christ, who, as John the Baptist said, had been given the Spirit without measure and thus perfectly displayed all the fruit of the Spirit (see John 3:34). Because of His meekness the Lord exhibited great *kindness* and infinite *patience*. In His dealings with men, Christ was never in a hurry but always had time for each individual who came to Him.

Jesus had a unique inner *peace,* which came from His absolute submission to the Father (meekness) and dependence on the Father (humility). He gives to all who follow Him a peace unlike the peace of the world—the quiet heart that enabled Him to sleep in the midst of the storm and enables us do the same (see John 14:27; Mark 4:37–38).

We have spoken of His *self-control* even in the midst of tremendous adversity, persecution, and rejection by men. But Christ knew the secret of composing and quieting His soul: a gentle submission to the Father's will (see Psalm 131:2). This enabled Him to control His emotions, His thoughts, His words, and His actions before men.

At the end of His public ministry, just before His great Passion, Jesus said, "'Now My soul has become troubled; and what shall I say, "Father, save Me from this hour"? But for this purpose I came to this hour. Father, *glorify Thy name'*" (John 12:27–28). Thus He submitted to all the abuse men could pour on Him.

We see His *faithfulness* in His willingness to go all the way to the cross; His *goodness* in the unassuming purity of His purpose; His *joy* in His loving obedience to the Father, which required quiet submission while in the hands of those who would kill Him (see John 15:10–11; Hebrews 12:2).

But of all the fruit of the Spirit, it is *love* in which we most clearly see the meekness of our Lord. He loved with a tender yet magnanimous, big-hearted, generous love that rises above pettiness and selfishness. Such love speaks intensely of meekness; that quiet, gentle, yet powerful disposition of the heart which willingly surrenders to the dictates of love. If we would be like Christ, we must love as He loved.

Now this does not mean that we are to pretend or counterfeit the fruit of the Spirit. But as we are faithful to imitate Christ and follow lovingly in His steps, the Holy Spirit does something through us that we, by imitation, could never do: He manifests the actual life of Christ. This is transformation.

CHAPTER ELEVEN

CHRIST IN YOU

*That the life of Jesus also may be
manifested in our mortal flesh.*

2 CORINTHIANS 4:11

W e are to imitate Christ in all the fruit of the Spirit. Fixing our eyes on Jesus, we are to strive to love in the face of hatred, rejoice in the midst of heartache, and be at peace in the midst of the storm. But in this striving we must acknowledge that the task is too great for us and cry out to God for His grace.

WARP SPEED

Then something happens. We are chugging along at twenty miles per hour, spewing and sputtering as we go, when we suddenly discover that God has popped us into "warp speed." We find that we *are* loving in the face of hatred; we *do* have peace and joy in the midst of chaos and grief; we *can* control self by the power of the Holy Spirit.

This warp speed is actually *transformation,* God's response to our striving to imitate Christ in the fruit of the Spirit and our crying for help from a deep sense of inadequacy and humility. In the broadest sense, transformation is the result of all three aspects of beholding combined: devotion, consecration, and imitation. God transforms us into the image of the object of our beholding—the Lord Jesus Christ.

Now, this transformation is not constant. It is proportional to our beholding, which is often intermittent at best. Baby Christians are often much more efficient in this because they do not know enough to be self-reliant. They only know that they need God.

But after learning a few truths, they become puffed up and impressed with what they think they know. "Let Him who thinks he stands take heed lest he fall" (1 Corinthians 10:12). They eventually learn to return to that place of lowliness before God, humbly striving to imitate Christ in the fruit of the Spirit.

Thus this transformation is not a permanent, future state reached after years of beholding, but the ongoing result of our intermittent, sometimes unsteady focus on Christ. We may get discouraged by our inclination to distraction, but our failure must not be our focus. We will never be transformed by beholding ourselves, but only by beholding the glory of the Lord.

This process of beholding and transformation is not quite so hit-and-miss as it might seem. Transformation is a supernatural mystery of God, which cannot be explained in purely mechanical terms. Yet it *is* the result of our beholding.

We can develop habits of beholding, which become more natural as time goes on, even becoming subconscious. There is a level of maturity which may be reached, not sinless perfection, but a certain, real conformity to Christ based on a beholding that has become second nature. Thus the interplay between our beholding and His transformation signifies the life fully yielded to the Spirit's control. This truth enabled Paul to say, "Be imitators of me, just as I also am of Christ" (1 Corinthians 11:1).

To the Philippians he wrote: "Brethren, join in following my example, and observe those who walk according to the pattern you have in us" (Philippians 3:17). Yet, just a few verses before this, Paul had said:

> Not that I have already obtained it, or have already become perfect, but I press on in order that I may lay hold of that for which also I was laid hold of by Christ Jesus. Brethren, I do not regard myself as having laid hold of it yet; but one thing I do: forgetting what lies behind and reaching forward to what

lies ahead, I press on toward the goal for the prize of the upward call of God in Christ Jesus. (Philippians 3:12–14)

Paul knew his imperfection yet also the level of maturity he had attained.

Many men and women have reached heights of maturity of which most Christians have never dreamed: Augustine, Samuel Rutherford, Robert Murray McCheyne, Jonathan Edwards, David Brainerd, Hudson Taylor, George Mueller, Amy Carmichael, Oswald Chambers, and Jim and Elizabeth Elliot to name just a few. All are examples to us, and we do well to observe the pattern of their walks with God.

We also must be examples ourselves, but we shrink from this. We say with such seeming humility, "Oh, I am no example." Yet others look to us as examples whether we like it or not. Let us walk in such a way that we can say with Paul, "Follow my example, as I follow Christ."

ABIDING IN THE VINE

Another example is Christ's own imagery of a branch, *abiding* in the vine:

"I am the true vine, and My Father is the vinedresser. Every branch in Me that does not bear fruit, He takes away; and every branch that bears fruit, He prunes it, that it may bear more fruit. You are already clean because of the word which I have spoken to you. Abide in Me, and I in you. As the branch cannot bear fruit of itself, unless it abides in the vine, so neither can you, unless you abide in Me. I am the vine, you are the branches; he who abides in Me, and I in him, he bears much fruit; for apart from Me you can do nothing." (John 15:1–5)

Abiding in the vine involves the elements of intimacy: *love, trust, submission,* and *dependence.* These are also involved in walking by the Spirit (see Galatians 5:16). When we abide in a heart of love and trust toward Christ, we abide as branches in the vine and are thus enabled to bear the fruit of the Spirit.

We do not *produce* this fruit, though an imitation of it is part of our beholding. It is the fruit of the Spirit within us; we simply bear it. Thus we become channels for God's grace to flow to others. How liberating to know that if we abide in the vine the Holy Spirit will do the rest!

We must remember that love and trust toward God, rather than being passive, are expressed through our beholding, which involves action: *deliberate* devotion, *deliberate* consecration, and *deliberate* imitation. The result of this action is the supernatural, transforming work of God.

Now let us go back to the verse with which we began this discussion: "But we all, with unveiled face beholding as in a mirror the glory of the Lord, are being transformed into the same image from glory to glory, *just as from the Lord, the Spirit*" (2 Corinthians 3:18). In the freedom of open-faced communion with Christ, gazing intently on His glory as we are transformed into His glorious image the Spirit is the *agent* of this transformation.

But transformation is more than just the production of fruit in *likeness* to Christ. Thus Paul takes transformation a step further when he speaks of the very *life of Christ*, of which each believer is a partaker, *being manifested in our mortal flesh* (see 2 Corinthians 4:10–11). Christ actually imparts to us His own life! This is real Christianity—a spontaneous overflow of the life of Christ through us.

PERSONALITY

Now, transformation is not *annihilation*. Christ's life being manifested in us does not mean the end of our existence, but the true beginning of life abundant, which is resurrection life. Paul said, "'I have been crucified with Christ; and it is no longer I who live, but Christ lives in me; and the life which I now live in the flesh I live by faith in the Son of God, who loved me, and delivered Himself up for me'" (Galatians 2:20).

God does want each of us to *die* to self and thus to our *independence*, because true Christianity is a *union* of our souls with God. But He also wants *life*, a resurrection from the dead that brings the freedom of submission to Him. He does not make us clones of Christ with no uniqueness of our own.

Personality makes each of us different and distinct from everyone else. It derives from ancestry, language, and the influence of relatives, friends, and every person with whom we have ever come in contact. It also derives from experience, sexuality, physical and mental health, level of intelligence, temperament, emotional makeup, sense of humor, talents, abilities, desires, and aspirations. These all come together in a unique composition called personality.

But this does not mean that we have any true significance apart from Christ. Our significance derives from our union with Him and His church. Neither does our uniqueness negate our union with Christ or with other believers (see John 17:21–23). We have become part of a whole and are not meant to stand alone as islands in ourselves.

Yet each of us remains a unique part, for God does not want to crush the individual personality. He wants to set it free through the sanctifying work of the Holy Spirit: "Where the Spirit of the Lord is, there is *liberty*" (2 Corinthians 3:17). John records a moment in which Jesus speaks of this ministry of the Holy Spirit:

> Now on the last day, the great day of the feast, Jesus stood and cried out, saying, "…He who believes in Me, as the Scripture said, 'From his innermost being shall flow rivers of living water.'" But this He spoke of the *Spirit,* whom those who believed in Him were to receive. (John 7:37–39)

In manifesting the life of Christ in us, the Holy Spirit makes each of us a unique expression of that life—a part of the endless creativity of God.

THE GLORY OF THE MINISTRY

Now let us consider the word *manifestation,* which is what I call a "glory" word. It speaks of glory in the broad passage we have leaned so heavily upon: 2 Corinthians 3:17–18; 4:10–11 (the fuller context would expand to 2 Corinthians 2:14–5:7). Manifestation means a showing forth, a revealing. Glory is the outward manifestation of something *hidden within.*

The word *glory* is a common word in our songs and prayers, but few really know its meaning. The English word *glory* is a translation of both a Hebrew word in the Old Testament and a Greek word in the New Testament.

The root meaning of the Hebrew word is *heavy,* and it came to mean *impressive* in modern English. If we say that a conversation is *heavy* we mean it is weighty; it has made an impression on us.

The root meaning of the Greek word is *to think.* When we give glory to God, we are telling what we *think* about Him, extolling His reputation and worthiness.

Eventually, from these root meanings, the word *glory* came to mean not only a telling forth but a shining forth, or an *outshining*—an outward, visible manifestation of an inward reality. The inward reality with God is His deity.

In an extraordinary moment, Moses asked to see God's glory, and God granted his request. God picked Moses up, put him in the cleft of a rock, covered him over with His hand, and passed by. Then God took His hand away and let Moses see just His back (see Exodus 33:18–23).

God had said that no man can see Him and live (see Exodus 33:20). So did Moses see God? He saw what he asked to see: the glory of God, the outshining, the visible, outward manifestation of the inward reality of God!

When Moses came away from the presence of God, his face shone with a reflection of God's glory (see Exodus 34:33–35). The people were terrified, so Moses covered his face until the glory faded away. Paul called this the glory of the Mosaic covenant: God's covenant with the children of Israel in the wilderness, when He gave them the Ten Commandments (see 2 Corinthians 3:7).

But this covenant had an "if" clause (see Exodus 19:5–6), which the people broke, resulting in this statement from God:

"Behold, days are coming," declares the LORD, "when I will make a *new covenant* with the house of Israel and with the house of Judah, not like the covenant which I made with their fathers in the day I took them by the hand to bring them out of the land of Egypt, My covenant which they broke, although I was a husband to them," declares the LORD. "But this is the covenant which I will make with the house of Israel after those days," declares the LORD, "I will put My law within them, and on their heart I will write it; and I will be their God, and they shall be My people. And they shall not teach again, each man his neighbor and each man his brother, saying, 'Know the LORD,' for they shall all know Me, from the least of them to the greatest of them," declares the LORD, "for I will forgive their iniquity, and their sin I will remember no more." (Jeremiah 31:31–34)

Paul states in 2 Corinthians 3:6 that he is a *servant* or *minister* of this New Covenant. This statement is a celebration of triumph in Paul's heart, for his ministry had been sorely tested by the Corinthians' sinfulness but now was gloriously reaffirmed by their repentance and obedience.

The Corinthian church was very immature and problematic. The people were factious and elitist; there was gross immorality among them, to which they were quite indifferent; they were smug, greedy, stingy, worldly and shallow, and irreverent in observing the Lord's Supper. They were fascinated with the fantastic and sensational and filled with spiritual pride. And, as a consequence, they were poor in love.

Paul wrote 1 Corinthians to address these grievous sins. He was firm, yet he wrote with a broken heart. He was not content just to deliver the truth and have done with it. He agonized over them, not knowing what their response might be. He waited, and the wait was torturous: "Our flesh had no rest, but we were afflicted on every side: conflicts without, fears within. But God, who comforts the depressed, comforted us" (2 Corinthians 7:5–6).

Then, finally, he heard of their repentance, and his heart overflowed with joy. His primary reason for writing 2 Corinthians was to relate to them that joy. This wonderful book is not a theological treatise but a very personal letter, revealing more than any other what a heart for ministry must be.

In chapter 2, Paul begins to describe his waiting for their reply. Then suddenly, he cannot contain himself but bursts into praise and thanksgiving in his appreciation for the glorious ministry to which he has been called. Paul gushes for nearly six chapters before he returns to the narrative:

> For even when we came into Macedonia our flesh had no rest, but we were afflicted on every side: conflicts without, fears within. But God, who comforts the depressed, comforted us by the coming of Titus; and not only by his coming, but also by the comfort with which he was comforted in you, as he reported to us your longing, your mourning, your zeal for me; so that I rejoiced even more. (2 Corinthians 7:5–7)

Thus the verses between 2 Corinthians 2:14 and 7:5 have been called the "great digression." It is a parenthetical passage, unnecessary to the story but of immense value in revealing the heart of true ministry.

And so, in 2 Corinthians 2, after relating his distress over not finding Titus in Troas, Paul burst forth with these words:

> But thanks be to God, who always leads us in His triumph in Christ, and manifests through us the sweet aroma of the knowledge of Him in every place. For we are a fragrance of Christ to God among those who are being saved and among those who are perishing; to the one an aroma from death to death, to the other an aroma from life to life. And who is adequate for these things? For we are not like many, peddling the word of God, but as from sincerity, but as from God, we speak in Christ in the sight of God. (2 Corinthians 2:14–17)

A MINISTRY OF EVANGELISM

Here, without deliberate intent, Paul gives us one of the most profound New Testament expressions of what true evangelism is in the heart and life of a *true minister*—and that includes all believers. Both *lifestyle* and *proclamation* evangelism are represented here.

True lifestyle evangelism is *God-centered* rather than *man-cen-*

tered: "For we are a fragrance of Christ *to God"* (2 Corinthians 2:15). If we are walking in intimacy with Christ, the sweet smell of His presence in our lives rises first to the nostrils of God as a fragrant aroma. Then this fragrance disseminates to those around us: "among those who are being saved and among those who are perishing."

To some, the smell of Christ about our lives is too sweet; a stench in their nostrils. The sweetness of Christ is an affront to their pride and they are repulsed: "to the one, an aroma from death to death" (v. 16). To others, the smell of Christ attracts and they are drawn to Him more and more as they sense in us His reality: "to the other an aroma from life to life." Here is real lifestyle evangelism.

"And who is adequate for these things?" Paul asks. He answers a few verses later: "Not that we are adequate in ourselves to consider anything as coming from ourselves, but our adequacy is from God" (2 Corinthians 3:5).

Here we see an illustration of *glory.* The *reality* is an intimate knowledge of God through the indwelling presence of Christ in our lives; the *glory,* or the outward manifestation, is "the sweet aroma of the knowledge of Him in every place" (2 Corinthians 2:14).

Paul describes the glory revealed at conversion: "For God, who said, 'Light shall shine out of darkness,' is the One who has shown in our hearts to give the light of the *knowledge* of the *glory* of God in *the face of Christ"* (2 Corinthians 4:6).

But the gospel also must be *proclaimed*, and Paul includes that in this passage as well: "For we are not like many, peddling the word of God, but as from sincerity, but as from God, we speak in Christ in the sight of God" (2 Corinthians 2:17). Here Paul chastises those who use the gospel for personal gain as do, no doubt, many televangelists of our day.

Notice that proclamation evangelism also is *God*-centered rather than *man*-centered: "We *speak in Christ in the sight of God."* Our speech is in that sphere in which Christ is the center and the great fascination. The first emphasis is not man and his need, but Christ and His holiness. This is favorable to God.

Because of man-centered theology we have seen a watering down of the gospel in our day to make it more palatable to men. Our first appeal is often to men's self-love: "Come to God! He will get you off drugs and straighten out your finances, your marriage, and your work situation." We present God as a quick fix, with no mention of any responsibility to be holy.

Today, if we begin with the love of God, people are unmoved. They have the notion that God *ought* to love them; after all, they are "number one." They are what really matters.

We forget that God is at enmity with man, that man is an offense to God's holiness, and that God's holiness must be appeased (see Psalm 7:11–12). To be faithful to the Word of God, we should begin by showing men the holiness of God and by making it clear that they deserve no mercy and are headed for hell at lightning speed.

A great illustration of this is Jonah's preaching to the people of Nineveh. The message that God gave him was one of judgment (see Jonah 3:4). He did not tell Jonah to go and plead the love of God, but to go to Nineveh and *cry against them* (see Jonah 1:2). As a result the Ninevites repented, and God showed mercy to them, which was His full intent in the first place despite the consternation of Jonah (see Jonah 4:2).

Mankind's only hope lies in the mercy of God. Once they see this they are ready to hear of the great *love* of God. They must then be invited to repent of their sins and, in faith, surrender their lives to God—not merely to gain His blessing, but because they can no longer be an offense to this holy God who loves them so.

A MINISTRY OF LOVE

Jesus said: "'Greater love has no one than this, that one lay down his life for his friends'" (John 15:13). Perhaps the New Testament's next most beautiful verbal expression of love emanating from the heart of a minister, is Paul's sentiment toward the Corinthians:

> You are our letter, written in our hearts, known and read by all men; being manifested that you are a letter of Christ, cared for by us, written not with ink, but with the Spirit of the living God, not on tablets of stone, but on tablets of human hearts. (2 Corinthians 3:2–3)

The Corinthians were inscribed into Paul's own heart as a letter of love, not by Paul, but by Christ because of Christ's own love for them. This knowledge gave Paul great confidence on the one hand and great humility on the other (see 2 Corinthians 3:4–5).

A MINISTRY OF GLORY

Christ gave Paul this love, and Christ made him a minister of the New Covenant: "who also made us adequate as servants of a *new covenant*" (2 Corinthians 3:6). In 2 Corinthians 3, Paul draws a contrast between the Old and the New:

OLD COVENANT	NEW COVENANT
letters (v. 6)	the Spirit (v. 6)
death (v. 7)	life (v. 6)
condemnation (v. 9)	righteousness (v. 9)
glory (v. 7)	greater glory (v. 8–9)

In every way the New Covenant is superior to the Old. But Paul's main emphasis in these verses is on the superior *glory* of the New Covenant, superior because it *lasts:*

> But if the ministry of death, in letters engraved on stone, came with glory, so that the sons of Israel could not look intently at the face of Moses because of the glory of his face…how shall the ministry of the Spirit fail to be even more with glory? For if the ministry of condemnation has glory, much more does the ministry of righteousness abound in glory. (2 Corinthians 3:7–9)

The glory shining on Moses' face, as wonderful as it must have been, was not lasting. It faded away. And as a result of their unbelief, a veil was placed over the very hearts of the Jews, and it is removed only if they as individuals turn to Christ (see 2 Corinthians 3:14–16).

But the glory of the ministry of the New Covenant does not fade away. It is as permanent as the covenant itself (see Hebrews 13:20), and as permanent as the power and efficacy of the mediator, the Lord Jesus Christ Himself, to keep His covenant appointments (see Hebrews 9:15).

Second Corinthians 3:18 is the essence of this spontaneous overflow from the heart of Paul regarding the glory of the ministry. We will be transformed from glory to glory, and the actual life of Christ will shine forth from within us in love, joy, peace, patience, and all of the other fruits of the Spirit.

The genuineness of our Christianity is measured not as much by how we act, as how we react. Anyone can act rightly unprovoked, but what are we like when caught off guard? What comes out of our mouths when we are suddenly put-upon, inconvenienced, misused?

Amy Carmichael wrote, "If a sudden jar can cause me to speak an impatient, unloving word, then I know nothing of Calvary love…. For a cup of sweet water cannot spill even one drop of bitter water, however suddenly jolted."[1]

What does the lost world need to see? When men see a life from which flows the fruit of the Spirit; when they see reactions of love and forgiveness, patience and hope, endurance and stamina, joy in the midst of grief, peace so far beyond their own understanding that it grips their very souls—then they are confronted with Christ Himself.

They see what Paul called the manifested *"light of the knowledge of the glory of God in the face of Christ"* (2 Corinthians 4:6). This light they see only within us and only if *we* are beholding the glory of the Lord. Thus they are struck by the profound darkness in their own lives.

The ministry is not what we do for Christ. The ministry is *Christ,* and the *glory* of the ministry is *Christ's life manifested in our lives.* "Christ in you, the hope of glory," said Paul (Colossians 1:27). This is the glory of the ministry. This, too, is transformation.

PART FOUR

PLEASING GOD— THE FIGHT OF FAITH

And without faith it is impossible to please Him.

HEBREWS 11:6

Paul encouraged Timothy to "fight the good fight of faith" (1 Timothy 6:12). This is not some vague, nebulous admonition to be a good Christian. It is a specific call to arms to fight a particular battle, that of *faith*.

Love is the motivation for this deliberate, robust faith, and this fight of faith is the essence of true Christian living. This kind of faith pleases God.

J. C. Ryle said, "Justifying faith is a grace that 'worketh not,' but simply trusts, rests, and leans on Christ (Romans 4:5). Sanctifying faith is a grace of which the very life is action: it 'worketh by love' and, like a mainspring, moves the whole inward man (Galatians 5:6)."[1]

Our tendency is to doubt our beliefs and believe our doubts. Instead, let us determine to doubt our doubts and believe our beliefs. And we must believe with our whole hearts.

We have explored the varying components of an intimate walk with God, all of which are part of our striving to *know* Him. This striving to know God is a major part of our responsibility in the development of practical holiness.

Now, we move to the second part of that development, which is a striving to *please* God. This portion will be divided into two groups of chapters: the first dealing specifically with faith or trust, and the second dealing with love.

Chapter Twelve

Dealing with Temptation

*No temptation has overtaken you but such as is common to man;
and God is faithful, who will not allow you to be tempted
beyond what you are able, but with the
temptation will provide the way of escape also,
that you may be able to endure it.*

1 Corinthians 10:13

In fighting the good fight of faith, the Christian faces two struggles: a struggle *within* and a struggle *without*. Inside each of us is a conflict between the flesh and the indwelling Holy Spirit of God (see Galatians 5:17). In the flesh one cannot obey God, because the flesh is contrary to Him and is disposed to sin. Neither can the flesh please God.

We see both truths in Romans 8:7–8: "The mind set on the flesh is hostile toward God; for it does not subject itself to the law of God, for it is *not even able* to do so; and those who are in the flesh *cannot please God.*"

Yet Paul said, "Those who belong to Christ Jesus have crucified the flesh with its passions and desires" (Galatians 5:24). We have chosen against the flesh, and by that choice we have carried out a sentence of death on it. But there must be an ongoing echo of that crucifixion, a daily suppression and denial of its claims.

We must denounce sinful practices, choose against them in our hearts, and endeavor to abandon them in our actions. This determined endeavor, in turn, affects the desires of our hearts. As Henry Scougal said in *The Life of God in the Soul of Man:*

> We can never hope to have our hearts purified from corrupt affection, unless we cleanse our hands from vicious action.... We have some command of our feet, and hands, and tongue, nay, and of our thoughts and fancies too, at least so far as to divert them from impure and sinful objects, and to turn our mind another way: and we would find this power and authority much strengthened and advanced if we were careful to manage and exercise it.[1]

Paul told the Ephesians, "For our struggle is not against flesh and blood, but against the rulers, against the powers, against the world forces of this darkness, against the spiritual forces of wickedness in the heavenly places" (Ephesians 6:12). We have a formidable enemy, and he and his cohorts do all they can to tempt us.

Know Your Enemy

It is imperative to know something of our adversary. Satan has been a murderer since the beginning of creation. His heart toward Christ was a heart of hate and murder, and thus it is toward us as well. He is our mortal enemy and will stop at nothing to destroy us.

The Lord also said that Satan is "a liar, and the father of lies" (John 8:44). All deception comes from him. When he lies he is just being himself; deception is his very nature. And deception is also his primary strategy in dealing with men.

Growth in the Christian life is a process whereby we learn to recognize the lies of Satan, expose them to the truth of God, and decide whom we will believe: Satan or God. Tragically, even when we know the truth, we may choose to believe the lie because of habits of action, emotion, and indulgence. Knowing the truth is only half the battle; we have to choose to believe and act on it.

We may not like to admit it, but we have all been deceived by Satan innumerable times. It may very well be that, even at this moment, we are deceived about something. Yet we do not know we are deceived. If we believe a lie, we do not know we are believing a lie. Only as lies are exposed to the truths of God can we begin to walk in truth and really grow as Christians.

We are to stand firm against the *schemes* of the devil (see Ephesians 6:11). Those schemes are his many and varied deceptions. We stand firm by determinedly believing the truth of God. This is fighting the good fight of faith.

THE LIES OF SATAN

The lies of Satan are as innumerable as the sands of the sea. They come in three categories: lies about *God,* about *ourselves,* and about Satan *himself.*

LIES ABOUT GOD

One classic lie about God is that He is a cosmic killjoy who delights in getting people under His thumb so He can squash the life out of them. Satan tells us that all God really wants to do is ruin our fun and make life miserable; if we really trust God with our lives and futures, He will make us do something we would deplore.

But in His Word, which refutes and exposes Satan's lies, God tells us, "'For I know the plans that I have for you...plans for welfare and not for calamity to give you a future and a hope'" (Jeremiah 29:11).

A second picture that Satan paints is one of God as a distant CEO in the sky, an aloof superpower detached and too busy to be bothered with our insignificant problems. But Scripture presents God as intimately acquainted with all our ways (see Psalm 139:3), even knowing the number of hairs on our heads (see Matthew 10:30) and inviting us to cast all our cares on Him because He cares for us (see 1 Peter 5:7).

Yet another image of God, which Satan proposes, is that of a doting, sentimental old grandfather in the sky, benevolent and permissive and just a little out of touch. "All God really wants is for everyone to be happy and to love each other," says Satan. Thus God overlooks our transgressions.

But the Scripture clearly teaches that God does not overlook sin. "Do not be deceived, God is not mocked; for whatever a man sows, this he will also reap. For the one who sows to his own flesh shall from the flesh reap corruption, but the one who sows to the Spirit shall from the Spirit reap eternal life" (Galatians 6:7–8). God is the righteous judge, holy and immutable, the omniscient sovereign of the universe (see Isaiah 40). He is certainly not out of touch, but lives in absolute, immediate reality (see 1 Timothy 6:16). Everything besides God only properly exists as it touches Him.

Another satanic lie is that God is like a man. Satan would have us think that God relates to us impatiently and barely tolerates us; that His love is conditioned on our performance; that His posture is condemnation.

But God is not like a man. His thoughts are higher than our thoughts; His ways are higher than ours (see Isaiah 55:8–9). God is love and is infinitely patient (see 1 Corinthians 13:4); His patience does not wear thin; His love does not grow cold. God loved us while we were yet sinners, and He proved His love through the death of Jesus Christ (see Romans 5:8–10). In that death Christ bore our condemnation. "There is therefore now no condemnation for those who are in Christ Jesus" (Romans 8:1).

LIES ABOUT US

Satan's lies to us about *ourselves* are many and varied. For example, he would have us believe we are either completely *useless* or completely *indispensable.*

With respect to our being *useless,* we see Christ illustrating His teachings with an insignificant fig tree or a little child. He said that if the people would not praise Him the very rocks would cry out (see Luke 19:40). We even see God speaking to the prophet Balaam through his donkey (see Numbers 22:28–30)! If God can use these things He certainly can use any one of His children. This is not to say that we are worthy, but He graciously chooses to use us in spite of our unworthiness.

With respect to our being *indispensable, no* man is indispensable to God. Yet we Christians often become impressed with what we think we know or with what we have done for the kingdom. God tells us that if we think we know anything we are mistaken (see 1

Corinthians 8:2); and if we think we *are* anything we are also mistaken (see Romans 12:3).

Moses is an excellent illustration of both extremes. When called to his formidable task by God from the burning bush, Moses protested his inadequacy (see Exodus 3:11; 4:1, 10, 13). He thought he could be of no use to God. But *God had chosen him* to deliver His people from four hundred years of bondage.

Yet, although this most dramatic of callings was evidenced by great displays of God's power, a while later God met Moses on the way to fulfill his mission and sought to kill him because he had failed to obey God. Consider this fascinating scene:

> Now it came about at the lodging place on the way that the LORD met him and sought to put him to death. Then Zipporah [Moses' wife] took a flint and cut off her son's foreskin and threw it at Moses' feet, and she said, "You are indeed a bridegroom of blood to me." So He let him alone. (Exodus 4:24–26)

Circumcision of the firstborn sons of Israel was very important to God, although it apparently was not to Moses. It symbolized that God's people Israel were a holy nation set apart from others, as is the church today spiritually (see 1 Peter 2:9). But Zipporah was not a Hebrew. She did not understand this bloody rite; perhaps she saw it as pagan and cruel. But when God sought to kill Moses, she knew what was going on and saved his life.

This obscure episode demonstrates that even Moses was not indispensable to God, who could have raised up a thousand others, and neither are we. Sadly, this lie is often believed by ministers. Satan tells them they are God's men, indispensable to His Kingdom and hence immune to scandal. But pride comes before destruction. When those who think themselves indispensable indulge in immorality, they often find themselves sadly mistaken. How many ministers in our day have fallen to sexual immorality, tax evasion, or any number of offences, and God *has* let them be found out? No man is indispensable; God does not need any of us.

LIES ABOUT HIMSELF

One of Satan's most prevalent lies about himself is that he does not exist. But the plain sense of Scripture refutes this notion. Christ Himself spoke more than once of Satan as a literal being. His existence is encountered all through the Scripture: from the temptation of Eve in Genesis 3 to his foretold doom in Revelation 20.

In answer to whether he really believed in a literal devil, C. S. Lewis wrote

> Now, if by "the Devil" you mean a power opposite to God and, like God, self-existent from all eternity, the answer is certainly No. There is no uncreated being except God…. No being could attain a "perfect badness" opposite to the perfect goodness of God; for when you have taken away every kind of good thing (intelligence, will, memory, energy, and existence itself) there would be none of Him left.
>
> The proper question is whether I believe in devils. I do. That is to say, I believe in angels, and I believe that some of these, by the abuse of their free will, have become enemies to God and…to us. These we may call devils…the opposite of *angel* only as Bad Man is the opposite of Good Man. Satan, the leader or dictator of devils, is the opposite, not of God, but of Michael.[2]

This brings us to a second lie, again quite prevalent even in the church, which is that Satan is a *rival* to God. Satan cannot compare to God in any way. The very thought is ludicrous; God is infinitely superior to Satan. Three of the attributes of God will aid us in drawing a proper contrast.

First, God is *omnipresent*.

> Where can I go from Thy Spirit? Or where can I flee from Thy presence? If I ascend to heaven, Thou art there; if I make my bed in Sheol, behold, Thou art there. If I take the wings of the dawn, if I dwell in the remotest part of the sea, even there Thy hand will lead me, and Thy right hand will lay hold of me. If I

say, "Surely the darkness will overwhelm me, and the light around me will be night," even the darkness is not dark to Thee, and the night is as bright as the day. (Psalm 139:7–12)

In contrast, Satan can be in only one place at a time. He is probably in that place where he thinks he can do the most harm to the kingdom of God. Certainly, the average Christian has never had any contact with Satan himself. When we say that Satan tempts us, we mean that one of Satan's many demons tempts us as his representative.

Satan controls an intricate, sophisticated, Mafia-like network of demons waging war against mankind. But Satan and his demons are limited to space, as are all creatures, while God is present everywhere at once and is thus an ever present help to us in times of trouble (see Psalm 46:1).

I relegate Satan to the last verses of Romans 8, where Paul said: "For I am convinced that neither death, nor life, nor angels, nor principalities, nor things present, nor things to come, nor powers, nor height, nor depth, *nor any other created thing,* shall be able to separate us from the love of God, which is in Christ Jesus our Lord" (Romans 8:38–39). Satan is just another created being. But God is the Creator of all things.

Second, God is *omniscient.* All the acquired knowledge of modern man, God has known from all eternity. No secrets are hidden from Him. No repressed thoughts in the most obscure recesses of the most troubled mind can escape Him; He knows them before we think them, He knows our needs before we feel them (see Psalm 139:1–3).

By contrast, Satan knows only what God allows him to know. Satan and his agents do not know our thoughts; they cannot read our minds. But they study us and know our habits, likes, dislikes, strengths, and weaknesses. They know the buttons to push to entice us to sin.

If you really want to frustrate the devil, change! Repent! Then he has to regroup and find another mode of attack. That is one reason why we should walk in a *mode* of repentance; it keeps Satan off center.

Besides enticing us to sin, these messengers from hell can plague us with doubts and paranoia, paralyze us with fear, and convince us to accuse and condemn ourselves or to believe that God accuses and condemns us. But hear God's Word:

> If God is for us, who is against us? He who did not spare His own Son, but delivered Him up for us all, how will He not also with Him freely give us all things? Who will bring a charge against God's elect? God is the one who justifies; who is the one who condemns? Christ Jesus is He who died, yes, rather who was raised, who is at the right hand of God, who also intercedes for us. (Romans 8:31–34)

Third, God is *omnipotent.* I once overheard two little boys talking. One held up his forearm to reveal his bulging biceps, saying, "Satan's muscles are this big!" The other retorted, from a similar stance, "Yeah, but God's muscles are *this* big!"

I laughed, but then I thought of how perfectly that illustrates the typically false view that these are two relatively equal opposing forces locked in a struggle for power. Most believe that God will eventually win out in the end but Satan will give God a run for His money.

No! God is omnipotent. This means that *all power belongs to Him;* even Satan's power is borrowed and temporary. One day he will have to relinquish that power; meanwhile, he can do nothing without permission from the sovereign Lord of the universe.

Why then does God allow him to have such power? Suffice it to say that God has His own purposes, which are always wise and good.

RESIST THE DEVIL

I often hear the exhortation, "Resist the devil and he will flee from you" (James 4:7). But this command is sandwiched between two others: "Submit therefore to God" and "Draw near to God" (James 4:7–8). The second has a promise with it: "Draw near to God and *He will draw near to you."*

How are we to draw near to God? "Cleanse your hands, you sinners; and purify your hearts, you double-minded. Be miserable and mourn and weep; let your laughter be turned into mourning, and your joy to gloom. Humble yourselves in the presence of the Lord, and He will exalt you" (James 4:8–10).

Satan is indeed limited in power. He was, in fact, defeated at the cross. Nevertheless, we must be careful not to underestimate him; while he is loose on earth, he is immensely dangerous. Peter admonishes us, "Be of sober spirit, be on the alert. Your adversary, the devil, prowls about like a roaring lion, seeking someone to devour" (1 Peter 5:8). He devours by deceit, and whole societies are held in the grip of his lies.

But the Christian has a huge advantage over Satan. Aside from the indwelling and enabling of the Holy Spirit, the support of the Father with all His authority and power, and the intercession of Christ, the *truth* is on His side—the truth of *God's Word*. Paul calls this the *sword of the Spirit*. It is one of the weapons of our warfare and it is divinely powerful (see 2 Corinthians 10:3–5).

Another crucial weapon is the *shield of faith* "with which [we] will be able to extinguish all the flaming missiles of the evil one" (Ephesians 6:16). What are those flaming missiles? Lies. To *believe* the Word of God is to employ the shield of faith and to fight the good fight of faith.

A third weapon is *prayer*. But we must understand that prayer is talking to *God,* not to the devil. We are never instructed in Scripture to talk to the devil, but we are instructed to talk to God. We have no personal authority over the devil. Even Michael the archangel did not personally rebuke Satan but said, "The Lord rebuke you" (Jude 1:9).

When we stand firm in this spiritual warfare, God intervenes with His infinite power. We alone are no match for Satan, but he is no match for our God, and "greater is He who is in you than he who is in the world" (1 John 4:4). I love Martin Luther's wonderful hymn, written at a time of extraordinary personal combat on the spiritual plane:

> A mighty fortress is our God,
> A bulwark never failing;
> Our helper He, amid the flood
> Of mortal ills prevailing;
> For still our ancient foe
> Doth seek to work us woe;

His craft and power are great,
And armed with cruel hate,
On earth is not His equal.
And tho' this world, with devils filled,
Should threaten to undo us,
We will not fear, for God hath willed
His truth to triumph thro' us.[3]

Indeed, Satan's doom *is* sure: "And the devil who deceived them was thrown into the lake of fire and brimstone, where the beast and the false prophet are also; and they will be tormented day and night forever and ever" (Revelation 20:10)!

RECOGNIZE WHAT IS GOOD

Now let us look at a very instructive passage: "Let no one say when he is tempted, 'I am being tempted by God'; for God cannot be tempted by evil, and He Himself does not tempt anyone" (James 1:13). God does not tempt, but He, in His sovereignty, does allow temptation.

TEMPTATION IS POSITIVE

In 1 Corinthians 10:13, Paul said:

No temptation has overtaken you but such as is common to man; and God is faithful, who will not allow you to be tempted beyond what you are able, but with the temptation will provide the way of escape also, that you may be able to endure it.

When Paul declares that God will not allow us to be tempted beyond what we are able, he implies that God *will* allow us to be tempted within the parameters of what we are able, by His grace, to endure. Please note that this verse, though often used in reference to adversity, really refers to temptation to sin.

The Lord Jesus, foretelling Peter's denial of Him, said, "'Simon, Simon, behold, Satan has demanded permission to sift you like wheat; but I have prayed for you, that your faith may not fail; and you, when once you have turned again, strengthen your brothers'" (Luke 22:31–32).

Now look more closely at what Jesus said to Peter regarding the betrayal: "Satan has *demanded permission*...." The word *demanded* shows *impertinence*. Who is he to demand anything of God? But look at *what* he demanded: *permission*. That shows the absolute *sovereignty* of God.

God allows Satan to tempt. But Satan has no power to *make* the Christian sin. His only *direct* power over us is the power of influence and suggestion through deception, although his influence over other people may be used against us in an *indirect* way. Fellow Christians can be used by Satan if they are not walking with God. Any lost person may even be possessed by a demon, although I believe this is not possible for the believer. But neither Satan's deception toward us, nor his evil influence over others around us, can ultimately thwart the eternal purpose of God toward His child. Even these things become part of the "all things" of Romans 8:28 that God causes to work together for our good.

But *why* does God allow us to be tempted? Satan says God wants us to fail, but this is one of his most heinous lies. God allows us to be tempted so that we might *succeed*. Every temptation is an opportunity to sin but also an opportunity to *obey*. Henry Drummond wrote:

> Do not resent temptation; do not be perplexed because it seems to thicken round you more and more, and ceases neither for effort nor for agony nor prayer.... It is having its work in making you patient, and humble, and generous, and unselfish, and kind, and courteous. Do not grudge the hand that is molding the still too shapeless image within you. It is growing more beautiful, though you see it not, and every touch of temptation may add to its perfection.[4]

Satan is an unwitting pawn in the hand of almighty God to bring about God's own purposes. And God's primary purpose toward us is to conform us to the image of His Son (see Romans 8:29).

God uses the temptations we face to strengthen our faith and confidence in Him. When we obey God in the power of the Holy Spirit, we are encouraged by that obedience to rely on Him even more in the next temptation. If we *yield* to temptation we must suffer the consequences, but God will even use that to show us how much we need Him. Thus He develops our meekness and humility, and we become more compassionate toward others.

The struggle within is not between self and Satan. It is between the flesh and the indwelling Holy Spirit. He is our guide who maneuvers us through the mine fields of life. The mines are sins and sin is death, but the Holy Spirit will lead us through, one step at a time, if we trust and lean on Him. This is to "walk by the Spirit," with the result that we will not carry out the desires of the flesh.

Satan would have us reverse the order: "Don't carry out the desires of the flesh, and you will be able to walk by the Spirit." But this is getting the cart before the horse. We are to walk *by* the Spirit. That means a walk of intimacy with the Spirit from whence comes the ability to resist.

But where is our enabling if we begin with the flesh? By what power do we whip the flesh into shape? The flesh is in opposition to the Spirit, strong in rebellion against God (see Galatians 5:17) yet weak toward temptation. It rolls over into sin with great ease.

Jesus said: "'The spirit is willing, but *the flesh is weak*'" (Matthew 26:41). Our spirits would be willing to comply with God's desires if we only knew how! Paul declared, "For I joyfully concur with the law of God in the inner man" (Romans 7:22).

Two Sides of Temptation

There are two aspects of temptation. When we say "I was tempted," we may be speaking of the *outward* aspect of temptation, in which one of Satan's demons offers us an opportunity to sin. Or we may mean the *inward* aspect of temptation, in which we ourselves are enticed by that offer. The former was experienced even by Christ when Satan tempted Him in the wilderness. The latter belongs only to fallen man.

Sometimes, in theological discussions, the question whether Jesus could have sinned is entertained. But how could the pure, holy Lord of glory be disposed to anything that would displease His Father? Yes,

Jesus was tempted when Satan approached Him in the wilderness (see Hebrews 2:18; 4:15), but there was nothing within Him that responded to that temptation. Satan's temptation dealt with legitimate, natural needs. When Satan tempted Jesus to turn stones to bread, our Lord was no doubt hungry, but He was not tempted within Himself to meet that need with any provision other than what came from His Father (see Matthew 4:3–4).

We, on the other hand, have a sinful disposition. We are disposed to pride, rebellion, and unbelief. Therefore, there is within us that which is easily drawn away by the devil's enticements. Satan cannot make us sin, but he can deceive us into thinking that he can. He also tells us that we have no choice because our desires are so strong. We will eventually cave in anyway; we might as well go ahead now. But we *do* have a choice. No matter how strong the inward lust toward sin, we may still humble ourselves and rely on the enabling grace of God.

This inward enticement to sin is what James emphasizes: "But each one is tempted when he is carried away and enticed by his own lust. Then when lust has conceived, it gives birth to sin; and when sin is accomplished, it brings forth death" (James 1:14–15). For the Christian, sin is death to his sensitivity, credibility, and influence for the kingdom.

Temptation Is Not Sin

Contrary to the lies of Satan, *temptation itself is not sin. Yielding* is sin, but Satan would have us feel guilty just because we felt tempted. But we do not have to answer to our feelings; we have to answer to God. Martin Luther reputedly said, "You can't keep the birds from flying over your head, but you can keep them from building a nest in your hair."

GOD ALONE CAN MEET OUR NEEDS

Satan is not actually mentioned in James 1, which emphasizes that *inward* aspect of temptation, but he is definitely understood there. The next verse says, "Do not be deceived, my beloved brethren" (James 1:16). Satan is the father of lies, so he is the source of all deception.

But what are we not to be deceived about? The answer comes in verse 17: "Every good thing bestowed and every perfect gift is from above, coming down from the Father of lights, with whom there is no variation, or shifting shadow." We are not to be deceived about the origin of good things. They all come from God, not Satan.

Satan wants us to believe that he can meet all our needs, that his provisions are even superior to God's. This is the basis of all his temptations. He appeals to our desires and convinces us that he offers what we really need.

When we opt for Satan's provisions, we sin because we have believed a lie. We are products of God's creativity—does He not know best what we need, and how best to fulfill that need?

How do we know that God's provisions are the only good provisions? Because they come from "the Father of lights, with whom there is *no variation,* or *shifting shadow."* By "no variation" I take James to mean *no change.* God is immutable (see Malachi 3:6); therefore, His gifts and provisions do not change. They remain the same.

But with Satan, nothing remains the same. What may at first taste sweet soon becomes bitter; what may seem beautiful becomes distasteful; what we were sure would satisfy soon sickens us to the point of despair.

By "no shifting shadow" I take James to mean *no deception.* Satan dangles a shiny bauble in the shadows and entices us to come after it, but it is counterfeit, a cheap imitation of the real thing.

All perversion of what is right and good is a lie. The real thing belongs to God. With Him, what you see is what you get—no deception, no shadow, only the full sunlight of reality. Only God can satisfy our deepest longings, because only His provisions are *lasting and real.*

His Perfect Timing

Our own impatience tempts us to opt for Satan's counterfeits. We live in an instant-gratification society where everything is convenient and immediate. We don't want to wait. But waiting is a major part of the Christian life.

Waiting involves real trust in God and love expressed through patience. Do we love God enough to wait? Do we *trust* God enough?

We fail when we think that we know better than God what we

need and when we need it. God is sovereign and God is good. He will not withhold any good thing from those who walk uprightly (see Psalm 84:11).

If we do not have what we think we need, we must not really need it right now. We can do without until God sees fit to give. In that case, God's provision is the ample and abundant grace to do without.

"But wait a minute—that doesn't sound right. We shouldn't actually have to do without!" We think this way because we have been conditioned to believe that we must have what we want and have it right now. We even think we *deserve* what we want and, therefore, should aggressively pursue it. But such is not God's way.

And yet, if we trust God, when we least expect it, God will surprise us with a fulfillment very much worth the wait. The classic example is the Christian young person who abstains from sex before marriage, convinced that God's provision is worth waiting for. I have never known anyone to be disappointed by that decision.

Now we can see fairly easily how God can meet our spiritual, psychological, and emotional needs through His Word, prayer, the fellowship of the Holy Spirit, and identification with His church. But what about our physical needs?

We should know that if we trust Him, He will take care of food, clothing, and shelter. David said, "I have not seen the righteous forsaken, or his descendants begging bread" (Psalm 37:25). But what about the deeper physical need of affection, the legitimate, basic need for human touch? Some people's lives are filled with human touch through the network of family and friends. But some have little of either, yet they have the same need for affection.

How can God meet that need? Once I moved to a new city where I knew no one. For long periods of time I had no physical contact with any other person, not even a hug or a pat on the back. At one point I remember being so starved for a human touch that I actually found myself looking forward to getting my hair cut. But I decided that if I could trust God to meet other needs, I could trust Him for this need as well.

So I waited, and God gave me the grace to do without until one day He profoundly met that need. It came through a simple, innocent hug from a child. Such an ordinary thing—and yet in that hug, I sensed the arms of God. He surprised me by meeting my need when I least expected it, when I had no thought of even *having* the need. Oh, the warmth and satisfaction He brought! God can and will meet every need, no matter how great or small, if we will love Him enough to trust Him.

But we must look to God and not to other people. Although He does meet many needs through people, they are simply doing His work. Even in marriage, the one to look to is God. The ideal in marriage comes when each partner looks to God to meet his or her own needs and looks to the other partner with a heart to meet that partner's needs. Then they can both rejoice when God meets each of their needs through the other! This is *love* rather than *lust*.

His Greatest Provision

The deepest need that God has placed within each of us is the need for Him. God is all we really *have;* anything else can be taken away. God is all we really *need;* if we have Him, we have everything.

But it is a weighty matter, and one which determines our joy, that we come to the place of confessing that God is all we really *want.* In truth, each of us longs for true satisfaction and fulfillment, but we often do not know that we were created to find our satisfaction in Him. If He is the only real source of satisfaction, then He *is* all we really want, whether we know it or not.

We must learn to say with David, "Whom have I in heaven but thee? and there is none upon earth that I desire beside thee. My flesh and my heart faileth: but God is the strength of my heart, and my portion for ever" (Psalm 73:25–26, KJV). These are not words of resignation, but of joy.

GOD ALONE CAN SATISFY OUR DESIRES

One of the strongest physical desires is the desire for sex, and that is quite normal. But it is wrong to think that sex is the ultimate fulfillment of the body. What of those who remain single all their lives and never have sex? Can they never be fully satisfied physically?

In 1 Corinthians 6:13, Paul says, "Food is for the stomach, and the stomach is for food; but God will do away with both of them. Yet the body is not for immorality, but for the Lord; and the Lord is for the body." In other words, just as the stomach is for food, the body is for the Lord. As Paul says a few verses later, the body is the temple of the Holy Spirit (see 1 Corinthians 6:19). Further, as food is for the stomach, so the Lord is for the body. In other words, *the Lord is the satisfaction of the body!*

Now we are speaking of physical satisfaction, not sexual. There is an enjoyment of God physically which outshines sexual pleasure. Is not singing physical? Or kneeling or lifting one's hands to the Lord? Are not tears and laughter physical? What of prostrating one's self on the ground in repentance? Or shouting for joy?

The greatest physical ecstasy is not sex, as wonderful as that is in the context of Christian marriage, but rather those moments of deep spiritual intimacy with God that find their expression in the members of our bodies. This is true for all Christians, married or single. How sad for Christians to long for sex as the ultimate fulfillment of their very lives! Being thus deceived, many Christians feel overwhelmed by their passions and desires. Fueled by Satan's deceptions, the lust of the flesh and the lust of the eyes and the boastful pride of life become so strong that to resist is like trying to stave off a huge tidal wave from a grass hut on the beach. Try as they might, they cannot escape this torrent of desire.

But the Christian is not to stop desiring. He is simply to stop desiring the wrong things. He must stop loving the things in the world and start really loving God. Self-denial does not mean the annihilation of desire. Rather, it means losing interest in self, in an all-consuming desire for God. That is easy to say, but how is it done?

A clue is found in the words of C. S. Lewis: "Our Lord finds our desires not too strong, but too weak."[5] Our desires are so weak that we settle for something less than what will truly satisfy. God would have us desire so strongly that we could never be satisfied with anything less than Him. God does not want to douse the fire of desire in us; He wants to ignite it. But we must determinedly focus that desire on Him. Then all other, lesser, natural desires are brought into a right perspective.

Here is a little prayer that I have found helpful when temptation has seemed to loom larger than my faith:

> Please be big to me, my King
> And let me be small;
> Let me be nothing at all,
> But You be everything.

The Desire for Obedience

The encroaching cancer of self-indulgence threatens to envelop our hearts. Grace-enabled obedience is the only way to deal with this devourer. But do we want grace or sin? Here we must so exercise our love and our faith that we choose obedience no matter how we feel.

Two things happen when we step out in obedience. First, we discover that God's grace undergirds that step and, second, that our desires toward the particular temptation quickly dissipate, because obedience is an act of faith, and feelings follow faith. Yet here again, we must make a choice to believe and to obey God, and thus to reaffirm in our hearts that we are not our own, but His.

Sometimes we come to a place where this choice is particularly difficult; it goes beyond mere temptation and raises questions for which we have no immediate answers. We may not realize it, but we are in a crisis of faith. Satan tells us that this choice is not so significant, but it is of monumental significance because it determines whether we go forward or slink backwards. This is, in fact, our crucible in the development of practical holiness.

Reality demands an answer. Are we different? Are we holy? Suddenly, we are seized with fear. All is stripped away; it comes down to an honest, bare, essential dialogue with God. Perhaps this is precipitated by an overwhelming sin problem; perhaps by an assignment from God to which we feel overwhelmingly unequal. Or, perhaps some personal heartache threatens to overtake our soul. We are losing control.

Then comes an honest cry to God: "Oh, God, I can't handle this! It's too big for me. Is it *real,* this stuff about *enabling grace?* Is it true? Is it really true—even for this that is so much bigger than me?"

Then in the stillness, we become aware that an opportunity is present—an opportunity to sin or to obey, to indulge the flesh or deny it. So small a thing it is that, at a less sensitive moment, we might ignore the still, small voice of God. But now we hear it. He has our attention: "Just obey." And we respond, "This I can do."

The realization dawns that He has shown us, in this small opportunity, the answer to our great quandary. In this is surrender; in this is faith. It is leaping (however small the leap may seem) into the dark, trusting that we will have a safe landing. And in the quiet fall of submission, we find ease and know that it comes because of *grace*. Underneath are His everlasting arms.

The mist has cleared for a moment, and we see that He has shown us the solution to the big problem: We must deal with one opportunity to sin at a time, one opportunity to obey at a time. Thus we see the dynamic, the interplay between the choice of man and the sovereign grace of God.

Which comes first? We may think it is choice, but after we choose, we see that it was grace before and grace behind. And so the struggle goes.

The Desire to Possess

Often I ask young people to identify their greatest treasure. Sometimes they point to things like clothes and cars; sometimes they mention family and friends; if they get really "spiritual" they list the Bible and salvation.

Then I take them to the passage where Jesus said, "'Do not lay up for yourselves treasures upon earth, where moth and rust destroy, and where thieves break in and steal. But lay up for yourselves treasures in heaven, where neither moth nor rust destroys, and where thieves do not break in or steal; for where your treasure is, there will your heart be also'" (Matthew 6:19–21).

In this passage the Lord does not condemn possessiveness; instead, He exhorts the hearer not to possess the wrong thing. God has given us the desire to possess, but we must focus our possessiveness in the right direction. The ultimate possession is Jesus, our greatest treasure.

When I was a young person, I was not very focused on material possessions, but I was very possessive toward people. I was so afraid of losing them that I held on too tightly and tended to smother relationships. But through this passage in Matthew 6, the Lord taught me something invaluable: If I would focus all my possessiveness on Him, He would be enough for me. Everything and everyone else can be taken away, but Jesus cannot. He is my greatest treasure.

As I learned to possess Him and enjoy Jesus, I was able to let people go. I was set free to love people without smothering them, without being possessive, without projecting a demanding spirit. The only way to love people without demanding in return is to see Jesus as your all in all.

No matter what we say about our devotion to Christ, if our heart is fixed on something else, that is where our treasure lies.

Is Jesus our true heart's desire? To those who fix their hearts on Him, He gives the rarest of all treasures: Himself. Others may thirst for the trinkets of this world's store, drinking from broken cisterns that which does not satisfy. But our satisfaction is the Lord, the fountain of living water (see Jeremiah 2:13). He is our portion. He is enough.

> Riches I heed not
> Nor man's empty praise.
> Thou mine inheritance
> Now and always.
> Thou and Thou only
> First in my heart.
> High King of Heaven,
> My treasure, Thou art.[6]

Chapter Thirteen

Living in Reality

*And this is the message we have heard from Him
and announce to you, that God is light, and in
Him there is no darkness at all.*

1 John 1:5

Those who seek satisfaction apart from God are suffering under a kind of delusion and walking in *unreality*. To walk apart from God is to walk as the living dead. The lost do not know they are dead, but after regeneration they testify that they knew nothing of real life until Christ (see Ephesians 2:1–7).

Tragically, Christians today are so influenced by the world that they live with little awareness of the shimmering realities of eternal things. It takes too much effort to walk in realness with God. To live in the reality of His presence, we must be real about who *we* are, and we would rather not be that honest. But not to walk in the reality of God is to walk as children of darkness and thus to be entrapped by Satan.

Although we live in this world of tangible things, we are by faith to look beyond to the intangible, the eternal. The time each of us has been given must be invested in eternity. One day, time will be no more, but that which is eternal will remain. Three things are eternal: *God, His Word,* and *people.* The wise man pours his life out as an investment in these three eternal values. This is really living.

THE REALLY REAL

Is that which we experience through sight, sound, smell, taste, and touch real? Yes, but what we see with our eyes today may be gone tomorrow; what we touch with our hands soon perishes with the using. Surely what is eternal is more real than what is temporal.

God is more real than anything He has created. Time, matter, and space are all inventions of His. Before they had any existence, He was. God, by His very nature and existence, *defines* reality.

This is the meaning of the word *light* in 1 John 1:5: "And this is the message we have heard from Him and announce to you, that God is light, and in Him there is no darkness at all."

John Calvin said:

> When God…is called "the Father of lights" and "light," we first understand that there is nothing in Him but what is clear, pure and sincere…that He so enlightens all things by His brightness that He lets nothing vicious or perverted, no spots or filth, no hypocrisy or fraud, lie hidden.[1]

The New Testament contains only three "God is" statements, all given through the apostle John: "God is *spirit*" (John 4:24); "God is *love*" (1 John 4:8); and "God is *light*" (1 John 1:5).

God is spirit. These are Jesus' own words; God is intangible and eternal, not bound by space, time, or matter. He is totally other than anything He has created, including man. To describe God the Scripture writers used anthropomorphism, lending Him human, physical traits to describe the purely spiritual in terms to which man can relate. Thus they attribute to God certain physical traits.

For example, in 2 Chronicles 16:9 we read, "For the *eyes* of the LORD move to and fro throughout the earth that He may strongly support those whose heart is completely His." Other examples include hands, arms, a mouth, and so on. God has made man a spiritual being as well, but man is alive spiritually only if he is inhabited by God's Spirit. This is the Christian's link to God's holiness.

God is love. This statement is much stronger than saying that God loves. It says that, apart from God, love has no meaning and no existence. On that glorious day when all hope is realized and faith becomes sight, love will shine forth into all eternity (see 1 Corinthians 13:13).

God is light. With these words John is referring in the broadest sense to reality. God is the *ultimate* reality. By that I do not mean eventual, but immediate and essential reality. He is *the* immediate, essential, earthshaking, heart-stopping reality. And the Christian is to *live* in the reality of God. This realization strikes at the root of deception, which is Satan's great instrument of temptation.

WALKING IN UNREALITY: DECEPTION

We take the word *light* in 1 John 1:5 to mean *reality* because of its immediate context. The verses which follow verse 5 speak of *deception* or *unreality* as a contrast to walking in the light and so say a great deal about what it is to *live* in reality or unreality.

> If we say that we have fellowship with Him and yet walk in the darkness, we lie and do not practice the truth; but if we walk in the light as He Himself is in the light, we have fellowship with one another, and the blood of Jesus His Son cleanses us from all sin. If we say that we have no sin, we are deceiving ourselves, and the truth is not in us. If we confess our sins, He is faithful and righteous to forgive us our sins and to cleanse us from all unrighteousness. If we say that we have not sinned, we make Him a liar, and His word is not in us. (1 John 1:6–10)

In verses 6, 8, and 10, the words "if we say" are used to indicate deception. It is deceptive to say one thing and do another; here, the deception relates to sin.

DECEPTION NUMBER ONE

In verse 6, the deception is toward others: "If we say that we have fellowship with Him and yet walk in the darkness, we lie and do not practice the truth." Here is hypocrisy—pretending to be *in fellowship* with God when we are not.

Sin hinders our fellowship with God. So, to walk in darkness is to walk in sin; to walk in denial of our sin, hypocritically, before others.

Darkness in verse 6 contrasts with *light* in verse 5. God is light; if we would have fellowship with Him we must walk in that light as well. This is what verse 7 is saying: "But if we walk in the light as He Himself is in the light, we have fellowship with one another...."

To walk in the light means to be honest about our sins. If we walk in honesty we have fellowship with God and "the blood of Jesus His Son cleanses us."

Our relationship with God is not in question. Through the blood of Jesus we were released from all our sins: past, present, and future (see Revelation 1:5), and thus enabled to have a relationship with God. Our fellowship is nevertheless hindered by unconfessed sins, which must be dealt with all along the way. Christ's shed blood continues to cleanse us from the sins that hinder our fellowship with Him on a daily basis.

DECEPTION NUMBER TWO

In verse 8 we see a different kind of deception—*self*-deception: "If we say that we have no sin, we are deceiving ourselves, and the truth is not in us."

Indeed, if we say that we have no sin we do not know ourselves. Perhaps we define sin in terms of overt acts, such as theft or murder or adultery, but these are merely *fruit* sins. *Root* sins of heart and mind go much deeper than what we have *done;* they go to the depth of who we are. Fruit sins simply point to the deeper root sin inside.

Often, we Christians try to rationalize away our sins. We excuse them because of what we might call extenuating circumstances: "If you knew the kind of people I have to deal with"; "You don't understand the pressure I was under"; or maybe, "I do have certain needs that have to be met." We are saying that our sin is justified and not really *sinful* sin.

But verse 9 says: "If we confess our sins, He will forgive us our sins and cleanse us from *all* unrighteousness." Confession means dragging sin into the light of God where we can see it for what it really is, with no more rationalization. Confession is getting real, taking responsibility, and agreeing with God that *all* sin is wrong. Unless we are honest we will go on deceiving ourselves, and "the truth is not in us."

How do we draw the line between what is sin and what is not?

Sadly, this question is often asked because we want to sin rather than obey. The best rule I know is, *where there is a doubt, don't.*

Once a wealthy man was interviewing potential chauffeurs to drive his little girl to school on a dangerous mountain road. In each interview he asked: "How close can you get to the edge of a cliff without losing control and going over?" The first driver said he could get within one foot of the edge; the second, within six inches. The third driver said he would not care how *close* he could get to the edge, but how *far away from it he could stay*. Of course, that man was hired!

Christians often wonder how close they can get to sin without sinning. For example, young people want to know how far they can go with physical affection before it becomes sinful. They perhaps draw a line, but they stray so close to the line they inevitably go over the edge and engage in sexual intercourse. Here, a compelling question is: What does having sex really mean? If you have done everything but have actual intercourse, can you really say you haven't had sex?

Instead of seeing how close we can get to sin without sinning, we should be concerned with how close we can get to God. The test for sin should be, "Can I do this in the presence of God, in the reality of His holiness?" If not, it is sin, plain and simple.

One philosophy of ministry today asks how close we can get to the world without sinning, on the assumption that to win the world to Christ we must be as much like it as possible. But we are supposed to be a "peculiar people," distinctly different from the world. Until they see something different in Christians they will not be attracted to Christ.

DECEPTION NUMBER THREE

In verse 10 the final stage of deception is *calling God a liar*. "If we say that we have not sinned, we make Him a liar and His word is not in us."

How often do you hear words like these: "I know what the Bible says, but I just feel…"? Thus we call into question the very integrity of God. If He says something is sin, it *is* sin. If *we* say it is *not*, "we make Him a liar and His word is not in us."

The Word of God is our plumb line (see Amos 7:7–8). We are to measure every experience, feeling, and belief by God's Word. If it does not line up it is sin.

We have adopted much secular terminology, even in the church. One such word is *addiction*. This is a clinical term which implies something at least partially beyond one's control and thus not one's responsibility. So, when we use *addiction* in reference to pornography, sexual promiscuity and deviance, gambling, and theft, we are excusing what God calls *sin*—habits of sin, which have a binding effect on the sinner but still are the sinner's responsibility before God. To call sin an *addiction* and thus excuse it is to call God a liar. Thus we exonerate men from guilt in their minds, but not in reality.

There is also a popular trend in counseling, within the conservative, evangelical church, toward an emphasis on *deliverance*. This word *deliverance* is a Bible word (see Matthew 6:13; Luke 4:18; Galatians 1:4), but it is not applied in Scripture to specific sin habits. Some are even teaching that these sin habits represent an inherited predisposition in one's genes and are therefore beyond one's control.

We are all descendants from Adam and inherit from him our depravity (see Romans 5:14–18; 1 Corinthians 15:22). In addition, the influence a parent's sin has on a child can be devastating. Yet that child is responsible before God for his own actions; his sin is his own responsibility, not his parents' and certainly not God's.

We as Christians must take responsibility for our actions and the subsequent responsibility of confession and repentance of every sin. We were created for fellowship with God, but we cannot have fellowship with Him if we are not real about our sin.

WALKING IN UNREALITY: ESCAPISM

We as Christians have the awesome privilege of living in the reality of God. Yet the average Christian lives to a great extent as if there were no God. Often we are preoccupied with what we want but do not have, forgetting that we have in God the preeminent satisfaction of all our needs. Hence we continue to exchange fantasy for reality and lies for the truth.

Perhaps we want to enjoy the reality of God in our most holy moments, but we want freedom the rest of the time to pursue our desires. We think we can leave God in a sacred corner and run off into the shadows to do what we please, returning undetected and unscathed by sin. But sin separates us from God *within ourselves,* and we fall prey to our own deception.

> …Nigh and nigh draws the chase,
> With unperturbed pace,
> Deliberate speed, majestic instancy;
> And past those noised Feet
> A Voice comes yet more fleet—
> "Lo! naught contentest thee, who contest'st not Me."
> …Halts by me that footfall:
> Is my gloom after all,
> Shade of His hand, outstretched caressingly?
> "Ah, fondest, blindest, weakest,
> I am He Whom thou seekest!
> Thou dravest love from thee, who dravest Me."[2]

WAYS OF ESCAPE

Most people today are looking for escape from some reality in their lives, ranging from the overt and obvious to the subtle. Drugs and alcohol are usually first on the list, but many other escapes beckon.

Pornography in all its lurid forms is a huge and growing industry in our country, feeding the fantasies of millions. This perfectly illustrates the degradation involved in living outside the reality of God. Sexual fantasies, which can result not only from pornography, but also from undisciplined thought lives, are also escapes from reality. These unclaimed thoughts lead to deeply entrenched habits of unreality, such as masturbation and sexual role playing, which in turn can lead to perversions of every kind.

The word *iniquity* means a perversion or twisting of what is true and right into something unnatural and wrong. Sexual perversion is a twisting of what is natural into something unnatural. Therefore, it is a *lie.* To be convinced that the unnatural is natural is to be deceived. This comes from a refusal to honor God and yet a lust to worship something He has created. This worship is a form of idolatry, the worship of anything that is not God.

Consider an example. Despite all the talk about monogamous

homosexual and lesbian relationships, the vast majority of so-called "gays" have many sexual partners in their lifetimes, far more than even the most promiscuous heterosexuals. Homosexuality is an obsession with and a worship of the male or female body. It is idolatry.

To worship anything besides God is to walk in unreality and to greatly offend the only true God. Thus Paul said:

> Professing to be wise, they became fools, and exchanged the glory of the incorruptible God for an image in the form of corruptible man and of birds and four-footed animals and crawling creatures. Therefore God gave them over in the lusts of their hearts to impurity, that their bodies might be dishonored among them. For they exchanged the truth of God for a lie, *and worshiped and served the creature rather than the Creator,* who is blessed forever. Amen. (Romans 1:22–25)

This lie of idolatry soon leads to the lie of iniquity—that the unnatural is natural:

> For this reason God gave them over to degrading passions; for their women exchanged the natural function for that which is unnatural, and in the same way also the men abandoned the natural function of the woman and burned in their desire toward one another, men with men committing indecent acts and receiving in their own persons the due penalty of their error. (Romans 1:26–27)

Those who believe this lie are convinced that their only fulfillment comes in these unnatural practices. They wonder why such practices should be considered wrong. Given their beliefs, we can understand why they wonder. These practices are wrong simply because man was created to find his fulfillment in God and worship Him alone. Iniquity brings guilt, which eventually eats away at every illusion of happiness. Only through the blood of Jesus Christ can the guilt of this or any other sin be taken away.

Heterosexual promiscuity and infidelity is as much a lie as homosexuality; it is a worship of the flesh as well. Adultery is based on the fantasy that someone other than your spouse is, at least for a few moments of passion, your rightful partner. This contradicts the Word of God and is therefore a lie (see Malachi 2:14–16).

God takes marriage vows seriously, even if those who make them do not. There is more at stake in a marriage than just the relationship between two people or even the stability of a home. The Christian marriage represents the relationship of Christ and His bride, the church, so the very integrity of God's love is at stake. If the marriage fails, the credibility of God's own love is brought into question.

People become further entrapped by other, more subtle fantasies about doing something great or important, about relationships and intimacy. Most people in the world today, including Christians, live in just enough reality to function in society. The rest of the time they live in dream worlds. They do not like reality and escape from it whenever they can.

When we are not happy with the circumstances of our lives, we tend to fantasize about *different* circumstances. We imagine what it might be like to have a more attractive, attentive, sensitive mate; to have more money, more responsibility; to be more athletic, attractive, or talented.

We also tend to base our impressions of others on things we have imagined, which have no basis in reality. How many teenagers develop crushes on teachers or classmates they do not really know? We create scenarios in our minds, imagined conversations with people who rub us the wrong way or stroke our egos, and live in some imagined moment in the future. This is unreality.

At other times we live in the past, riding on past glories or remaining paralyzed by past fiascoes. It is good to both learn from our mistakes and enjoy our good memories, but we must let that enjoyment be a part of the present. We must not live in the past to escape from the present—*reality is God,* present with me right here, right now, in this moment.

Oddly enough, busy-ness may be an escape from reality. That may be why some people are workaholics. Often, Christians substitute busy-ness at church and commitment to "the program" for intimacy with God.

Noise can be a distraction from really thinking. Thus we turn on the radio as soon as we get in our cars; we switch on the television as soon as we walk into our homes. In silence and stillness we are more apt to come face to face with the reality of who God is and who we are. If there is unconfessed sin in our lives we may not want to be that real. But silence is a joy to the clean heart and serenity the garden of a clean mind.

Materialism, shopping, making and spending money—all these can also be ways to escape reality, attempts to fill our lives with *things,* which we wind up worshiping rather than God. We substitute the gift for the Giver, and our blessings become our curses. Things are not God. This is unreality.

All forms of entertainment—theater, movies, television, escapist fiction—are ways to escape reality. Even hobbies, recreation, and sports can be escapes. We live in an entertainment-crazed society, running from one form of entertainment to another because we are subconsciously running from God. We abhor boredom, and Satan has convinced us that God is boring.

This is the most ridiculous lie that Satan has ever perpetuated! *Nothing is more enjoyable than God;* nothing else can compare with Him. "O taste and see that the LORD is good," said David (Psalm 34:8). No enjoyment is more fulfilling or more lasting. To this we were predestined. We fulfill our reason for being by enjoying God, because through this enjoyment we glorify Him.

WALKING IN REALITY

So are we never to have hobbies or play sports or watch television or read a book? None of these things are wrong in themselves, if they are wholesome. But they must be enjoyed *with* God, *in the presence* of God, not as an escape *from* Him.

> All which I took from thee I did but take,
> Not for thy harms,
> But just that thou might'st seek it in My arms.[3]

Play golf with God; read a magazine with God; watch a movie with God. Of course, that will mean a more discriminating choice in what you read or watch. It also means you must walk in a mode of repentance and appreciation of His presence. The result is a clear conscience and the sweet enjoyment of His fellowship.

We are meant to laugh and play at times, and we certainly may appreciate all forms of artistic expression that are uplifting and wholesome. Part of our enjoyment of God is enjoying every aspect of His creation in His company and in His fellowship. As a matter of fact, that is the *only* way of true enjoyment. But we must never use His creation as an escape from Him or as a substitute for Him.

God is the most magnificent of all beings. How can anything corruptible even begin to compare in beauty to the incorruptible God? Yet if God *is* reality, any escape *from* reality is an escape from God. Why would anyone want to escape from God, unless he believes that God is not enough? Each of us must make a deliberate choice to live in the reality of God. It is amazing how many unworthy things go out of our lives when we make that choice.

How much better to walk consistently in reality than to be jerked back into it from a fantasy world! We may play with fantasy, thinking that no one is hurt by it. But if fantasy is in our hearts, soon it will show in what we say and do. Francis Paget said:

> That inner world of willful imaginations and of cherished desires is not so wholly hidden from others as we may sometimes fancy. We may believe that we can keep it quite apart from our outward life—that we can huddle it all out of sight when we meet and deal with our fellow-men; but the habits of the mind will quite surely tell, sooner or later, more or less clearly, on those subtle shades of voice and bearing and expression by which, perhaps, men most often and most nearly know one another.[4]

Satan's enticements are escapes from God. When we yield, we are saying that God is not enough for us. When temptation comes, look away to Jesus. Flee to Him, believing that He alone can satisfy. Only thus can you walk in the bright reality of His presence and love.

CHAPTER FOURTEEN

ESCAPING ANXIETY

Be anxious for nothing,
but in everything by prayer and supplication
with thanksgiving let your requests be made known to God.

PHILIPPIANS 4:6

Christ used some of His most vivid, winsome language when speaking of worry and anxiety. Of the Father's care for His children, Christ spoke of the birds of the air who neither sow nor reap nor gather into barns yet are daily fed by God, who values His children far more (see Matthew 6:26).

He then asks: "'And which of you by being anxious can add a single cubit to his life's span?'" (Matthew 6:27). In asking this He shows us, in a humorous yet sobering way, that we are not in charge of the future, *God is*. Indeed, it is foolish to imagine that worry could alter anything in a positive way.

Next Jesus points to the lilies of the field, which neither toil nor spin, and yet are clothed in more splendor than even Solomon in all his glory. How much more will God clothe His children than these temporary grasses of the field (see Matthew 6:28–30)?

Christ also speaks of the little sparrows that die and fall in the woods each day, and there is no man to notice. But God notices. God cares for us as well and knows the number of the very hairs on our heads. We are worth more to Him than many sparrows (see Matthew 10:29–31).

We find a compelling admonition in Christ's words: "'But seek first His kingdom and His righteousness; and all these things shall be added to you.'" Then He adds: "'Therefore do not be anxious for tomorrow; for tomorrow will care for itself. Each day has enough trouble of its own'" (Matthew 6:33–34).

Christ gives us the incentive to change the way we live our lives. We need not be governed or hampered by anxiety if we are under the sovereign rule of God. We must simply love God and fight the good fight of faith *one day at a time*.

THE COMMAND

Worry and anxiety are part of everyone's experience. Though we may see clearly the potentially devastating results of worry, both physically and emotionally (ask any doctor), we may be blind to its destructive effect on our spiritual life. Anxiety is a cancer that eats away at our flesh and our faith. It must be dealt with properly lest it devour us completely.

We excuse worry and even laugh it off as being hereditary or just part of being human: "Oh, I'm from a long line of worriers." We see it as a very light thing, just a weakness.

But worry is a *sin,* and not a minor one. It is the fruit of unbelief and thus an affront to God, a slap in His face. It is saying that God is not worthy of our trust. What do others think of our God when they hear us complain and whine?

We know that anxiety is a sin from Paul's admonition: "Be anxious for nothing, but in everything by prayer and supplication with thanksgiving let your requests be made known to God" (Philippians 4:6). This is not a suggestion but a command; to break any of God's commands is sin.

However, Paul does not give us only a negative, but a positive. He gives us something with which to replace that worry: don't worry about anything; instead, *pray about everything*. We must replace our worry with prayer. This refers to great perplexities, heartache, and adversities, plus the nagging little concerns of everyday life. In everything, pray.

However, it takes a specific kind of prayer to replace worry. We can pray and worry at the same time. Sometimes our prayers are no more than complaints to God about whatever is worrying us. Such prayer does not replace worry; it makes matters worse.

The prayer that replaces worry is prayer "with thanksgiving." *Thanksgiving is our only escape from anxiety, our only way out.* Yet this word is easily snatched from the Christian's mind, as though Satan erases it from our spiritual vocabulary as we would erase a word from paper.

Now, notice that Paul does not speak of prayer with thankfulness, but with thanksgiving. Our instruction is to give thanks, and we must do so even when we do not feel thankful. We must do so in faith—faith in God's Word, that when He gives a command, He also enables us to keep it. We also give thanks in obedience, just because God said to.

Here is a sample of how such a prayer might go:

"Father, You have told me to give thanks, yet I don't feel very thankful. But I am going to give thanks anyway. *Thank You.* Thank You that I can see with my eyes, I can hear with my ears, I can walk with my feet. Thank You that I have air to breathe, food to eat, a place to lay my head. Thank You that You are God and I am not. Thank You that You are my Father and that I can cast all my cares on You. Thank You that You are both sovereign and good and that nothing touches my life that is not filtered through Your fingers of love. Thank You that all suffering is temporary, that Jesus is coming back, and I will spend eternity with Him. Thank You for His blood, for forgiveness, for eternal life. Thank You that You are working to conform me to His image and that one day I will awake in Your glorious presence, clothed in His righteousness, and see You face to face! Thank You, Father!"

In this act of obedience our faith is stretched and strengthened, and our confidence renewed. We begin to actually *feel* thankful. Feelings follow faith. Thus *thankfulness* is the result of *thanksgiving.* And worry and genuine thankfulness cannot abide in the same heart.

THE REWARD

Thanksgiving is an act of obedience, the reward for which is wonderful: "And the peace of God, which surpasses all comprehension, shall guard your hearts and your minds in Christ Jesus" (Philippians 4:7). In response to thankful prayer, the peace of God acts as a sentry over a city gate, standing guard between our hearts, our minds, and any anxious thoughts.

Now, this is an extraordinary kind of peace, which is indeed beyond comprehension. It is the peace of God, a supernatural, inner peace of which the world knows nothing. This peace characterized the earthly life of Christ, and He freely gives it to those who follow Him: "'Peace I leave with you; My peace I give to you; not as the world gives, do I give to you. Let not your heart be troubled, nor let it be fearful'" (John 14:27). The peace of the world is the absence of conflict; when not at war, we are at peace. But the peace of God is peace in the midst of conflict.

I love the story of the artist who was commissioned to paint a picture that would illustrate peace. He was given freedom of subject matter as long as peace was its expression. The day came for the unveiling, and all were filled with excitement. But when the veil came back, everyone gasped. Here was a dark, foreboding scene at the edge of the ocean, waves billowing and spray tossing in the air. Lightning streaked across the sky, and torrents of driving rain descended at a slant.

The man who commissioned the painting protested that this certainly did not illustrate peace. But the artist told him he was not looking closely enough. He looked again and saw that over on one side of the canvas was a black, jagged cliff. Out on the edge of that cliff, barely hanging on, was a naked, twisted little tree. Another look revealed a nest in that tree's uppermost branch, and in that nest a little bird sang its heart out. *That* is the kind of peace God gives His children: the ability to sing in the midst of the storm.

> Thou art the Lord who slept upon the pillow
> Thou art the Lord who soothed the furious sea,
> What matter beating wind or tossing billow
> If only we are in the boat with Thee?
> Hold us in quiet through the age-long minute
> While Thou art silent, and the wind is shrill:
> Can the boat sink while Thou, dear Lord, art in it?
> Can the heart faint that waiteth on Thy will?[1]

Yet sometimes it seems that the boat *has* sunk, as when we face the death of a spouse or a child or some great disappointment so crushes our spirit that we feel paralyzed. In truth we are still afloat; God is faithful. He will still enable us to say to our souls, "Hope in God, for I shall yet praise Him, the help of my countenance, and my God" (Psalm 42:11).

Though the waves of grief, perplexity, and doubt beat about you, be of good courage; He is still "in the boat with thee." At these times the Christian may most profoundly know the incomprehensible wonder of supernatural peace, the safe haven of the soul.

But what if we are in a black cave and do not know the way out? "Thy word is a lamp to my feet, and a light to my path" (Psalm 119:105). This light does not illumine the mountain range before us, but we need only enough for the next step, and God provides that in His Word. Yet we must persevere and take those steps to emerge from the darkness into sunlight again.

THE MAINTENANCE

Sometimes, even though we have prayed with thanksgiving and the peace of God has been granted, we find that our minds are under unusual attack from Satan, and there is a potential threat to that peace. When worrisome thoughts creep back in, we can replace them with meditation on God's Word or thoughts about Jesus or wholesome thoughts about the ordinary "stuff of life."

Thus Paul's familiar admonition: "Finally, brethren, whatever is true, whatever is honorable, whatever is right, whatever is pure, whatever is lovely, whatever is of good repute, if there is any excellence and if anything worthy of praise, let your mind dwell on these things" (Philippians 4:8).

Sometimes, in extreme moments of intercession, it becomes hard to discern between worry and a burden from God to pray. The test is releasing the burden back to God in prayer. If, after we have earnestly prayed all that we know to pray, our hearts are still plagued with worry, we must confess that worry as sin and deliberately give *thanks* to God in faith and obedience. Then we must replace the faithless thoughts with thoughts of the faithfulness of God. This will certainly dispel the darkness and bring to the heart that restful peace it so craves.

THE BIRTHRIGHT

In Philippians 4:9, Paul says, "The things you have learned and received and heard and seen in me, practice these things; and the God of peace shall be with you."

Let me end with a provocative question. Which would you choose, the *peace of God* or the *God of peace?* For me there would be no question; I would choose the God of peace. I would have the God I love, plus the hope that, when this life is over, I would have His peace for all eternity.

But the Christian does not have to choose; he can have both! Peace is our birthright; let us claim and enjoy it. We can if, by faith and obedience, we always give thanks to God.

CHAPTER FIFTEEN

KNOWING GOD'S WILL

'For I know the plans that I have for you,'
declares the LORD, 'plans for welfare and not for calamity
to give you a future and a hope.'

JEREMIAH 29:11

Discerning God's will is a matter of *faith*. We would like for God to hand down His directions from the sky, but He does not. Instead, He teaches us to trust Him primarily by revealing His will through means which cannot be attested by signs and wonders.

Many questions we have concerning God's will are answered for us clearly in His Word. Then we need look no further. God will never contradict through any other means what He has already revealed; therefore, it is incumbent upon us to know the Word.

Yet many questions regarding specific decisions are not directly dealt with in Scripture, though every decision is addressed indirectly through scriptural *principles*. This chapter presents a time-honored method of discerning God's will in specific decisions.

GOD'S WILL FROM GOD'S PERSPECTIVE

The only right perspective is God's. The first step in seeing God's will from His perspective is simply to see it as *what He wants,* to see it as His desire, pure and simple and not filtered through our own desires. Too often when Christians speak of God's will, their concern is not so much with pleasing God as with pleasing themselves.

As we grow to know God, we begin to see that, because of His love, His desires toward us are for our good. We begin to trust Him, to see that He wants only what is best for us. Thus we seek His will all the more fervently, which is what He wants us to do. However, whether we realize it or not, often our concern is more with fulfilling our *own* desires than the desires of God. We want what God wants because we believe it is best for us.

But the *best* reason for seeking God's will is simply the fact that it *is* God's will. We ought to seek it because we want Him to have His way. Yet none of us can ever be sure that our motives are completely pure in anything, let alone in seeking the will of God. There is in us an undercurrent of selfishness and pride, even when we are closest to God. Thus God has made very special provisions for the accomplishment of His will, as is revealed in Romans 8:26–29:

> And in the same way the Spirit also helps our weakness; for we do not know how to pray as we should, but the Spirit Himself intercedes for us with groanings too deep for words; and He who searches the hearts knows what the mind of the Spirit is, because He intercedes for the saints according to the will of God. And we know that God causes all things to work together for good to those who love God, to those who are called according to His purpose. For whom He foreknew, He also predestined to become conformed to the image of His Son, that He might be the first-born among many brethren.

The contextual theme in this passage is the will of God. It tells us that the Holy Spirit prays for us according to the will of God. He dwells within each believer, and there He intercedes, praying for the Father's will to be accomplished in that life. Why? Because "we do not know how to pray as we should." The Father hears and answers the prayer of the Spirit, because He prays in perfect harmony with the Father's heart.

We also see that God actively causes *all* things, good and bad, to work together for good in the lives of those who love Him and are called according to His purpose. All believers love God and are called according to His purpose. This is our holiness positionally.

What is God's will concerning us? In a single word, *Christlikeness.* "For whom He foreknew, He also predestined to become *conformed to the image of His Son*" (Romans 8:29). If we want to know the all-consuming desire of God toward us, it is that we be conformed to the image of Christ.

At this point one may well ask if God has a preference in all the personal decisions we must make in life, both major and minor. Obviously, God's desire is that we choose right over wrong, good over bad; we determine the difference according to the principles of righteousness in the Word.

But what about decisions between two or more good things? How do we determine what is *best?* What about important decisions that are simply not mentioned in the Bible: "Whom do I marry?"; "Where do I go to college?"; "Do I take this job?" Does God really have a preference in such things?

Some say He does not, that we are free to choose on our own as long as our choices do not conflict with the clear teaching of Scripture. I do not agree. I believe this view is an understandable "pendulum swing" away from those who flippantly say things like, "God told me to do it." However, to think that God has no preference in the particular decisions of our lives is letting the pendulum swing too far.

It is impossible to reconcile this idea with the infinite interest that God has in each of His children. The psalmist said,

> O LORD, Thou hast searched me and known me. Thou dost know when I sit down and when I rise up; Thou dost understand my thought from afar. Thou dost scrutinize my path and my lying down, and art intimately acquainted with all my ways. Even before there is a word on my tongue, behold, O LORD, Thou dost know it all. (Psalm 139:1–4)

Jesus told His followers that "'the very hairs of your head are all numbered'" (Matthew 10:30). And 1 Peter 5:7 says, "Casting all your anxiety upon Him, because He cares for you." God *does* care about even the smallest things in our lives. Surely He has a preference in the particular decisions we must make.

Yet we must learn to see these decisions from God's perspective. God's will is that we be conformed to the image of Christ. This truth must be foremost in our thoughts. If we lose sight of this we lose perspective. So often we tend to see the will of God as just a series of right choices, of right decisions. We think that if we determine His preference in each particular, we have found the will of God.

But this is seeing each particular as an *end in itself*. God sees them as means toward a greater end, our conformity to the image of Christ. The particulars are secondary. They are important, and God does have preferences, but they are not nearly as important as the ultimate goal of attaining Christlikeness. They are the tools He uses to mold and shape us toward that end.

Indeed, being redemptive by nature, God also uses *wrong* choices, blunders, and even deliberate disobedience to bring about His purposes. "God causes *all* things to work together for good."

We hear the phrase, *the perfect will of God;* and we assume that, unless we always make perfect choices, we blow our chance at really knowing and doing His will. We might say that God's perfect will is that we never sin. But if we speak thus, have we not all missed it thoroughly? Is there any hope then for any of us to know the will of God?

God would have us come up to His vantage point. We must learn to see each particular choice—good and bad, right and wrong—as something He can use toward His ultimate end. *God will* bring His purposes about.

As Paul said, "For I am confident of this very thing, that He who began a good work in you will perfect it until the day of Christ Jesus" (Philippians 1:6). God has begun a good work in us, which He will continue to perfect, in spite of our sin, until the Lord returns or we are taken home.

That work will not be fully realized until we stand before Him in glory. The psalmist said, "As for me, I shall behold Thy face in righteousness; I will be satisfied with Thy likeness when I awake" (Psalm 17:15). Until that day the Holy Spirit will continue to pray for us according to the will of God, and God will continue to cause *all* things to work together toward His ultimate goal.

GUIDANCE VERSUS PERMISSION

From God's perspective the particulars are means toward Christlikeness rather than ends in themselves. Nevertheless, *God does have a preference in the specific decisions of our lives,* and He wants us to know that preference. Let us take a look at two prerequisites to knowing His will in the particulars.

PREREQUISITE ONE

First, we must realize that, when we are truly seeking the will of God, *He will not reveal that will to us as an option.* Some would have God lay His will out on the table, along with all the other options. But they reserve the final decision for themselves. Though they definitely want to know God's will, they will follow it only if they think it is their best option. Their major concern is their own will, not God's. Before they can know God's will, they must be willing to follow it no matter what it might be.

A minister who was also an accomplished pianist once stood before his congregation for a moment of silence, then walked over to the piano and began to play a beautiful melody. As he played, he began to sway back and forth and to say, "Yes, Lord." As the music swelled, the congregation, being looser than most, began to join in little by little until every voice resounded in conviction, "Yes, Lord!" Then the minister stopped playing, walked to the pulpit again, and said, "Well, Lord, You have heard our answer. Now, what is the question?"

That should be our attitude. Our answer should already be yes to whatever God's will may be. After all, how can you say, "No, Lord"? Those two words are mutually exclusive.

When we discussed a method for using quiet time, we emphasized the importance of fixing our hearts on God every morning. If we do not, we go into the day with our hearts unfixed, and they will fix on the next thing that comes along. This is extremely important in knowing and doing the will of God.

We are constantly bombarded with choices. Opportunities arise each day, small and large, which might seem enormously appealing but which might not be God's will for us. If our hearts are not fixed on God, and if we do not endeavor to keep them fixed on Him throughout the day, when an opportunity comes along, our hearts will fix on that instead.

Then, if we go to God about it at all, we go to Him for *permission* rather than *guidance*. Seeking guidance from God reveals a love for God's desire, for His good pleasure. Seeking permission reveals a heart for what *we* want, in which case we cannot discern the will of God.

Often, when a Christian is faced with a decision, his friends and acquaintances ask the standard question, "What do you really *want* to do?" They ask this as though discerning one's own desire is the way to discern God's. My answer is always, "It doesn't matter what I want; what matters is what God wants!" What we want often changes from day to day. We are fickle. When we do get what we think we want, we often discover that we don't really want it after all.

We must learn to have no preference in our hearts before we can know God's preference. Though we might be attracted, through logical deduction, to certain aspects of one choice over another, we must keep our hearts from getting bound up with that choice.

George Mueller said, "I seek at the beginning to get my heart into such a state that it has no will of its own in regard to a given matter."[1] We must have *only one preference,* and that one preference is *God.* "When one is truly in this state," says Mueller, "it is usually but a little way to the knowledge of what His will is."[2]

PREREQUISITE TWO

Second, we must realize that *God wants us to know His will more than we want to know it ourselves.* He never plays games with us, as Satan would have us believe. He does not lure us into a maze and then disappear before we get close enough to find Him. If we believe this lie we simply do not know God's character. God loves us; He does not delight in confusing us; He delights in our trust of Him.

Sometimes God delays revealing His will because He is waiting for the proper timing. He may remain silent for a time to prove our faith and to purify our love. Nevertheless, His silence is temporary and does not indicate indifference, but rather His intense care for us.

God's Preference in the Particulars

Now we are ready to consider specific ways in which God speaks to us concerning specific decisions that we must make. I owe a particular debt to George Mueller for the following principles.[3]

A "Word from the Word"

First of all, and most important, God speaks through His Word. God will never lead us to do anything that contradicts His written Word. That is why we must follow Paul's instruction: "Be diligent to present yourself approved to God as a workman who does not need to be ashamed, handling accurately the word of truth" (2 Timothy 2:15).

Not only must we *know* it, we must *obey* it. Any Christian, under the right circumstances, might be tempted to follow his feelings rather than the Bible. But we must never exalt feelings or limited human reasoning above the written Word of God, and we must guard our hearts against such a treasonous act.

In decision making, we may ask God to speak to us directly *through some verse or passage* of His own choosing, which might or might not specifically relate to the decision we face but can have an application when illumined by God's Spirit. This has been called a *word from the Word.*

This word must not come through our manipulating Scripture, trying to make it say what we want it to say. Any verse or passage has only one legitimate interpretation, though it may have many applications. We are responsible to know the proper interpretation. Then we may trust God to apply the Scripture to our particular decision as He sees fit. This requires patience and faith on our part.

It is best not to go scrambling through the Bible with a particular decision in mind, but to stay in the Word faithfully each day, praying that God, in His own time will illumine the verse or passage we need.

Neither should we avoid passages in which we know God speaks in a *general* way to our specific decision, fearing that we might manipulate these verses more easily than others. God can speak through even a seemingly obscure verse or passage, and quite often does. But He may also choose to speak in the context of more general instruction on the specific matter at hand, as when a man seeks to know whether

God would have him propose marriage to a certain lady. He should not avoid passages like Proverbs 31, which gives a striking picture of a godly woman.

Now, we need not expect goose bumps to accompany this illumination. Our initial response can be simple surprise: "God, is this really You?" But this may soon be followed by a settled but trembling confidence that God *has* spoken. This is faith.

Finally, it is important to have checks and balances. We should not make a decision based solely on a single "word from the Word" but must look for God to confirm it through other means. This protects us against even subconscious manipulation of the Scripture.

CIRCUMSTANCES

Second, God speaks to us through *circumstances*. Circumstances are always subject to God because He is the sovereign of the universe. Our circumstances are engineered by Him; even adversity is part of His sovereign plan. God often uses circumstances to refine the timing. Thus at times, He removes barriers so we can move ahead, or erects barriers so we will stay put.

However, to make a decision based on circumstances alone is perilous and premature. This is the way of the impetuous and unbelieving. We must always remember that a situation may look tailor-made for us and still not be God's will. This possibility must be weighed in the balance.

I suggest making two lists of circumstances under the headings "pros" and "cons." Then compare the two, asking the Holy Spirit to show you from each heading what needs to be scratched off and what needs to remain. This can be very enlightening, as one side of the list begins to outweigh the other.

On rare occasions our lists may look very puzzling after being scrutinized by the Holy Spirit. Factors arise that do not seem compatible with human reasoning and might even seem to contradict conventional logic. Then it seems that the Holy Spirit scratches everything off the list except an inner prompting in a certain direction from which we cannot get free. In rare and unusual times our faith can be tested to the maximum. What God seems to be saying sounds illogical to human ears, yet it also seems to be His direction for us.

Again, others will tell us that our thoughts make no sense. Satan will taunt us with questions like, "What do *you* know about the will of God? Do you think you are more spiritual than everyone else?" All around us will be voices, sometimes screaming that we are headed in the wrong direction. All of this should produce in us humility; for what *do* we know about the will of God? But when we get alone with Him, His still, small voice quietly assures us that we are on the right track.

It takes faith to obey God when His direction seems illogical. But after we have obeyed, we look back and see that it was the most logical thing we could have done. God sees the future, and we can trust it to Him. When we make the choice to go forward in what we feel is God's direction, although our circumstance list is almost blank yet is dominated by the supreme voice of God, confirming circumstances then begin to fall into place.

An example of this comes when God calls a man to the ministry or missions. At first the call seems fantastic and unfeasible. Yet, though many logical objections may appear on the "cons" list, they must ultimately be scratched off. Perhaps God has spoken through a "word from the Word" or perhaps through a recognizable voice deep within, and this factor, on *His* list, outweighs every other.

Faith is the key—the choice to obey in faith is the only one that brings peace, which leads directly into our next topic.

A SENSE OF PEACE

Third, God reveals His will through a sense of *peace* from the Holy Spirit or the absence of a check in our spirits. This is not to be confused with an emotional feeling. It is deeper than emotion; it lies in the realm of conviction and resignation to God. Often, this sense of rightness or peace comes in conjunction with a "word from the Word."

However, this sense of peace should *never be trusted alone*. So many things can affect our moods, from outward pressures to internal chemistry. What we sense through this factor must be confirmed through the others as well.

In addition, it is never wise to make a decision based on any one or two of these three factors. God is infallible, but we are not. Without meaning to, we may manipulate the Scripture, misinterpret our circumstances, or experience a deceptive sense of euphoria that we mistake for the peace of God. But if all three factors line up and point in the same direction, it is safe to say that we believe God has spoken, and we have discerned His will.

Now, this is not an attempt to reduce God's guidance to a formula. God cannot be put in a box, and He does not have to lead in the same way every time. In Scripture He sometimes guided people through dreams and signs. However, God does want us to seek His will in the wisest and most responsible way possible, for to "'everyone who has been given much shall much be required'" (Luke 12:48).

Remember the two prerequisites. First, we must *commit* to His will even before we *know* it. Second, He wants us to know His will even more than we want to know it ourselves. Thus we can be assured that we will find His will if we are faithful to seek it.

THE PERFECT TIMING

One widely accepted school of thought concerning the will of God, which I believe is wrong however popular it might be, goes like this. If you do not know God's preference in a specific decision, but there seems to be an open door in front of you, just step out in faith and trust that God will close the door if it is not His will.

I believe this to be dangerously presumptuous. This is not stepping out in faith; it is stepping out in impatience, ignorance, and unbelief.

Impatience reveals a fear that the opportunity will pass us by if we do not act. This further reveals a heart fixed on the opportunity rather than God. Yet if God is silent until an opportunity passes, He has answered. His silence means *no*.

By *ignorance* I mean stepping out without yet knowing God's overall direction. This is foolish and premature and can have devastating results. This is certainly not acting in faith but in *unbelief*. Faith must have an object, and if we are ignorant of the preference of God, we have no adequate object in which to put our faith.

Those who choose God's *mercy* as the object of their faith—which they really see as tolerance or permissiveness—presume upon His kindness, thinking that He will not let them walk through a wrong door. They forget that God's ultimate goal for them is Christlikeness. God may very well let them go through a wrong door to teach them patience, wisdom, and faith and to make them more submissive and dependent. Sometimes pain is necessary.

It is wise to be very cautious about open doors—not fearful or unbelieving—but cautious and wise. We do not know what is on the other side. What looks like a greener pasture could be the back side of the desert.

However, if we walk through an open door into the desert and thereby see that we have been foolish and sinful, God will provide springs in the desert if we confess that sin. He will even *use* us in the desert, and He will use the desert in us. Yet He may, by His providential will, keep us there for quite some time.

Thus we must not run ahead of God. We must not take things into our own hands. When in darkness concerning God's will, we must not light our own fire. There is a solemn warning in the Scripture concerning this:

> Who is among you that fears the LORD, that obeys the voice of His servant, that walks in darkness and has no light? Let him trust in the name of the LORD and rely on his God. Behold, all you who kindle a fire, who encircle yourselves with firebrands, walk in the light of your fire and among the brands you have set ablaze. This you will have from My hand; and you will lie down in torment. (Isaiah 50:10–11)

We may revere the Lord and be very teachable and submissive to those to whom God has given charge concerning us, and yet be in the dark about His will in a particular decision. There is nothing wrong with that. We are right where God wants us. We must simply trust Him and remain in the darkness until *He* lights a fire.

But again, what if an opportunity is passing by, and God has not lit a fire? If God does not speak, rather than try to make things happen on our own, we must *trust Him* and *let the opportunity go*. God *has* spoken in His silence. His answer is *no*.

However, if we insist on lighting our own fires and walking in the light of those fires, God will in His providence allow it, but we will "lie down in torment" and only God knows for how long.

> Thou hast enough to pay thy fare?
> Well, be it so;
> But thou should'st know, does thy God send thee there,
> Is that it all? To pay thy fare?
> There's many a coin flung lightly down
> Brings back a load of care.
> It may cost what thou knowest not
> To bring thee home from there.[4]

Note that any decision, no matter how much deliberation it necessitates, will ultimately be made in an instant. God is sovereign and holds the future in His hands; He has ordained a moment, somewhere in the future, in which He intends to reveal His preference in whatever decision is before us. If we agree that this is true, we must make sure that we are in God's will *in this moment.*

We do this by communicating constantly with Him and by obeying the guidance we already have. If we live in God's will in this moment, the next, and the next, by the time we get to the most critical moment, we will be ready.

God loves us so much. If we desire to do His will, He will make certain that we know it. But only God knows when the timing is just right; we must trust that to Him.

PART FIVE

PLEASING GOD— THE FIRE OF LOVE

But the greatest of these is love.

1 CORINTHIANS 13:13

The wellspring in each of our lives is love—either love for God or love for self. If the spring welling up in us is the putrefaction of self-love, it will manifest itself as an attempt to usurp all that is exclusively God's. If it is a surge of love to God, it will be manifested in all that is holy, noble, and true.

In conversion, initial repentance is a response of love from a heart that has been conquered by God's love. Even faith issues forth as a river of love from His fountainhead of love. John 3:16 says, "'For God so loved the world, that He gave His only begotten Son, that whoever believes in Him should not perish, but have eternal life.'" To believe in Christ is to say yes to His overtures of love. We love because He first loved us.

The bottom line in holy Christian living is love, first for God and then for men. Love is the only basis for true, practical holiness. Paul said to the Corinthians, "But now abide faith, hope, love, these three; but the greatest of these is love" (1 Corinthians 13:13). One day, faith will become sight and hope, reality; but love will remain.

God has *commanded* that we love, and to disobey that command is sin. Must we be commanded to love? Yes, because love for God and for our neighbor is not without a struggle. God has a rival for our love; that rival is self. An inordinate self-love is the origin of all sin because it signifies a lack of love for God.

To *love* God is to *obey* Him, but disobedience is spiritual adultery. So let us strive to love God with burning hearts, remembering His great love for us. Let the blaze of our love be obedience.

"'For love is as strong as death...its flashes are flashes of fire, the very flame of the LORD. Many waters cannot quench love, nor will rivers overflow it'" (Song of Solomon 8:6–7). This is practical holiness. This pleases God.

CHAPTER SIXTEEN

YOU SHALL LOVE

*"'YOU SHALL LOVE THE LORD YOUR GOD WITH ALL YOUR
HEART, AND WITH ALL YOUR SOUL, AND WITH ALL YOUR MIND.'
This is the great and foremost commandment."*

MATTHEW 22:37–38

In sending forth His dear Son, God the Father dealt a death blow to sin. The instrument of death was the cross of Jesus Christ. The Cross represents God's righteous judgment on sin, but it is also the way to life for the sinner because the essence of the Cross is love.

What a heartbreaking thing is this extraordinary love of God, the immensity thereof lavished on such pitiful objects as are we! Yet God has "sent forth the Spirit of His Son into our hearts, crying, 'Abba! Father!'" (Galatians 4:6). Thus we can say with John in amazement, "See how great a love the Father has bestowed upon us, that we should be called children of God" (1 John 3:1)!

Is there anything that humbles us more than the dear love of God? The holiness of God exposes to us our wretchedness before Him, but when the awesome truth that this holy God has loved us in spite of our wretchedness begins to dawn on our souls, our arrogance shrivels in the dust of shame.

It is an amazing thing to gaze upon our Lord, the beloved of the Father, and to contemplate the love that He displayed on Calvary.

Jesus! why dost Thou love me so?
What hast Thou seen in me
To make my happiness so great,
So dear a joy to Thee?
Ah, how Thy grace hath wooed my soul
With persevering wiles!
Now give me tears to weep; for tears
Are deeper joy than smiles.[1]

Such a heartfelt cry of intermingled pain and joy comes from our earnest contemplation of the Cross.

LOVING GOD

Love is the greatest thing in the world! It is the "more excellent way" (1 Corinthians 12:31). Thus we are commanded to love, the first object of that love being God Himself. This command shines a blinding light into our hearts and exposes the selfishness so evident there. Yet we do love God, however small that smoldering ember may seem. But embers can be coaxed into sparks and sparks fanned into flames.

WITH ALL YOUR HEART

The command is first addressed to the *heart*. If the Lord is our God, we must exercise our love with a full heart fiercely focused on Him. This speaks of devotion and worship. It begins with fixing our hearts at the beginning of each day, remembering His beauty and delighting therein. Then we must strive to keep our hearts fixed all through the day, guarding against any worldly distractions.

The more we see His love, the more we grow in the exquisite joy of intimacy. Augustine wrote, "What do I love when I love Thee?… I love a certain light, and a certain voice, a certain fragrance, a certain food, a certain embrace when I love my God."[2] There is something so comfortable about loving God.

Similarly, God commands love by His very nature. Those who know Him cannot help but love Him, He is so perfectly, infinitely lovely. We may grieve the Holy Spirit by saying yes to sin, but this does not diminish His love. You can only grieve someone who truly loves you. We may quench the Spirit by saying no to His promptings, but this does not cause Him to withdraw and stand aloof. He simply waits for the time to woo again, working in us all the while to change and soften our hearts.

With All Your Soul

The command is also to love God with all one's soul. This means with all our life, with all the energy of the inner man, and with every outward manifestation. We do this primarily through the consecration of our bodies and of the lives we live in those bodies. Thus active obedience in the Christian life is the supreme expression of love to God.

With All Your Mind

In addition, the command is to love God with all one's *mind*. This means to give our thought life to Him, renewing our minds with Scripture and focusing our minds on good, high, and noble things. To develop our minds to the glory of God is to love Him with our minds.

Any number of things in our culture can discourage real thinking, from the theft of our children's creativity by a failed school system, to the mesmerizing influence of the media, to the trend toward "dumbing down" everything we read, including the Bible. But the Christian must not succumb to these pitfalls. The business of loving God requires stretching all our faculties to their outer limits, including our mental powers.

In Preeminence

According to Christ's command, to love God is *foremost*. This means that our love for God must be preeminent in our lives. All other loves must pale in comparison to this first love. This truth compelled our Lord to use strong language in alluding to the love that His followers must have toward Him.

No Rival

In Luke 14:26, Jesus said, "'If anyone comes to Me, and does not hate his own father and mother and wife and children and brothers and sisters, yes, and even his own life, he cannot be My disciple.'" These words seem shocking, yet they serve to stress the necessity of Christ's supremacy in our hearts. Our love for Him must be so preeminent that all other loves are as hatred.

No Refusal

In Luke 14:27, He said, "'Whoever does not carry his own cross and come after Me cannot be My disciple.'" The Cross represents sacrifice and submission to the will of God. To love Christ is never to refuse any sacrifice that love might require.

No Retreat

When we come to Christ, we must count the cost, and there is a cost to love. Once we set our hand to the plow, love demands that we not look back (see Luke 9:62). If we love Christ, we will follow Him to the very end:

> "For which one of you, when he wants to build a tower, does not first sit down and calculate the cost, to see if he has enough to complete it? Otherwise, when he has laid a foundation, and is not able to finish, all who observe it begin to ridicule him, saying 'This man began to build and was not able to finish.' Or what king, when he sets out to meet another king in battle, will not first sit down and take counsel whether he is strong enough with ten thousand men to encounter the one coming against him with twenty thousand? Or else, while the other is still far away, he sends a delegation and asks terms of peace." (Luke 14:28–32)

No Reservation

Finally, in verse 33, Christ adds, "'So therefore, no one of you can be My disciple who does not give up all his own possessions'" (Luke 14:33). Nothing can be of more value to us than Christ. There must be nothing, temporal or eternal, which in any way threatens His preeminence in our hearts and lives.

In Obedience

To love God is to *obey*. Our obedience is directly proportional to our love. If we do not obey, how can we say that we love? None love God flawlessly, and the result of flawed love is flawed obedience. But we must at least *want* to love and obey God perfectly.

Self-Examination

Do you want to sin? Our answer is no. The Christian has in his heart a growing desire to obey God, although the insatiable appetites of self often take over. Thus he does what he does not wish to do in his inner man.

If the above is true of you, why do you *not* want to sin? The best answer is that you love God. However, some might indicate *fear of displeasing* God. Christian fear is a good thing; it is not being afraid of God as though He were a monster out to get us. God's perfect love casts out all fear of that nature (see 1 John 4:18). Our fear of Him is a reverential awe, perhaps even a dread of His reality and His holiness. But also, Christian fear is the *fear of hurting the God we love*. Love to the point of fear lest we offend is a great deterrent to sin.

The third question might seem a little surprising: Do you like being told what to do? Or, in an even more piercing way: Do you *love* being told what to do? God does not suggest; He commands. Do we love instruction? Then we love being told what to do, even if our instruction comes through other people, as long as we know that it comes from God.

Do you love righteousness? God does, and we must love what He loves. Over and over in Psalm 119, David exclaims, "I love Thy Law!" Do we love God's law, or is there within us a resistance to every discussion of it, even as a rule of life? David said of the laws of the Lord that they rejoice the heart; "They are more desirable than gold, yes, than much fine gold; sweeter also than honey and the drippings of the honeycomb" (Psalm 19:10).

Do you specifically love the Ten Commandments and see them as positives for God's glory or as negatives that weigh you down? Loving the moral law is not difficult if we love God, because the law of God represents His desires, and we should love what *He* desires. Thus we delight in obeying His law.

Hence we determine in our hearts that: (1) we will have no other God but Him; (2) we will refuse to be more impressed with any man or any other part of God's creation than with Him; (3) His name and all it represents will be sacred and honored in our lives; (4) we will joyfully set aside a day devoted only to rest, reflection, and the joy of corporate worship.

Thus we will love the Lord our God with all our hearts, souls, and minds.

In addition, (5) we will honor all men but especially our parents, who must hold a special place of honor in our hearts, our conversation, and our lives; (6) we will so value the lives of others that we will nurture and preserve them rather than snuff them out; (7) we will honor marriage vows as sacred to God; (8) we will deal in honesty and integrity; (9) not defrauding, misusing, or robbing; and (10) rejoice in others' blessings without envy but with real contentment, even though those blessings might be more substantial than our own.

Thus we will *love our neighbors as ourselves.*

These are high standards but not too high for love. Yet we are so often unloving and selfish, both in our relationships with God and with men. We choose self and betray the righteousness of Christ. This brings us to the final question:

Though we are often self-seeking, do we at least to some extent hunger and thirst for righteousness? The proof that we are alive spiritually is not that we are *full* but that we are *hungry.*

What is it, then, to hunger and thirst for righteousness? Let me offer a short, six-part test.

1. Do you long to be free from the *power* of sin? Paul said, "'I have been crucified with Christ'" (Galatians 2:20). And again, "He who has died is freed from sin" (Romans 6:7).

2. Do you long to be free from the *love* of sin? Any Christian who is truly honest with himself will acknowledge that there is within him a love of sin. But there will also be a longing to be free from that love, a weariness of sin, and a growing attraction to Christ.

3. Are you beginning to *hate* the sin in you because it is an offense

to God? As we grow in our love for God, we begin to abhor all that is abhorrent to Him. We begin to see sin for what it really is—hatred toward God and exalting self as God.

4. Do you *hunger for* God, not merely for the things of God, but for God Himself? The psalmist said, "As the deer pants for the water brooks, so my soul pants for Thee, O God" (Psalm 42:1); and, "O God, Thou art my God; I shall seek Thee earnestly; My soul thirsts for Thee, my flesh yearns for Thee, in a dry and weary land where there is no water" (Psalm 63:1).

5. Do you long to *know* God in a deeper intimacy than ever before? Paul said that greatest value to him, which he chose at the loss of everything else, was to "know Him, and the power of His resurrection and the fellowship of His sufferings" (Philippians 3:10).

6. Do you long to be *like* Jesus? When you see Christ's zeal, His courage, His selflessness, and His humility, do you long to be like him? When you hear Jesus say, "'I always do the things that are pleasing to Him'" (John 8:29), do you want to always please the Father as well?

If your answer is yes to these questions, even if that yes is weak, you *have* a hunger and thirst for righteousness. This hunger, generated by the indwelling Holy Spirit, is the earnest of being filled. "You *shall* be filled" and filled and filled again. Thus we fulfill the greatest of all commandments, to love the Lord our God.

CHAPTER SEVENTEEN

SELF-OBLIVION

"The second is like it,
'YOU SHALL LOVE YOUR NEIGHBOR AS YOURSELF.'"

MATTHEW 22:39

M atthew 22:39 has been used to promote an insidious false philosophy, which has stealthily crept into the church and become so pervasive that our whole view of self is askew. Indeed, the traditional biblical view of self has been virtually overturned within the church, and yet Christians are often unaware of this deception and have adopted the worldly view as contemporary Christian doctrine.

INORDINATE SELF-LOVE

This false philosophy is a misplaced focus on self, which encourages an inordinate self-love. We are told that if we do not love ourselves, we cannot love God or our neighbor; thus Christ is teaching us to love ourselves. *No!* He is not teaching us to love ourselves; He is teaching us to love our *neighbor.*

Christ does not *condemn* self-love; nor does He *commend* it. He simply *acknowledges* it. He takes it for granted that we all love ourselves. God has built into each person a certain kind of self-love: an instinct for survival, a desire to avoid pain and enjoy pleasure, an interest in personal development, and a desire to improve.

Thus Paul said, "For no one ever hated his own flesh, but nourishes and cherishes it, just as Christ also does the church" (Ephesians 5:29). No one really needs to be taught to love himself. It just comes naturally.

Now, we may not always *like* ourselves, for one reason or another. We may even dislike ourselves to the point of hatred. But this self-loathing, even to the point of suicide, comes from a deep dissatisfaction with self, which is actually a sick form of self-love. I do not mean to be insensitive to any whose lives have been touched by suicide, as has my own. But we must see that suicide is the result of this morbid self-absorption. Anyone who goes to this extreme simply loves himself too much to live with himself any longer.

PROPER SELF-RECOGNITION

Now we *do* need to be taught to recognize ourselves for who we are. We must as Christians have two estimations of ourselves. We must see who we are *apart* from Christ and who we are *in* Christ. Apart from Christ we are all depraved, wretched sinners. In Christ we are heirs of God and joint heirs with Christ (see Romans 8:17), set apart from the world, objects of God's everlasting love. This biblical perspective fosters true humility and gratitude, but without this proper estimation we grow more and more selfish and less and less holy.

THE WORLD'S VIEW OF SELF

In our society we attach to the word *self* many words that demonstrate a worldly view, yet by many Christians these *self-exalting* ideas are considered compatible with the teaching of Scripture, rather than contradictory. For example:

Self-*confidence*. But the Bible says, "For the LORD will be your confidence, and will keep your foot from being caught" (Proverbs 3:26).

Self-*dependence*. But the Bible says, "Not that we are adequate in ourselves to consider anything as coming from ourselves, but our adequacy is from God" (2 Corinthians 3:5).

Self-*promotion*. But Jesus said, "'Blessed are the meek: for they shall inherit the earth'" (Matthew 5:5, KJV). Rather than elevating self, the Christian exalts Christ and esteems others.

Self-*acceptance*. By this I mean excusing self, saying, "Well, that is just the way I am." But we do not need to be just like we have always been. The Bible says, "Be imitators of God" (Ephesians 5:1). We are supposed to be like Jesus.

Self-*defense*. Yet Peter said, "But if when you do what is right and suffer for it you patiently endure it, this finds favor with God" (1 Peter 2:20).

Self-*preservation*. But the psalmist said that the Lord was his rock and redeemer (see Psalm 19:14), his refuge and shield (see Psalm 119:114), his defender (see Psalm 6:4), and his deliverer (see Psalm 17:13).

Self-*esteem*. But Paul said, "Esteem others as better than [more important than] themselves" (Philippians 2:3, KJV).

Self-*help*. The largest section in almost any Christian bookstore today is called "self-help." But the psalmist said, "My help comes from the LORD, who made heaven and earth" (Psalm 121:2; see also Psalm 46:1; 94:17).

Self-*discipline*. But the Bible says, "'THOSE WHOM THE LORD LOVES, HE DISCIPLINES'" (Hebrews 12:6). According to Paul we are to discipline ourselves unto godliness (see 2 Timothy 4:7–8), and we are to recognize the importance of disciplining our thought life. However, self-generated discipline without a true dependence on the Holy Spirit promotes pride and independence. The best disciplines for self are *meekness* and *humility*, through which we discipline ourselves unto godliness. Then all our self-discipline or striving will be empowered by His grace. That leaves no room for boasting except in God Himself.

These terms all suggest an unhealthy focus on *self*, which fosters self-indulgence and leads even to self-worship. This is not what Scripture endorses concerning self.

SELF-DENIAL

Christ attached only one word to self: *deny*. In Luke 9:23, He said, "'If anyone wishes to come after Me, let him deny himself, and take up his cross daily, and follow Me.'" To deny self is not to deny things to self, but to deny self to self, to turn the back on self. When Peter denied Christ, he said, "'I do not know the man'" (Matthew 26:72). To deny self is to say of self, "I do not know the man.'"

Christ says that we are to take up our cross daily. This is the cross upon which self must be crucified daily. *Take up* is what we do; *crucify* is what God does. Often, I have heard one of my heroes, Dr. B. Gray Allison, say that we are to put self up on the cross daily and then ask God to kill it.

When a Christian sins, it is because he has lost his awareness of the reality of God. His spiritual vision and focus have been impaired. What's more, he has been deceived. Indeed, he has deceived himself, and this deception is willful. He *wants* to believe the lie because he wants what he wants and will have it no matter the cost (see John 3:19). This shows us that there is something even deeper.

When a Christian sins, in essence, he has *gone mad!* However, he cannot plead temporary insanity as though he were not responsible for his actions. But there is something quite insane about a Christian's sinning. After he has confessed, in the clear light of day, he wonders in shame, "How could I so easily have chosen self above God? I must have been mad!"

Faber, in his poem entitled "Self-Love," hits the mark convincingly:

Oh I could go through all life's troubles singing,
Turning earth's night to day,
If self were not so fast around me, clinging
To all I do or say.
My very thoughts are selfish, always building
Mean castles in the air;
I use my love of others as a gilding
To make myself look fair.[1]

Thus we must daily and sometimes hourly turn away from self, for we are self-loving creatures. Though we cannot escape from self in this life, we can by the grace of God deny its power to control our lives. We can, over and over again, deliberately choose Christ over self.

When Christ declared the two great commandments, He knew what was in the heart of men (see John 2:24–25). Jesus knew that no man needs to be encouraged to love himself but that he does need to be encouraged to love his neighbor.

THY NEIGHBOR AS THYSELF

This subject might have little appeal to many because it is not about them; it is about their neighbor. But herein lies a fundamental aspect of this book's overarching theme. Holiness is separation not only from the world and sin, but also from self, and this is nowhere more evident than in Christian charity.

Who is our neighbor? Jesus answered this question with the parable of the Good Samaritan (see Luke 10:29–37). Our neighbor is anyone in need, regardless of his race or nationality. This includes the stranger as well as the friend, the lost as well as the saved.

For the sake of clarity, we will divide our neighbors into two categories: *others* and *brothers*.

OTHERS

We cannot say that we love God if we do not love anyone He allows to touch our lives. As we observe the life of Christ, we see true love in action. No one ever loved as Jesus loved. He was never too tired, too busy, or too distraught.

He loved not only the lovely, the lovable, and the loving, but also those who were outcasts because of poverty, race, deformity, or disease; those who were hard to love, the cruel, self-seeking, and hard-hearted; those who did not love in return.

So must we love those who are rejected by society; we must take them into our bosoms as did Christ. So must we love the mean-spirited, the cruel, even the murderers, the adulterers, and all other haters of God and users of men. These, we must look upon as Christless sinners who are where we would be apart from the grace of God and love them as did our Lord. So must we love those who do not love us back, who squander our love, who disdain to be loved and reject all our overtures. In these as well, we must see ourselves before the love of Christ was shed abroad in our hearts, and we must love.

Only a focus on Christ and His selfless love enables us to love indiscriminately. When we see Christ in the midst of the multitude, we are attracted not to the multitude, but to Christ. This requires an opening of our hearts, a deliberate choice to express love even at the risk of rejection. We must not force ourselves on people. But we must come to the settled conclusion that everyone wants to be loved, no matter what they project outwardly, and it is our responsibility to love them.

A major part of imitating Christ is walking in this love for others. After saying "Be imitators of God as beloved children," Paul said, "and walk in love, just as Christ also loved you, and gave Himself up for us, an offering and a sacrifice to God as a fragrant aroma" (Ephesians 5:1–2). This is a self-forgetful, self-oblivious love that finds both its origin and inspiration in the overwhelming love of God.

> Our love is but a rising mist
> Created by that rush,
> Which plunges to the rocks beneath
> And sanctifies the just—
> The just made just to sanctify
> The Lord within the heart,
> That love may be a testament
> To Love's exquisite art.

When we are stretched to our limit, we must remember that love is a fruit of the Spirit. It is the single most significant manifestation of the holy life of Christ in us. We must depend on the Spirit, for He teaches us how to love even as He enables us.

"We cannot help it," says Henry Drummond. "Because He loved us…we love everybody. Our heart is slowly changed. Contemplate the love of Christ, and you will love."[2]

Love is at the heart of our new nature. To be Christian is to love. We are to love all men, even those who are our enemies. Jesus said:

"You have heard that it was said, 'YOU SHALL LOVE YOUR NEIGHBOR, and hate your enemy.' But I say to you, love your enemies, and pray for those who persecute you in order that you may be sons of your Father who is in heaven; for He causes His sun to rise on the evil and the good, and sends rain on the righteous and the unrighteous. For if you love those who love you, what reward have you? Do not even the tax-gatherers do the same? And if you greet your brothers only, what do you do more than others? Do not even the Gentiles do the same? Therefore you are to be perfect, as your heavenly Father is perfect." (Matthew 5:43–48)

Love for others motivates us to live holy lives. Paul wrote, "And may the Lord cause you to increase and abound in love for one another, and for all men, just as we also do for you; so that He may establish your hearts *unblamable in holiness* before our God and Father at the coming of our Lord Jesus with all His saints" (1 Thessalonians 3:12–13).

If we truly love others we will take no thought of ourselves but will do whatever we must to commend them to Christ. By so doing, we fulfill the law of love and become like Christ Himself.

> *Lord, help me live from day to day*
> *In such a self-forgetful way*
> *That even when I kneel to pray*
> *My prayer shall be for others.*[3]

The Christian must be *God*-centered, not *man*-centered. That is, we are never to opt for sympathy with men over a zeal for the honor of God and the integrity of His Word. I do not mean that we are to be unsympathetic. All our dealings with men must be in the context of love. But love must be in the context of *holiness*—the holiness of God.

Yet while the above premise is true, the Christian must be *people*-oriented rather than *time*-oriented. In other words, people are more important than our schedules. This is difficult for those who are driven by goals, tasks, and time, but it is not impossible. We must train ourselves to really listen to people, to give them all the attention they need. This means that sometimes our schedules must fall by the wayside. If that seems impossible, then we are slaves to our schedules and are simply too busy.

Do people have access to our lives? This is what ministry is really all about. Do we care about people and look on them with compassion? Or are we condescending, superior, critical, and judgmental? This is self-righteousness, the supreme counterfeit to holiness. Self-righteousness allows us to despise, to condemn, to criticize, to gossip, to elevate ourselves, and to refuse to forgive; it is that ugly *self* with which we are supposed to finish.

Do we abuse people with biting humor to demonstrate our own cleverness? Any humor at the expense of another is wrong, no matter how playful or harmless it might seem. A person may pretend not to be hurt and might even be able to hold his own with us, but deep inside he is wounded by what we have said. Is this love? When we indulge in this kind of humor, we are not living in an awareness of the presence of Christ.

Love requires that we tell the truth, even if the truth hurts. A true Christian is thus a minister of the Word. But do we have a zeal for the truth because we love the *truth* or because we love *being right?* Is ministry to others just delivering to them the truth and then saying, "Well, I've done my part. Now you can take it or leave it." No. We must by our love *show* them the truth.

Are we *redemptive* toward people as He is redemptive, with true meekness and humility, earnestly pointing them in the right direction? Paul said, "Brethren, even if a man is caught in any trespass, you who are spiritual, *restore* such a one in a spirit of gentleness; each one looking to yourself, lest you too be tempted" (Galatians 6:1). We are spiritual only if we can point others aright without an air of superiority and condemnation. When we are no longer surprised by our own depravity, we are not surprised by another's either.

Is our heart to help those whom the Lord has entrusted to us, as was the heart of our Lord Himself (see John 17:12)? Or, as some have done, do we tell those whom we cannot easily lead to "saturate the place with their absence"? How clever that sounds but how unlike Christ!

Paul told Timothy, "But the goal of our instruction is love from a pure heart and a good conscience and a sincere faith" (1 Timothy 1:5). Do we only offer people instructive doctrine, or do we communicate Christ to them? If we would give them Christ, it must be in love and in true humility.

BROTHERS

In Galatians 6:10, Paul wrote, "So then, while we have opportunity, let us do good to all men, *and especially to those who are of the household of the faith.*" Thus our love for our fellow believers goes even deeper than the general love which we must possess for all mankind (see 1 Thessalonians 4:9–10).

Toward fellow believers, we are not to be content with brotherly love alone (Greek: *phileo*), but to go beyond it to a God-kind of love (Greek: *agape*). Peter made a clear distinction when he said that in our brotherly kindness *[phileo],* we should supply love *[agape]* (see 2 Peter 1:7). In other words, love your brother with the same selfless love with which you have been loved by God.

Again, Peter said: "Since you have in obedience to the truth purified your souls for a sincere love of the brethren *[phileo],* fervently love *[agape]* one another from the heart" (1 Peter 1:22). Without an understanding that these are two different kinds of love, these verses sound confusing. But with it, one can see that Peter is stressing a deep commitment between fellow believers, a love that goes beyond mere filial love.

John had much more to say about this God-kind of love: "If someone says, 'I love God,' and hates his brother, he is a liar; for the one who does not love *[agape]* his brother whom he has seen, cannot love God whom he has not seen" (1 John 4:20). And again, "Beloved, let us love *[agape]* one another, for love is from God; and everyone who loves is born of God and knows God. The one who does not love does not know God, for God is love" (1 John 4:7–8).

Christ told His disciples: "'A new commandment I give to you, that you love *[agape]* one another, even as I have loved you, that you also love one another. By this all men will know that you are My disciples, if you have love for one another'" (John 13:34–35).

Love must be action that reflects an investment of our very lives. It requires generosity and sacrifice. It also requires that we be open and transparent, honest and real. Yet we must love responsibly, with wisdom, discernment, and real knowledge as our guides (see Philippians 1:9–10). We must love enough to give our brother the truth even when the truth hurts, but only while hurting right along with him.

Love costs—sometimes our comfort, sometimes our very lives. Is that not what love cost our Lord? Shortly before His crucifixion He said to the disciples, "'Greater love has no one than this, that one lay down his life for his friends'" (John 15:13).

Thus John again wrote in his first epistle: "We know love *[agape]* by this, that He laid down His life for us; and we ought to *lay down our lives for the brethren.* But whoever has the world's goods, and beholds his brother in need and closes his heart against him, how does the love of God abide in him? Little children, let us not love with word or with tongue, but in deed and truth" (1 John 3:16–18).

These words compel us to love beyond our comfort zones; indeed, to love with the sacrifice of our very lives. And this refers to *every* brother in Christ, not just those for whom we have a personal affinity. Our human nature rebels against this. Thus is set the tension that can only be relieved as we look to our Savior and rely on the Spirit, who alone produces the fruit of agape love.

Laying down our lives for the brethren means more than dying for them physically. How often are we called to do that? It means that each of us will be a servant to them for Christ's sake, will think of them as more important than ourselves, will labor in prayer for them, and will put their best interests above our own. Only thus will we fulfill what James called the royal law of love: "'YOU SHALL LOVE YOUR NEIGHBOR AS YOURSELF'" (James 2:8).

CHAPTER EIGHTEEN

THE ART OF FORGIVENESS

A man's discretion makes him slow to anger,
and it is his glory to overlook a transgression.

PROVERBS 19:11

I n an old cemetery not far from New York City, there is a grave-
stone on which is written a one-word epitaph. There is no name,
no date, only a single word—*forgiven*. Whose remains could be
in that grave? Perhaps they are those of a prodigal son or an unfaithful
spouse or perhaps someone whose life had been restored through the
great love of God.

Apart from the word *Jesus,* surely the word *forgiven* is the most
precious in the English language. What relief, what freedom, what joy,
and what reverence and broken-heartedness are engendered by this
word!

> "Forgiven!" one brief glimpse He gave;
> 'Twas all that I could bear;
> Enough to bring me to His feet—
> Enough to keep me there.
> For then the shadows of my heart
> By His own hand were riven,
> As on its darkest page He wrote
> One shining word, "Forgiven!"[1]

The basis of this wonderful gift is the redemptive work of our Lord; its evidence is our own ability to forgive. Forgiveness is love in action. Christ's death and resurrection was God's greatest expression of love toward man. But this gift was given that He might forgive. When we forgive others, we also demonstrate love in action. Thus to forgive is to be like our heavenly Father.

HEART FORGIVENESS

When wronged we must genuinely forgive *from the heart,* no matter how great the offense, remembering all that we ourselves have been forgiven of.

> And so, as those who have been chosen of God, holy and beloved, put on a heart of compassion, kindness, humility, gentleness and patience; bearing with one another, and forgiving each other, whoever has a complaint against anyone; just as the Lord forgave you, so also should you. (Colossians 3:12–13)

This means opening our hearts toward the offender and rising above the offense to a big-hearted, God-kind of love, which does not take into account a wrong suffered. This does not mean necessarily that the hurt goes away or that we can yet fully trust the offender once again. But it does mean that the bitterness is removed and is replaced with humility and love.

Bitterness is death to our souls, the result of unattended spiritual wounds. Forgiveness cleans these dirty wounds. For our own sakes and for the sake of the kingdom, we must forgive.

The deepest, most profound wound I have ever sustained came from an individual whom I loved and still love more than life itself. But this precious person went through a period of rebellion and hatred toward me. Yet, though I felt a deep spiritual responsibility, after a long struggle ended in a rift in the relationship I could no longer carry out my assignment. I felt that I had certainly failed and that all my prayers and all the investment of my heart were lost. This caused me to doubt everything, even my faith!

In that experience I learned a great deal about myself and my own offense before God. Outwardly, I was careful to not present a demanding spirit, but I soon discovered a demanding spirit within. Besides disappointment almost to the point of despondency, I also felt anger and even rage. I felt used and abused.

Now, we cannot help how we feel, but we can help what we do with those feelings. It is not wrong to be hurt or to wish we were better treated, but to *demand* better treatment reveals a deeper problem still. Thus God used this experience in my life to show me my depravity once again.

A demanding spirit reveals an indignation, not just toward the person, but toward God, which is presumptuous and impertinent. Because of our own great sinfulness, we are surely as depraved as the brother who has wronged us. This is not to excuse his sin, but to acknowledge our own wretchedness as well as his.

I also learned through this experience, more profoundly than ever before, that real love always involves pain. But it is worth it—if for no other reason, because it gives us a chance to identify with our Lord. How real His pain becomes to us, and how small is our hurt compared to His.

For me, there was a progression of hurt during the turbulent time. First, I felt utterly *despised,* so I went with a heavy heart to God and said, "Father, I cannot be despised." But He sweetly replied, "He was despised" (Isaiah 53:3). So I relented, "Well, then, I can be despised."

Then the problem escalated to the point of total *rejection,* and again I went to God, saying, "Father, I cannot be rejected." Again the answer came: "He is despised and rejected" (KJV). Hence my sad response was, "Well, then, I *can* be rejected."

After the rejection I was devastated, and though I did not deliberately flaunt my grief it was obvious to all who knew me that I was hurting. Some of my closest friends interpreted my pain as spiritual immaturity and weakness. They expected me to just bounce back, but I could not. This caused me great anxiety; again, I went to my Father with it, and again He brought the Scripture to my conscious mind, "He is despised and rejected of men; *a man of sorrows, and acquainted with grief* " (KJV).

I was comforted! These were deep lessons about loving and about the heart of Christ that I could never have learned apart from a crushing grief.

I also took great comfort in the experience of Paul with the Corinthians. Paul was not unspiritual when he agonized almost to the point of despair over whether they would respond to his rebuke with repentance. Some might have said that Paul cared too much, but if our love is godly, can we ever care too much? No one, not even Paul, has perfect love within himself. But each of us can be a channel of God's perfect love.

Happily, I can say that God was redeemed in my relationship. I was enabled to truly forgive from the heart, and though for a long time there was no repentance on the part of this loved one, it did eventually come. Today, that redeemed relationship is one of the greatest joys of my life.

In some cases, however, there is never any repentance of the other person. Perhaps that person has died without asking for forgiveness. We must not wait for the other's repentance before we forgive from the heart. Ephesians 4:32 does not have an "if" clause.

Responsible Forgiveness

Christ said to His disciples, "'Be on your guard! If your brother sins, rebuke him; and if he repents, forgive him'" (Luke 17:3). Here, there *is* an "if" clause. Does this contradict everything we just said? No. To forgive from the heart does not mean that we excuse a person from his responsibility to repent. That would be immoral and irresponsible on our part.

Though we hold no bitterness toward this brother, we must love him enough not to let him off the hook. This can be difficult and painful. If he knows that he has sinned, it is not necessary to remind him of his responsibility to repent. He already knows. But if he has built a wall of pride, he is the one who must tear the wall down.

Then the Lord makes an even more challenging statement: "'And if he sins against you seven times a day, and returns to you seven times, saying, "I repent," forgive him'" (verse 4). Seven is not a magic number. Jesus used it symbolically to emphasize the necessity of a *heart* of forgiveness. No matter how many times your brother sins, if he repents, take him at his word and forgive him. If he is lying, that is between him and God.

Notice now the disciples' response: "And the apostles said to the Lord, 'Increase our faith!'" (verse 5). This is a protest: "Lord, you must be kidding! We can't forgive that way; it would take a lot more faith than we have."

Christ then responded with one of the strongest rebukes in Scripture: "'If you had faith like a mustard seed, you would say to this mulberry tree, "Be uprooted and be planted in the sea"; and it would obey you'" (verse 6). In other words, the disciples already had all the faith they needed to obey Jesus' command.

The disciples were missing Christ's whole life message. If we find it difficult to forgive from the heart, our problem is a deficiency in *love*. We grow in love for others just as we grow in love for God, by appreciating God's love for us. "In this is love, not that we loved God, but that He loved us and sent His Son to be the propitiation for our sins. Beloved, if God so loved us, we also ought to love one another" (1 John 4:10–11).

First John 4:19 says, "We love, because He first loved us." Notice that this verse does not name the object of our love. That object can be God, but it might also be our brother.

The disciples needed a fresh look at their own depravity, as do we. When we feel our shame and evil and then see the generous forgiveness of God made possible only through the blood of Christ (see Hebrews 9:22), we "cannot help but go softly thereafter, as one lately shriven, passionately loving as one much forgiven."[2]

When we are confronted with a brother who has wronged us before, who seeks to be reconciled again, we will humbly, lovingly forgive as unto the Lord and hope that, for his sake, his repentance before God is genuine.

We must not hold onto the wrong, saying, "Well, I forgive, but I won't forget." To forgive does not mean that our memory is wiped clean or that we are not to hold others to their responsibility to repent. It does not mean to trust them blindly in the future, without expecting them to prove themselves true.

But it does mean that we take them at their word, though they say

"I repent" seven times a day. Such forgiveness is possible only through that magnanimous, Spirit-produced love that does not keep a record.

Is this forgiveness, then, not a large portion of our obedience to the royal law of love? When we ourselves sin, do *we* not long for forgiveness? And when we receive it, are *we* not profoundly grateful? If so, when we forgive another we are truly loving our neighbor *as ourselves*.

Chapter Nineteen

The Heart
of Worship

"For such people the Father seeks to be His worshipers."

John 4:23

Recently, there was a secular seminar at a large university entitled "Why Can't We All Just Get Along?" I don't know what that seminar was actually about, but when I heard the title, I imagined it in the context of the modern North American church.

Is that not quite often the cry heard today from different realms of Christendom? If we really love one another, we will be tolerant of all our differences, even whatever doctrinal disputes we may have, putting them all away for the sake of harmony. This concept is quite appealing to the man-centered church of today, which borrows freely from the world's philosophy of "live and let live."

Though we must be loving and patient with one another, we dare not forfeit doctrinal integrity. I am not waving a denominational banner, but I am emphasizing the necessity for doctrinal purity. This reflects a zeal for the integrity of God Himself.

It seems that today people are scurrying around in every direction, all doing their own thing and all frantically searching for satisfaction from every dry well in sight. If challenged by a call to holy living, or to a strict adherence to biblical standards, they cry pitifully, "Why can't we all just get along?" But this question does not take into account the holiness and justice of God.

This example brings to mind the very visual images of Psalm 2. Imagine the people in this psalm as ants:

> Why are the nations in an uproar, and the peoples devising a vain thing? The kings of the earth take their stand, and the rulers take counsel together against the LORD and against His Anointed [Christ]: "Let us tear their fetters apart, and cast away their cords from us!" (Psalm 2:1–3)

What a ludicrous scene: nations of ants seeking to overthrow the supreme God of the universe! Obviously, this is ludicrous to God as well: "He who sits in the heavens laughs, the Lord scoffs at them" (verse 4).

But this laughter is based not on humor, but on irony: "Then He will speak to them in His anger and terrify them in His fury" (verse 5). What God says to these ant nations and their kings is that He has installed His King on His holy mountain (see verse 6). This king is Jesus, the legitimate ruler of the nations (see verses 7–9). Next comes a warning to the ant kingdoms:

> Now therefore, O kings, show discernment; take warning, O judges of the earth. Worship the LORD with reverence, and rejoice with trembling. Do homage to the Son, lest He become angry, and you perish in the way, for His wrath may soon be kindled. How blessed are all who take refuge in Him! (verses 10–12)

This is sound advice: *Worship* the Lord with *fear;* rejoice with trembling; humble yourselves in subservience to God's Anointed; take refuge in Him. This view of Christ stands in stark contrast, but not in contradiction, to the gentle and humble servant of the Gospels. Yet hear Christ's own words:

> "I have come to cast fire upon the earth; and how I wish it were already kindled! But I have a baptism to undergo, and how distressed I am until it is accomplished! Do you suppose that I came to grant peace on earth? I tell you, no, but rather

division; for from now on five members in one household will be divided, three against two, and two against three. They will be divided, father against son, and son against father; mother against daughter, and daughter against mother; mother-in-law against daughter-in-law, and daughter-in-law against mother-in-law." (Luke 12:49–53)

This does not sound like Jesus intends for everyone to just get along. This is a Lord to be worshiped in fear. The division of which He speaks is produced by this fear. Some fear the Lord and some do not, even in the same family. Thus the fear of the Lord is a line of demarcation. It is also a symbol of holiness.

Worship in the Fear of the Lord

The fear of the Lord is a posture of reverence in the quiet solemnity of sacred things. It is a trepidation lest we offend, a hatred of all offense toward the God we love (see Proverbs 8:13). It is a horror of living independently from Him lest we become an offense ourselves. But this loving fear is actually a deterrent to sin: "And by the fear of the LORD one keeps away from evil" (Proverbs 16:6; also Proverbs 19:23; 23:17).

The fear of the Lord is the posture of true worship. Worship is bowing the heart to love. It is to be filled with wonder and awe; to be wrapped up in, captivated by, enraptured with. Worship means being so preoccupied with the object of worship that, at least for an instant, we can think of nothing besides.

Worship is also being dazzled by the *worth* of its object. Thus we hear from the battlements of eternity:

"Worthy art Thou, our Lord and our God, to receive glory and honor and power; for Thou didst create all things, and because of Thy will they existed, and were created." (Revelation 4:11)

"Worthy is the Lamb that was slain to receive power and riches and wisdom and might and honor and glory and blessing." (Revelation 5:12)

But worship is not reserved for stratospheric "mountaintop" experiences. The most common moments of life in the valley are sacred and holy opportunities for worship. Every ordinary element of life, if lived to please God and bring honor to Him, is an expression of worship. Worship is a submissive focus, not only of our attention, but of our very lives on God.

WORSHIP IN THE BEAUTY OF HOLINESS

We are instructed to "worship the LORD in the beauty of holiness" (Psalm 29:2, KJV). How lovely is true holiness in the believer, a life set apart only for God! This is the heart of worship. But what makes holiness beautiful?

Well, holiness in man is a reflection of the only truly Holy One. But when the holiness of God is extended to us in Christ, what is that character in Christ—that hidden pearl of beauty reflected in us—that is the inestimable beauty of holiness? It is *humility*.

Humility is self-forgetfulness. There is nothing so unattractive as arrogance and pride; conversely, there is nothing more appealing than genuine self-forgetfulness. Humility is thus that self-oblivion that so characterizes love. *If holiness is separation from self, and humility is this beautiful self-forgetfulness, then humility must be the beauty of holiness.*

What causes us, then, to forget about ourselves? Only one thing: a preoccupation that relegates self to the insignificant. When directed toward others, this preoccupation is sacrificial love; when directed toward God, it is worship.

Hence worship and humility are inseparable. *Worship is being so focused on God that we forget about ourselves. Humility is forgetting about ourselves because we are so focused on God.* Thus we truly worship God only in humility, which is the beauty of holiness.

PRIVATE WORSHIP

Each of us must learn to worship God in private. This is the essential part of intimacy with God, of secrets shared with God. It begins with an appeal to God to examine our hearts: "Search me, O God, and know my heart; try me and know my anxious thoughts; and see if there be any hurtful way in me, and lead me in the everlasting way" (Psalm 139:23–24). This is followed by confession of any known or revealed sin. Then we exercise faith that we have been forgiven and now have free, open fellowship with our God.

In the personal, private enjoyment of that communion, there are often precious moments of pure delight in which we seem to lose ourselves completely. There is, as A. W. Tozer said, the "ability to withdraw inwardly to meet God in adoring silence."[1] This is worship.

This self-oblivion does not happen by our trying to *forget self,* but by our trying to *remember God.* Worship is simply a fascination with Him that causes us to lose interest in, and sometimes even consciousness of, all else besides.

Thus when we experience worship privately, our focus is not on our experience, but on God. This should be true in corporate worship as well. Worship is an experience. But we have not really worshiped, either privately or corporately, until we have forgotten about our experience. If our focus is on having an experience, we may have that very thing but not have God. Worship comes when, in the process of beholding, we lose ourselves and the pervading sense of our immediate experience and are caught up in the wonder of God. When we become conscious of the experience, our worship is impaired.

Now, I am not speaking of some hyperspiritual, out-of-body epiphany, but of something I believe is much more common and frequent than we realize, yet it is nevertheless an encounter with God. It is simply a fascination, even if only a momentary fascination, with God.

CORPORATE WORSHIP

Corporate worship, in the truest sense, happens when God does something or reveals something to a *group of believers at once,* which causes them corporately to bow before Him, to be in awe of Him, to be preoccupied with Him. This is quite unusual in the church of our day. There seem to be many hindrances to corporate worship.

For one thing, we have a wrong approach. We think that worship is for us, for our enjoyment; so we go to church to see what we can get out of it. No. Worship is for *God. He* is what worship is about. We benefit immensely from worshiping Him, but our benefit is not the primary purpose (see Psalm 103).

Our approach to corporate worship is often very sterile. Henry Blackaby has well said that we come to church and sit down with the same mindset we have when sitting in front of the television. We have been conditioned by the media to look for *entertainment* and *information,* and we apply these expectations to worship.

Entertainment

The average Protestant church service in America is filled with entertainment, especially in the form of music. Music *can* be an aid to worship, but more often than not it seems to be a hindrance. This is because so much music is geared toward impressing men with performance rather than honoring and extolling God.

This entertainment mode is indicative of the worldliness so prevalent in the church. We should be different from the world—this is holiness. But instead, we take our cues from the world and imitate *it* rather than Christ.

Music has more and more been taken out of the hands of the congregation and put into the hands of soloists and praise teams. But music should primarily be a way for the congregation to communicate with God, not a way for the musicians to communicate with the congregation.

When and if, in our churches, the people *are* given an opportunity through music to communicate with God, it is often through simple, repetitive choruses. This repetition may aid in stimulating our emotions, but it does not necessarily foster true worship, nor does it challenge our minds. Where is loving God with our *minds?*

I am not saying that choruses are necessarily bad. Many choruses are great blessings, especially those which are pure Scripture (if the context is not compromised). And I am encouraged to see that our young people are often singing choruses which are much deeper in meaning than what has commonly been sung in the recent past. But choruses often present only one thought. More often than not, such repetition just promotes a feel-good sensation, and this is often confused with worship. Worship is not goose bumps, tears, or laughter.

There has of late been a tragic trend toward discarding the great hymns of the church. Although this would be an enormous loss, it is understandable; it is a reaction to years of dead, mindless hymn singing. But this is no fault of the hymns themselves. How we need to rediscover our heritage! The hymns of one hundred years ago and beyond were written primarily by theologians who loved God and His Word. Thus the hymns were filled with sound doctrinal truth and wonderful allusions to Scripture. They represent deep meditation on the truths of God.

C. H. Spurgeon is reputed to have said that the common man gets his theology from the songs he sings. What an indictment this is on the church of today! It is still true that the average church member gets his theology from what he sings, but most of the songs he sings or hears sung in church teach him no sound doctrine, and for his own part, he is basically biblically illiterate.

It is also true that the songs we sing *reflect* the theology of the day. Here is another indictment of the American church. Modern songs and hymns, with few exceptions, are generally very shallow doctrinally and are often based on *wrong* theology. They are primarily driven by emotion and are often man-centered rather than God-centered. Thus most of the songs we sing are about us—our blessing, our benefits, our redemption. We are bored by any complete emphasis on God, such as in the hymn "Immortal, Invisible God Only Wise," because it is not about us.

We tend to fall in love with certain songs and are often enamored with their recording artists as well, treating them like the world treats pop stars. But we cannot afford to have a love affair with any song. I have been a singer for many years, and I have had to lay aside songs to which I had a sentimental attachment because I came to see that something in them was not doctrinally sound.

How we need men and women who know the Word and the God of the Word! We need talented musicians who have an immense integrity about doctrinal soundness, who can also use their minds to produce creative and poetic verse rather than catchy, gimmicky senti-mentality. And we need melodies, harmonies, and accompaniments which do not steal the message from the listener's ear.

Until that day comes, we would do well to teach our people to love the rich hymns of old. But that means we must learn to love them ourselves. This can be accomplished best through learning and emphasizing the hymns' scriptural allusions and quotations, and by citing and celebrating illustrations of doctrinal value in them.

For instance, in the hymn "Come Thou Fount of Every Blessing," the second verse uses a word which is not common to our everyday language but is a significant word in Scripture. "Here I raise my Ebenezer / Hither by Thy help I'm come."[2] What in the world is an *Ebenezer?* This question, rather than being seriously considered today, is laughed at and discarded because we are bored by thinking.

But with a little effort we discover a precious gem. Ebenezer means "stone of help." It was a memorial stone erected by Samuel when God delivered him and the Israelites from the Philistines. Samuel called the stone *Ebenezer* because God had *helped* them (see 1 Samuel 7:12).

How much more substance and lasting power has this than some emotionally stimulating yet mindless repetition? The hymns can and do stimulate our emotions, but they also give us meat to chew on and help us appreciate more the deeper things of God.

Worship is a time to fix our affections on God, and I certainly do not wish to invalidate the significance of emotion in worship. Thus emotion of great proportion may and often does accompany worship, both private and corporate. Indeed, in worship one may often laugh or cry and sometimes even do both at once. But we should never confuse emotion with worship. These are two very different things. We are foolish if we think that, just because we have felt something, we have worshiped.

Neither is music synonymous with worship. Yet I often hear some of our brightest and best young people refer to the music time of the service as the "worship time." That is perhaps an innocent mistake, but it *is* a mistake. Worship, both personal and corporate, may occur as a result of some truth communicated through music, but it may also occur during the prayer time, or the preaching, or the giving, or the Scripture reading. When God speaks to us, impressing on our minds some aspect of who and how wonderful He is, we worship spontaneously, with perhaps no conscious thought. This can and does occur in the hearts of individuals at any time during a service.

Satan would completely obliterate worship if he could. He does anything possible to confuse the issue. As a result, God's people often have a warped view of worship. They want to worship, but they also want to feel something. They have that mistaken idea that worship is for them.

What is more, we ministers believe that we have to cater to what the people want. No. Again, worship is not for the people; it is for God. And the people are rarely in tune with what God wants. Thus it is all the more imperative that ministers be in tune and put God's desires above those of anyone else.

Pastors must teach their congregations what real worship is and how it is performed. Shepherds must lead their flocks to develop a God-centered approach to worship, seeking first *His* pleasure. The people must come to see that they themselves are the performers—not the preacher or the musicians—and that God is the audience.

Ministers must possess enough courage and humility to admit when we have gone in a wrong direction. We must teach people to have a right heart about worship. We can do all the right things, but if our hearts are not set to please God, it will all be for naught.

Doing this may require the removal from our services of some of the trappings that spell performance, including hand-held microphones and taped accompaniment tracks, which make even an inexperienced young person sound like a seasoned performer rather than a worshiper. This is not to say that these things are evil in themselves. Nor is it to pass judgment on anyone who uses them: Only God sees the heart.

But it is to say that we need to avoid all appearance of evil and make no provision for the flesh. Anything that fosters a performance mentality, in either the hearer or the singer, is a provision for the flesh. Now I know that, to some, I am treading on hallowed ground with these comments, but this is how I see it.

In addition, we should avoid any musical accompaniment that has an obviously secular sound or a tempo which distracts from the message of the song, be it piano or organ accompaniment, sound track, or orchestra. The words are the most important part of any good song. Music is merely a framework for a message, and any aspect of the framework that distracts from the message should be discarded.

Also, any songs that have a poor message or fail to exalt Christ must be excluded. And, in addition, those who sing must have more than talent; they must be pursuers of holiness.

Applause is another worldly practice which we would do well to remove from our services. I know that this sounds behind the times, but the church ought to be behind the times in some things. The applause of today is not the clap offering of the Israelites in the Old Testament; it is a secular expression of appreciation for a performance, which fosters a performance mentality and imitates the world. The church ought to be distinctly different from the world.

Humor is also a wonderful gift from God, and it has its place. So, we ministers should not be stiff and sour, but neither should we be stand-up comedians. That undermines the dignity of God and trivializes sacred things. It is time for the church to grow up and face maturely the awesome responsibility of God-focused, self-forgetting worship. If this sounds boring, we simply do not yet know what true worship is.

I believe we need to return to purity and simplicity in corporate worship. We should *together* sing praises to God from trembling hearts of love; we should *together* pray and read the Scriptures; and we should hear the gospel preached with a sense of our personal responsibility to respond in a godly way to what we hear. We should do all this with no kind of gimmickry or polish, just for the sake of attracting men. The more the church focuses on God alone, the more the world takes notice.

Rather than trying to be like the world, on the false assumption that by this we will win the world, we need to try to be like Jesus. When the lost come to church, they do not need to see the world. They need to see Christ. This does not mean that the lost will be comfortable in our services. Indeed, they should be very *un*comfortable in the presence of our holy God, but this may lead to life eternal. They will see Christ and be drawn to Him only if we lift Him up in the beauty of holy worship.

Information

We live in what has been called the information age. We have more information than most of us are mature enough to handle. Cynicism has made its mark on the church to the point that many conservative Christians doubt even God's ability to truly affect our age.

We are a worldly church, and this is nowhere more evident than in the media's influence on our approach to worship. The media has conditioned us to treat the worship service as if it were a television broadcast, looking for entertainment and information. When we go to church, we expect to receive some information, but we have no real sense of responsibility to do anything positive with that information, such as to pray, seeking to know God's perspective on it. Thus we are not changed by what we hear.

This fosters a detached, observational approach to worship rather than a participatory one. How different this is from the New Testament teaching on body life (see 1 Corinthians 12:12–27)! Oh, we shake hands and smile, but we are so self-contained, independent, and individualistic. Each of us is in his or her own little bubble, and all the bubbles line up side by side on the pew but never really touch. Do we know the person next to us? Do we care?

Appeasing Conscience

Some professing Christians go to church out of habit or a sense of duty. Their sacrifice to God is this little snippet of time on Sunday morning, and their conscience is cleared by their nod toward God.

Others go to get their emotional fix for the week. Their sacrifices are their tears and their shouting. But does this affect how they live their lives? Many take the same self-indulgence they display in church back into the world and feel exonerated from guilt, even over some habitual sin. Their consciences are appeased by their public displays of emotion; thus they deceive even themselves.

Do we trifle with sin, mock God, abuse His grace, and then really expect to worship Him? True worship is performed only in *holiness;* anything less offends Him.

Indeed, in Amos 5:21–24, God said to those who had forsaken holiness but had embraced ritualism and emotionalism:

"I hate, I reject your festivals, nor do I delight in your solemn assemblies. Even though you offer up to Me burnt offerings and your grain offerings, I will not accept them; and I will not even look at the peace offerings of your fatlings. Take away from Me the noise of your songs; I will not even listen to the sound of your harps. But let justice roll down like waters and righteousness like an ever-flowing stream."

I believe God is saying this to the church of America today as well. All that we have just described is an insufficient, warmed-over appeasement offering to God. I believe this elicits from God the same response that He gave to the Israelites in Malachi's day. They had despised and profaned His name, dishonored Him with inferior sacrifices (see Malachi 1:6–8), and scoffed at worship, saying, "'My, how tiresome it is!'" (Malachi 1:13). Hear God's passionate response to them:

> "Oh that there were one among you who would shut the gates, that you might not uselessly kindle fire on My altar! I am not pleased with you…nor will I accept an offering from you. For from the rising of the sun, even to its setting, My name will be great among the nations, and in every place incense is going to be offered to My name, and a grain offering that is pure; for My name will be great among the nations." (Malachi 1:10–11)

Now, given all of the above, perhaps I have painted a bleak picture of the state of the American church. Yet I believe there is great reason to hope; first, because God is a redemptive God, and second, because it seems that the true people of God are becoming more and more dissatisfied with the status quo. In less than a century we have gone from dead ceremonialism to self-gratifying emotionalism, looking for what A. W. Tozer called *the lost spirit of worship.*[3] But we have not found it. Why not try simply focusing with all our hearts, souls, and minds on God, in loving fear and true humility?

Jesus said that those who worship God must worship in *spirit,* that is, in spiritual life and in truth (see John 17:17). The true worshiper chooses an allegiance to the living Word of God rather than to His own feelings and to those of others.

This means that, though he loves others, he may not always be able to "just get along." Love does not always equal harmony. Meekness does not mean cowardice. Worship is not about fellowship, unless there is a oneness of spirit in a corporate allegiance to God's Word. We must be willing to address the misconception of worship, even within our own congregations, with kindness but also with fortitude and zeal for the honor of God.

God deserves the best we have to give: the best attention and the best response. By response, I do not mean an "amen" every now and then, but a life focused on God. This is true worship. Thus God is pleased with our public worship only if the pursuit of holy living is part of our daily experience.

The great preparation for corporate worship is private worship. How this needs to be stressed from our pulpits! If it is not, our people will continue to go to church unprepared for corporate worship, having given no thought all week to this awesome privilege and responsibility. How can a people hear from God corporately if they do not corporately worship Him? And how can a people corporately worship God if they do not responsibly prepare their hearts all through the week?

Worship is work and a very rewarding work, indeed. Yet were there no rewards, it would be of no matter, because worship is for God, not for us. Worship is *our* work; we *must* worship God; for this purpose we were created (see Revelation 4:11). God has built into each of us a longing to worship. If we do not worship Him we will worship self in one way or another. This is death. But to worship God is our very life.

THE OBJECT OF WORSHIP

How big is God! How small are we! Yet God condescends to look upon us with compassion and seek our worship. Isaiah's moving depiction of God as "'the high and exalted One who lives forever, whose name is *Holy*'" (Isaiah 57:15) is of a God who has something to say!

And this is what He says: "'I dwell on a high and holy place, and also with the contrite and lowly of spirit in order to revive the spirit of the lowly and to revive the heart of the contrite'" (Isaiah 57:15). God is present everywhere, but He is at home in only two places: in a *high and holy place* and *with the humble of heart*. "Humble self-abandonment is quite enough to give us God," said Evelyn Underhill.[4]

This means that God does not live with the proud. The proud cannot praise and worship God because only the humble can worship in holiness, and God requires holiness of His worshipers. Indeed, God *inhabits* the praises of His holy ones (see Psalm 22:3).

But God does not exist for our praise. If we become silent, "'the stones will cry out!'" (Luke 19:40). Yet even if they do not, nothing in God is diminished or depleted. God is self-existent, self-contained, and self-fulfilled. Even if nothing else glorifies Him, He glorifies Himself.

THE GLORY OF GOD

In his remarkable book, *Desiring God,* John Piper sets forth this premise: "The chief end of God is to glorify God and enjoy himself forever."[5] If by the word *end* in this statement, he means God's chief goal, I heartily agree with him. "God's own glory is uppermost in His own affections," Piper goes on to say.[6] And again, "God's ultimate goal, therefore, is to preserve and display His infinite and awesome greatness and worth, that is, His glory."[7]

God does glorify Himself, but He does not *exist* to glorify Himself. That puts glory above God. God glorifies Himself because He alone *is* glorious. There is glory in the sunset, glory in a single flower; there is even glory in man. But these are all reflected glories, as the moon is to the sun.

God *will be* glorified by *all creation*. In this little thing, this invention of God called "time," there is some temporary resistance to glorifying God. But Paul said that one day every knee will bow and every tongue confess that Jesus Christ is Lord, to the glory of God the Father (see Philippians 2:10–11).

Time is not a measurable part of eternity, as though eternity were time itself. Eternity is eternal. Time and space and matter are all inventions of God for His glory. This whole experiment of creation is simply God being God. And to simplify it further, we come to the bottom line of all existence: *God is*. Thus He revealed Himself to Moses as "'I Am'" (Exodus 3:14). All reality is wrapped up in that one supreme statement: "I Am."

Thus all of creation, both temporal and eternal, points to His reality. The psalmist said of material creation, "For He commanded and they were created. He has also established them forever and ever; He has made a decree which will not pass away" (Psalm 148:5–6). All of creation can exist for only one purpose: to testify to His existence and to bring glory to Him. "For His name alone is exalted; His glory is above earth and heaven" (Psalm 148:13).

"For in him we live, and move, and have our being," said Paul (Acts 17:28, KJV). We have no existence apart from Him. Thus man's proper function is certainly to glorify God (see Isaiah 43:7). And this is his fulfillment as well.

Nevertheless, man's fulfillment is not the central thing, certainly not to God and rightfully not to man. Yet we have the twisted idea that God exists for our pleasure, that we are the center of His universe. No. We exist for His pleasure, and He alone is the center.

We must realize that we are not what it is all about. We have been included in something which is so much bigger than our little lives. My life is not about me. My ministry is not about me. It is about God and His glory.

We think that we are each some great painting, and in one sense we are each a new creation, a work in progress (see Ephesians 2:10). But the *kingdom* is the big picture. We are merely brush strokes on that canvas. To see this is to see the joy of submission. And what will the end product be? What the unveiling? The bride of Christ; the kingdom of God.

Yet even the kingdom is not really what it is all about. The kingdom is God's great masterpiece by which He brings glory to Himself, but He is what it is about. The bride in all her beauty does not eclipse the glory of her husband—at least not the heavenly husband. He is the attraction. He alone is the center.

This does not mean that God is God-centered in the way that man is self-centered. God is naturally centered on Himself simply because He *is* the center. God is not self-absorbed as men are self-absorbed, with little or no interest or feeling for others, except as it benefits them.

Thus from the beginning, God involved Himself in His experiment of matter, space, and time. He fully invested Himself in His creation, making man the primary object of His love there. But this was for *His* glory, not for ours. For His own glory He poured out Himself selflessly at the cost of enormous pain. Thus He lavished on us His wondrous love.

What is more glorious than a love which caused the infinitely Holy to sacrifice Himself for the infinitely sinful? This is God *being!* And this is really all there is. We are swallowed up by this. If we love Him, even our own existence does not ultimately matter to us, only that He exists. If we were to disintegrate or had never been, it would change nothing in God. He would go on flawlessly in His every perfection.

Here is actually the purest form of worship. It is right and good to worship and praise God for what He has done and, further, for who He is. But we have not fully worshiped until we have also been captivated by the *fact* that *He is*. When we are caught up in the wondrous awareness of this reality, worship becomes so simple.

THE JOY OF TRUE WORSHIP

This is the delight and joy of the Christian. Thus Piper's other modification of the old creed, replacing the conjunction *and* with *the preposition by,* is also true: "The chief end of man is to glorify God *by* enjoying Him forever."[8] And there is no enjoyment comparable to the enjoyment of God!

The Lowest Place

But in the true enjoyment of God we forget about ourselves. This is true humility, that self-abandonment which comes with the realization that God is all. But this self-abandonment is itself part of the joy of loving hearts. Henry Scougal speaks eloquently of this same joy:

> It is impossible to express the great pleasure and delight which religious persons feel in the lowest prostration of their souls before God, when, having a deep sense of the Divine majesty and glory, they sink, if I may so speak, to the bottom of their beings, and vanish and disappear in the presence of

God…when they understand the full sense and emphasis of the Psalmist's exclamation, "Lord, what is man?" and can utter it with the same affection.[9]

True worship in the presence of God is a spontaneous bowing of both knee and heart in exquisite delight.

The Son of God

What a joy is true worship! Worship is not some disinterested fulfillment of an obligation; it is a delight. And the chief object of our delight is not only the Father, but also the Son. As John recorded in Revelation, "'To Him who sits on the throne, *and to the Lamb,* be blessing and honor and glory and dominion forever and ever'" (Revelation 5:13).

Paul said of Christ:

And He is the image of the invisible God, the first-born of all creation. For by Him all things were created, both in the heavens and on earth, visible and invisible, whether thrones or dominions or rulers or authorities—all things have been created by Him and for Him. And He is before all things, and in Him all things hold together. He is also head of the body, the church; and He is the beginning, the first-born from the dead; so that He Himself might come to have first place in everything. For it was the Father's good pleasure for all the fullness to dwell in Him, and through Him to reconcile all things to Himself, having made peace through the blood of His cross; through Him, I say, whether things on earth or things in heaven. (Colossians 1:15–20)

There is none to compare with Jesus. He is the pearl of great price, the radiance of the Father's glory, the chief cornerstone, the prince of peace, the beginning and the end. He is our friend, our brother, our Lord, and our God; the fairest of ten thousand, the bright and morning star, the lily of the valley. He is the beloved of the Father, the Redeemer, the Advocate, the propitiation for our sins. He is our joy!

Oh for a thousand tongues to sing
My great Redeemer's praise
The glories of my God and King
The triumphs of His grace![10]

We will be adoring Him throughout the ages. What a glorious prospect! Hallelujah! But here and now, He must so captivate our hearts that we actually *become* a praise, a fragrance of Christ to God.

Fairest Lord Jesus,
Ruler of all nature,
O Thou of God and man the Son;
Thee will I cherish,
Thee will I honor,
Thou my soul's glory, joy, and crown.[11]

Jesus is more than our delight, more than the joy of our hearts. He is the very atmosphere in which we live. To worship Him is to really live.

The Holy Spirit

The Holy Spirit is a Person. Indeed, He is the third Person of the Trinity, and His very real presence within us is the most personal aspect of intimacy with God. Yet today it seems that He is thought of more as a power or force than a sentient being. People use words like *it* and *what* and *that* when speaking of Him.

This may be due in part to a poor interpretation of Ephesians 5:18–19: "And do not get drunk with wine, for that is dissipation, but be filled with the Spirit, speaking to one another in psalms and hymns and spiritual songs, singing and making melody with your heart to the Lord." In verse 18, the definite article *the* is not used in the Greek, nor the word *holy* to precede the word *Spirit*. The Greek word here translated as *with* may also be translated as *in*. Thus the command could be, "Be filled in spirit." This might be a reference to man's spirit.

In Colossians 3:16, Paul said, "Let the word of Christ richly dwell within you." Paul goes on in both passages to speak of singing and making melody in the heart and of having a heart of thanksgiving. So perhaps Paul is saying, "Don't be drunk with wine, but be filled to overflowing in your spirit with praise and thanksgiving and with the living Word of God."

If Ephesians 5:18–19 is speaking of the Holy Spirit, the parallel between wine and the Spirit must not be seen in terms of a substance. The Holy Spirit is not a divisible quantity of which we may have some, none, or all. This imagery is poor and lends itself to statements like, "We get filled up, but then we leak." You do not have part of a person. To be filled with wine does not mean to be filled as a glass is filled, but to be under the influence and control of wine. In the same way, we are to be influenced and controlled by the Holy Spirit. This requires submission on our part and full surrender to His leading. If we do not thus respond we grieve Him (see 1 Thessalonians 5:19) and quench Him like dousing a fire (see Ephesians 4:30).

This certainly does not mean that we can in any way diminish His power. Nor does it mean that we can extinguish His love, causing Him to draw away from us. But it does mean that we can hinder the flow of His power within us. Just as sin interrupts our fellowship with God, sin interrupts the flow of God's power in our lives. The solution to both problems is confession and obedience.

All that we have said indicates that we need a relationship of intimacy with the Spirit. He is our Comforter and Companion, our Defender, our Intercessor, our Teacher, our Nurturer, and our Guide.

Each of us has the Holy Spirit if he or she is a child of God (see Romans 8:9), but does the Spirit have us? Does He have us to the extent that we do not quench Him? If not, He cannot use us. He will use His Word, but He will not use us. We must walk in holy communion with the Spirit if His power is to be manifested in our lives.

MEMORIZING SCRIPTURE

S cripture memorization is often thought of as just for children in Bible school. But Scripture memorization is for every serious child of God, no matter how old he or she might be. There are many reasons why we should memorize God's Word.

1. Scripture memorization helps keep us from sin. Psalm 119:9 says, "How can a young man keep his way pure? By keeping it according to Thy word."

2. The Word of God gives us guidance. Psalm 119:105 says, "Thy word is a lamp to my feet, and a light to my path." Psalm 119:130 says, "The unfolding of Thy words gives light; it gives understanding to the simple." Psalm 119:24 says, "Thy testimonies also are my delight; they are my counselors."

3. The Word of God gives wisdom. Psalm 119:97–100 says, "O how I love Thy law! It is my meditation all the day. Thy commandments make me wiser than my enemies, for they are ever mine. I have more insight than all my teachers, for Thy testimonies are my meditation. I understand more than the aged, because I have observed Thy precepts."

4. The Word of God equips us for our Christian duties. Second Timothy 3:16–17 says, "All Scripture is inspired by God and profitable for teaching, for reproof, for correction, for training in righteousness; that the man of God may be adequate,

equipped for every good work." Second Timothy 2:15 says, "Be diligent to present yourself approved to God as a workman who does not need to be ashamed, handling accurately the word of truth." Scripture memorization gives us confidence in witnessing.

5. Scripture memorization is important to the Holy Spirit's work in our lives. We limit that work if we don't memorize Scripture. Jesus said in John 14:26, "'But the Helper, the Holy Spirit, whom the Father will send in My name, He will teach you all things, and bring to your remembrance all that I said to you.'" But how can He bring to our remembrance something which we have not memorized?

6. Luke 4 shows us that Jesus memorized Scripture. That is reason enough to memorize it ourselves; He is our example. He used the Word to divert Satan's temptations.

7. The memorized Word is used by the Holy Spirit to change our disposition. Colossians 3:16 says, "Let the word of Christ richly dwell within you, with all wisdom teaching and admonishing one another with psalms and hymns and spiritual songs, singing with thankfulness in your hearts to God." James 1:21 says, "Therefore putting aside all filthiness and all that remains of wickedness, in humility receive the word implanted, which is able to save your souls."

HOW DO YOU MEMORIZE SCRIPTURE?

There are several approaches to Scripture memorization. Some people memorize individual verses on specific topics. Others memorize whole passages or chapters. Some take on entire books, which is really a challenge but a very rewarding one if done in humility.

Here are some basic rules to follow that will make the memory work go smoothly.

1. Memorize in humble dependence on God. He is the one who empowers you by His grace. Don't get puffed up or impressed with yourself or with what you are doing. Only be impressed with God.

2. Choose the Bible translation you want to memorize from and don't deviate from it. It should be a translation and not a paraphrase. The translation I recommend is the New American Standard Bible (NASB).

3. Use Scripture memory cards. Each verse should be written on a blank card, either business or index size.

4. The reference should go on the front and back of the card. On the front the verse should be written, with the reference at the beginning and at the end. On the back, only the reference should be written.

5. Make sure that you understand the verse before trying to memorize it. It is good to read the verse slowly, phrase by phrase, and concentrate on its meaning.

6. The reference must be learned as part of the verse. Every time the verse is quoted the reference should be quoted as well. This may seem unnecessary, but if the reference is not learned as part of the verse, it will more than likely be forgotten. The reference is the address; it is always important to know where a verse can be found.

7. Writing out the verse helps. You might want to write it several times, perhaps phrase by phrase.

8. Say each phrase of the verse several times to yourself. Say the first phrase and second phrase together several times. Then add the third phrase, if there is one, and the fourth and fifth.

You might also use a tape recorder or make up a tune to go with the verse or ask a friend to quiz you or be an accountability partner and memorize with you.

HOW DO YOU REVIEW MEMORY VERSES?

Each memory verse must be reviewed daily, or it will be lost. When a verse is learned, it should go into a review system. If, for instance, you are memorizing two verses a week, a good way to incorporate memorization and review is to memorize one of the verses on Monday, add it to the review on Tuesday, memorize the second verse on Wednesday or Thursday and add it to the review on Thursday or Friday.

When reviewing a group of cards, look only at the reference on the back. If the reference has been learned as part of the verse, it will immediately bring to mind the verse. This will make review much faster and easier. If you have trouble remembering part of the verse, turn the card over—but only as a last resort. Then review that verse again at the end of the stack.

Scripture review should be quick and easy. The only thing that will make it hard is neglecting it for a time. Consistency is the key. Be consistent with review even if you are unable to be consistent in memorizing new verses.

The publisher and author would love to hear your comments about this book. *Please contact us at:*
www.multnomah.net/becausewelovehim

Notes

Part One
Developing Practical Holiness

1. Jerry Bridges, *The Pursuit of Holiness* (Colorado Springs, Colo.: NavPress, 1978), 14.

2. Ibid.

Chapter One
An Appeal to Love

1. Of self-denial, Handley Moule says: "Take the New Testament and try the case by the words 'deny' and 'denial' in successive passages. I think it will be seen that self denial is not self control. In all cases…'to deny' much more resembles…'to ignore' than to control. It means to turn the back upon, to shut the eyes to, to treat as nonexistent. 'Let him deny himself…' (Luke 9:23)—that is, let him ignore self; let him say to self, 'I know thee not….'" Hadley Moule, *Practicing the Promises* (Chicago: Moody Press, 1975), 20. Hence the self-denial which Jesus points to in Luke 9:23 is not "to deny things to myself, but to deny myself to myself. It is to say no to self and yes to Christ." John Stott, *Basic Christianity* (Grand Rapids, Mich.: William B. Eerdmans Publishing Company, 1986), 111.

2. Elisabeth Elliot, *Discipline: The Glad Surrender* (Old Tappan, N.J.: Fleming H. Revell Company, 1982), 151.

3. A. W. Tozer, *The Knowledge of the Holy* (San Francisco: Harper & Row, 1961), 105.

4. J. I. Packer, *Keep in Step with the Spirit* (Old Tappan, N.J.: Fleming H. Revell Company, 1984), 110.

5. Ibid.

6. John Calvin, *Calvin's Commentaries,* vol. 22, *Commentaries on the Catholic Epistles* (Grand Rapids, Mich.: Baker Book House, 1993), 164.

7. A. W. Tozer, *The Christian Book of Mystical Verse* (Camp Hill, Pa.: Christian Publications, 1963), 123. The stanza is from "In

Immanuel's Land," a nineteen-stanza poem by Mrs. Anne Ross Cousin based on the letters of Samuel Rutherford. Some of this poem may be recognized in the hymn "The Sands of Time Are Sinking."

8. James L. Snyder, *In Pursuit of God: The Life of A. W. Tozer* (Camp Hill, Pa.: Christian Publications, 1991), 123.

9. Tozer, *The Christian Book of Mystical Verse,* 66. The stanzas quoted are from "Jesus, Thy Boundless Love to Me," by Paul Gerhardt.

CHAPTER TWO
DISCIPLINE

1. How is this teaching harmonized with what was said in chapter 1 about man's depravity continuing after conversion? Herein lies the tension, to which Paul referred in Romans 7:15–23 and Galatians 5:17, between the principle of sin within and the Holy Spirit's work of sanctification within. The change that the Holy Spirit produces begins with a growing desire to know God and please Him. But this desire must not be confused with any inherent, fundamental goodness. As Paul bemoans, "Nothing good dwells in me, that is, in my flesh" (Romans 8:18). Yet this distress itself shows a change of desire that signifies a newness of life.

2. D. Martyn Lloyd-Jones, *Studies in the Sermon on the Mount* (Grand Rapids, Mich.: William B. Eerdmans, 1982), 196.

3. Packer, *Keep in Step with the Spirit,* 65–66.

4. Stephen F. Olford, *The Way of Holiness* (Wheaton, Ill.: Crossway Books, 1998), 22.

5. Lawrence J. Crabb, *Inside Out* (Colorado Springs, Colo.: NavPress, 1989), 145.

6. Amy Carmichael, *Thou Givest...They Gather* (Fort Washington, Pa.: Christian Literature Crusade, 1960), 59–60.

7. Julian of Norwich, *Revelations of Divine Love* (Westminster, Md.: Newman Press, 1927), 49.

8. D. H. S. Nicholson and A. H. E. Lee, eds., *The Oxford Book of English Mystical Verse* (Oxford: The Clarendon Press, 1917).

9. John Rippon, comp., *A Selection of Hymns from the Best Authors, Intended to Be an Appendix to Dr. Watts' Psalms and*

Hymns (London: 1787). From "How Firm a Foundation."

10. Amy Carmichael, *Gold Cord* (Fort Washington, Pa.: Christian Literature Crusade, 1983), 63.

11. Amy Carmichael, *Toward Jerusalem* (Fort Washington, Pa.: Christian Literature Crusade, 1988), 10.

12. Frank E. Gaebelein, ed., *The Letters of Samuel Rutherford* (Chicago: Moody Press, 1980), 135.

13. Joseph H. Thayer, *The New Thayer's Greek-English Lexicon* (Lafayette, Ind.: The Book Factory, 1979), 5485.

14. John W. Peterson, ed., *Great Hymns of the Faith* (Grand Rapids, Mich.: Zondervan, 1973), 355. From "Every Stormy Wind That Blows" by Hugh Stowell.

CHAPTER THREE
STRIVING

1. *Favorite Hymns of Praise,* (n.p., n.d.), 466. From "A Mighty Fortress" by Martin Luther.

2. F. B. Meyer, *Devotional Commentary on Philippians* (Grand Rapids, Mich.: Kregel Publications, 1979), 168.

3. A. T. Robertson, *Paul's Joy in Christ: Studies in Philippians* (Grand Rapids, Mich.: Baker Book House, 1980), 194.

4. Carmichael, *Gold Cord,* 182.

5. *Favorite Hymns of Praise,* 361. From "Am I a Soldier of the Cross?" by Isaac Watts.

6. Frank L. Houghton, *Amy Carmichael of Dohnavur* (Fort Washington, Pa.: Christian Literature Crusade, 1979), 42.

7. Elisabeth Elliot, *Shadow of the Almighty: The Life and Testament of Jim Elliot* (San Francisco: Harper & Row, 1979), 15.

8. Oswald Chambers, *My Utmost for His Highest* (New York: Dodd, Mead & Company, 1935), 295.

PART TWO
KNOWING GOD—FIRST STEPS

1. Chambers, *My Utmost for His Highest,* 31.

CHAPTER FOUR
SALVATION

1. John Flavel, *The Works of John Flavel* (Carlisle, Pa: The Banner of Truth Trust, 1982), 1:58–59.

2. Does the doctrine of election, which teaches that only God Himself can choose whom He will call to be His own, hinder us from a zeal for the lost? It should not. Yet we may be overwhelmed by the depravity of man and thus have a negative attitude toward the possibility of man's ever perceiving the narrowness of the road. This causes us to be skeptical about every conversion and thus discourages us from witnessing. That skepticism is *unbelief*—unbelief in God's ability to save, which is a denial of the sovereignty of God—the very foundation of the doctrine of election. But the doctrine of election, truly understood in light of God's sovereignty and omnipotence, should *excite* us with the possibility that any person we share with might be chosen of God.

3. Thomas Watson, *The Doctrine of Repentance* (Carlisle, Pa.: The Banner of Truth Trust, 1994), 31.

4. Chambers, *My Utmost for His Highest,* 97.

5. Tozer, *The Christian Book of Mystical Verse,* 36–37. A poem by John S. B. Monsell.

6. Watson, *The Doctrine of Repentance,* 23.

7. Ibid., 7.

CHAPTER FIVE
SECURITY

1. Andrew Thomson, *The Life of Samuel Rutherford* (Glasgow, Scotland: Free Presbyterian Publications, 1988), 198.

CHAPTER SIX
DEVOTION

1. Walter Hines Sims, ed., *Baptist Hymnal* (Nashville, Tenn.: Convention Press, 1956), 306. From "How Tedious and Tasteless the Hours" by John Newton, verse 3.

2. G. H. Morling, *The Quest for Serenity* (Dallas, Tex.: Word Publishing, 1989), 52.

3. Peterson, *Great Hymns of the Faith,* 355.

4. Sims, *Baptist Hymnal,* 208. From "Love Divine, All Loves Excelling" by Charles Wesley.

5. For further reading on the presence of God, consider Brother Lawrence's time-honored book from the seventeenth century: *The Practice of the Presence of God* (White Plains, N.Y.: Peter Pauper Press. Inc., 1963).

6. A. W. Tozer, *The Pursuit of God* (Harrisburg, Pa.: Christian Publications, 1948), 97.

CHAPTER SEVEN
CONSECRATION

1. Sims, *Baptist Hymnal,* 144. From "When I Survey the Wondrous Cross" by Isaac Watts.

2. B. B. McKinney, ed., *The Broadman Hymnal* (Nashville, Tenn.: Broadman Press, 1940), 112. From "Alas! And Did My Saviour Bleed?" by Isaac Watts.

3. John Phillips, *Exploring Romans* (Chicago: Moody Press, 1981), 182.

4. Robert Murray McCheyne, *From the Preacher's Heart* (Scotland: Christian Focus Publications, 1995), 14.

5. Frances R. Havergal, *Kept for the Master's Use* (Wheaton, Ill.: Victor Books, 1986), 5.

6. From "The Great God of Heaven" by Henry R. Bramley.

7. William G. Blaikie, *The Inner Life of Christ* (Ireland: Tentmaker Publications, 1995), 6.

8. Ibid.

9. Ibid., 9–10.

10. Jeanne Guyon, *Madame Guyon's Spiritual Letters* (Augusta, Maine: Christian Books Publishing House, 1982), 22.

CHAPTER EIGHT
THE RENEWING OF YOUR MIND

1. Francis Paget, *The Spirit of Discipline* (London: Longmans, Green, & Co., 1893), 71.

2. Ibid., 73.

3. Ibid., 77–78.

CHAPTER NINE
IMITATION: PART ONE

1. J. C. Ryle, *Holiness* (England: Evangelical Press, 1979), 36.

2. Blaikie, *The Inner Life of Christ,* 92.

3. Robert Law, *The Emotions of Jesus* (Ireland: Tentmaker Publications, 1995), 12.

4. Henry T. Blackaby and Claude V. King, *Experiencing God* (Nashville, Tenn.: Broadman & Holman Publishers, 1994), 32.

5. Blaikie, *The Inner Life of Christ,* 106–107.

6. Carmichael, *Toward Jerusalem,* 85.

CHAPTER TEN
IMITATION: PART TWO

1. Sims, *Baptist Hymnal,* 342. From "Rock of Ages" by Augustus Montague Toplady.

2. S. D. Gordon, *Quiet Talks on Power* (New York: Grosset & Dunlap, 1903), 95–99.

3. Andrew Murray, *Humility* (Springdale, Pa.: Whitaker House, 1902), 54.

4. Elisabeth Elliot, *Keep a Quiet Heart* (Ann Arbor, Mich.: Servant Publications, 1985), 18.

CHAPTER ELEVEN
CHRIST IN YOU

1. Amy Carmichael, *If* (Fort Washington, Pa.: Christian Literature Crusade, 1938), 46.

PART FOUR
PLEASING GOD—THE FIGHT OF FAITH

1. Ryle, introduction to *Holiness,* xviii–xix.

CHAPTER TWELVE
DEALING WITH TEMPTATION

1. Henry Scougal, *The Life of God in the Soul of Man* (Harrisonburg, Va.: Sprinkle Publications, 1986), 95–96.

2. C. S. Lewis, preface to *The Screwtape Letters* (New York:

MacMillan Publishing Co., Inc., 1975), 3.

3. Sims, *Baptist Hymnal*, 8. From "A Mighty Fortress" by Martin Luther.

4. Henry Drummond, *The Greatest Thing in the World* (New York: Grosset & Dunlap, n.d.), 29.

5. C. S. Lewis, *The Weight of Glory and Other Addresses* (Grand Rapids, Mich.: Eerdmans, 1965), 94–95.

6. Sims, *Baptist Hymnal*, 60. From "Be Thou My Vision."

CHAPTER THIRTEEN
LIVING IN REALITY

1. Calvin, *Calvin's Commentaries*, 22:163

2. Francis Thompson, *The Hound of Heaven and Other Poems* (Old Tappan, N.J.: Fleming H. Revell Company, 1965), 15, 18.

3. Ibid., 18.

4. Paget, *The Spirit of Discipline*, 71–72.

CHAPTER FOURTEEN
ESCAPING ANXIETY

1. Carmichael, *Toward Jerusalem*, 36.

CHAPTER FIFTEEN
KNOWING GOD'S WILL

1. Mrs. Charles E. Cowman, *Springs in the Valley* (Grand Rapids, Mich.: Zondervan Publishing House, 1964), 308.

2. Ibid.

3. Ibid., 20.

4. Carmichael, *Gold Cord*, 190.

CHAPTER SIXTEEN
YOU SHALL LOVE

1. Tozer, *The Christian Book of Mystical Verse*, 103–104.

2. St. Augustine, *Confessions: Text and Translation* (London: Loeb Classical Library, 1919), x. 6.

CHAPTER SEVENTEEN
SELF-OBLIVION

1. Tozer, *The Christian Book of Mystical Verse,* 48.

2. Drummond, *The Greatest Thing in the World,* 31.

3. McKinney, *The Broadman Hymnal,* 77. From "Others" by C. D. Meigs.

CHAPTER EIGHTEEN
THE ART OF FORGIVENESS

1. Morling, *The Quest for Serenity,* 21.

2. Carmichael, *Toward Jerusalem,* 91.

CHAPTER NINETEEN
THE HEART OF WORSHIP

1. Tozer, preface of *The Knowledge of the Holy,* vii.

2. Sims, *Baptist Hymnal,* 15. From "Come, Thou Fount of Every Blessing" by Robert Robinson.

3. Tozer, preface of *The Knowledge of the Holy,* vii.

4. Evelyn Underhill, *Light of Christ* (Wilton, Conn.: Morehouse-Barlow Co., Inc., 1989), 18.

5. John Piper, *Desiring God* (Portland, Ore.: Multnomah, 1986), 30.

6. Ibid., 31.

7. Ibid., 32.

8. Ibid., 23.

9. Scougal, *The Life of God in the Soul of Man,* 81–82.

10. comp./ed. *Favorite Hymns of Praise,* 456. From "Oh for a Thousand Tongues to Sing" by Charles Wesley.

11. Sims, *Baptist Hymnal,* 176. "Fairest Lord Jesus" from *Munster Gesangbuch,* 1677.